About This Book

The Age of Jackson is the Pulitzer-Prize-winning story of the rancorous struggle, one hundred to one hundred and twenty years ago, as to who was going to run the United States of America, and for what purpose and to whose benefit. General Jackson's election in 1829 cast a pall of gloom and despair over most of America's best and most influential people. He was called a man of "bad character," his election was an "effrontery" and could only result in the rule of the "mob." Men in high places despaired of being able to find leaders for "a revolution." This was the sort of talk that ushered Jackson into the White House. It would have discouraged most well men —but Jackson was sick in body though not in mind, nor was he weak in heart. He fought and licked not only bankers but also the banking system. He took the best ideas of Hamilton and Jefferson and forged a Democratic Party. Like Roosevelt a hundred years later he collided with the courts, and won. Depression, panic and the struggle of the working man for justice marked this age. Yet out of this pessimism and confusion came a great philosophy and movement of equity and justice and opportunity. Gone forever was the Hamiltonian idea that society could best be governed by the aristocracy, and gone also was the Jeffersonian idea that large urban populations were just so many "sores" on the social body. Jackson had faith not only in America but also in the people of America—all of them. Lincoln owed much to Jackson. Franklin D. Roosevelt did. And you do, too.

This is a convenient abridgment of the whole book done especially for The New American Library; all the words are those of the author, Arthur M. Schlesinger, Jr., and constitute about one third of the original.

DONALD PORTER GEDDES

Special Editor—Abridged Mentor Edition

MENTOR Books of Related Interest

GEORGE WASHINGTON: MAN AND MONUMENT
    by Marcus Cunliffe
This brilliant study of the first President of the United
States presents a realistic picture of Washington's life
and times, stripped of the myths and fictions which
have obscured his great and lasting achievements.
                                              (#MP536—60¢)

JEFFERSON (revised and abridged) *by Saul K. Padover*
The story of Thomas Jefferson as farmer, philosopher,
architect, statesman and President of the United States.
                                              (#MP408—60¢)

THE LIFE OF ABRAHAM LINCOLN *by Stefan Lorant*
A unique text and picture biography of the great and
beloved American President, with hundreds of illus-
trations.   (#MT323—75¢)

THE AMERICAN PRESIDENCY *by Clinton Rossiter*
A clear account of the history and evolution of the
Presidency and the President's current duties and re-
sponsibilities.   (#MT454—75¢)

To Our Readers

THE AGE OF

JACKSON

(ABRIDGED)

by

Arthur M. Schlesinger, Jr.

A MENTOR BOOK

Published by The New American Library

TO
MARIAN

The feud between the capitalist and laborer, the house of Have and the house of Want, is as old as social union, and can never be entirely quieted; but he who will act with moderation, prefer fact to theory, and remember that every thing in this world is relative and not absolute, will see that the violence of the contest may be stilled.

—GEORGE BANCROFT

Foreword

THE WORLD CRISIS HAS GIVEN NEW URGENCY TO THE question of the "meaning" of democracy. If democracy is indeed to be the hope of the future, we know now that we must have its lineaments clearly in mind, so that we may the more surely recognize it and the more responsibly act upon it. For some the questioning has taken the form of a search for the immutable moral abstractions of the democratic faith. Such an inquiry meets profound human needs, even if it rarely succeeds in getting far along its own path. But, for the student of history, the "meaning" of democracy is likely to assume a form at once far more simple and far more complex. The key to that meaning is rather to be sought in the concrete record of what democracy has meant in the past. What range of possibilities has it, in fact, unfolded? What methods has it found legitimate? What have been its values and its resources?

The world after victory will contain internal, as well as external, perplexities of the utmost difficulty and importance. We do not yet know how in detail the American democracy will move to meet them; but this we do know, that, if it is to remain a democracy, its moods, methods and purposes will bear a vital relation to its attack on similar (if less intense) crises of its past.

Democracy has recommended itself above all other modes of organizing society by its capacity for the peaceable solution of its internal problems. Its flexible political and social structure, with the premium placed on tolerance, bargaining and compromise, has on the whole kept alive enough hope for discontented minorities to deter them from taking up the option of revolution. The great exception in our history was a question so crucial that perhaps it could have been solved in no other way. (We know now that it is an illusion that wars have always been unnecessary.)

But the crisis of the second order—the time of bitter social tension which somehow escapes the final flare-up—constitutes democracy's great triumph. The resources which have enabled the American democracy to surmount such crises in the past will be drawn on to the full in the near and shadowed future. The actual issues, political and economic, of Jackson's day have now an almost Arcadian simplicity. Nonetheless they went to the roots of many of the democratic ambiguities, opening up and probing questions whose recurrence a century later testifies to their continuing significance for a free society.

The heritage of Andrew Jackson, as President Roosevelt has said, is "his unending contribution to the vitality of our democracy. We look back on his amazing personality, we review his battles because the struggles he went through, the enemies he encountered, the defeats he suffered and the victories he won are part and parcel of the struggles, the enmities, the defeats and the victories of those who have lived in all the generations that have followed."

In the days of Jackson, as in all periods of rapid social adjustment, there was a close correspondence between the movement of politics and the movement of ideas. This work attempts to examine the politics more or less in terms of the ideas; and, in the course of the study, it has seemed that Jacksonian democracy, which has always appeared an obvious example of Western influence in American government, is not perhaps so pat a case as some have thought; that its development was shaped much more by reasoned and systematic notions about society than has been generally recognized; and that many of its controlling beliefs and motives came rather from the East and South than from the West.

The clash of ideas in these years reveals, moreover, a number of characteristics of democracy in transition. It may help perhaps in building up a conception of the peaceable "revolution" by which our democracy has, save for the tragic exception, thus far avoided the terror of violent revolution.

History can contribute nothing in the way of panaceas. But it can assist vitally in the formation of that sense of what is democratic, of what is in line with our republican traditions, which alone can save us.

ARTHUR M. SCHLESINGER, JR.

May 7, 1944
Washington, D.C.

Acknowledgments

THIS BOOK IS THE OUTGROWTH OF A series of lectures entitled "A Reinterpretation of Jacksonian Democracy" delivered at the Lowell Institute in Boston in the fall of 1941. I am profoundly indebted to my father, Arthur M. Schlesinger, for his wise counsel and keen criticism. Bernard DeVoto, Frederick Merk and my mother, Elizabeth Bancroft Schlesinger, have contributed to my understanding of the pre-Civil War period. I wish also to express my gratitude to the Society of Fellows of Harvard University, which made my researches possible, and in particular to Lawrence J. Henderson and to A. Lawrence Lowell, who greatly enriched my insight into the interplay of historical forces. Although I cannot believe they would altogether have liked my conclusions, I hope that they would have respected the methods by which they were reached. I am grateful to Charles A. Beard, who generously placed at my disposal his notes on the Jacksonian era. The librarians of the Harvard College Library, the Massachusetts Historical Society, the Library of Congress and the New York Public Library were of great assistance. My wife, Marian Cannon Schlesinger, has been a source of inestimable help and encouragement at all times.

A. M. S., JR.

Contents

I	Prologue: 1829	11
II	End of Arcadia	15
III	Keepers of the Jeffersonian Conscience	23
IV	Background for Revolution	25
V	The First Year	35
VI	The Men Around the President	39
VII	Beginnings of the Bank War	45
VIII	Veto	52
IX	Counterattack	60
X	Hard Money	67
XI	Credo of the Workingmen	75
XII	Stirrings in the Bay State	80
XIII	George Bancroft and Radicalism in Massachusetts	84
XIV	Radicalism in New York	87
XV	Rise of the Locofocos	93
XVI	The Pattern of Locofocoism	96
XVII	The Third Term	98
XVIII	Panic	104
XIX	Divorce of Bank and State	109
XX	The Southern Dilemma	115
XXI	Radicalism at High Water	118
XXII	The Whig Counterreformation	122
XXIII	1840	125
XXIV	Jacksonian Democracy as an Intellectual Movement	128
XXV	Jacksonian Democracy and the Law	134
XXVI	Jacksonian Democracy and Industrialism	138
XXVII	Jacksonian Democracy and Religion	142
XXVIII	Jacksonian Democracy and Utopia	144
XXIX	Jacksonian Democracy and Literature	145
XXX	Tyler Too	151
XXXI	Minorities and Majorities	153
XXXII	Cloud on the Horizon	156
XXXIII	Gathering of the Storm	157
XXXIV	Free Soil	160
XXXV	The Storm Approaches	162
XXXVI	"Our Federal Union . . ."	164
XXXVII	Traditions of Democracy	174

I *Prologue: 1829*

FOR THE WHITE HOUSE THE NEW YEAR BEGAN IN
gloom. The President's wife spent a sleepless and painful night,
and Mr. Adams, waking at daybreak, found the dawn overcast,
the skies heavy and sullen. He prayed briefly, then fumbled for
his Bible and turned to the Book of Psalms, reading slowly by
the yellow light of his shaded oil lamp. "Blessed *is* the man that
walketh not in the counsel of the ungodly, nor standeth in the
way of sinners, nor sitteth in the seat of the scornful." On he
read to the ultimate assurance. "For the Lord knoweth the way
of the righteous: but the way of the ungodly shall perish."

The familiar words assuaged disappointments of four years.
To an Adams, the first psalm seemed almost a personal pledge.
"It affirms that the righteous man is, and promises that he shall
be, blessed," he noted with precise gratification in his journal,
and went to his desk for his usual early-morning work. As his
pen began to scratch across the paper, the lamp, its oil low,
flared for a moment, then flickered out. Mr. Adams sat in the
gray light.

It was no year for righteous men: everywhere they sat in
darkness. Two months before, General Andrew Jackson had
been elected President of the United States. The ungodly were
now in the ascendancy, and those who walked not in their
counsels had little but Scriptures for consolation. "There is
more effrontery," Samuel Clesson Allen, retiring Congressman
from Massachusetts, had exclaimed, ". . . in putting forward a
man of his bad character—a man covered with crimes . . .
than ever was attempted before upon an intelligent people."
The good Reverend Robert Little, pastor of the Unitarian
Society of Washington, sadly chose his text: "When Christ
drew near the city he wept over it."

The retiring President put on a brave front at his last reception; but, too weary for his walks along the Potomac, he now
sought his exercise on horseback, while his wife prepared to
move from the executive mansion. The appearance of Mr.
Clay, the Secretary of State, shocked the capital. One visitor,
on a January afternoon, found the small drawing room in the
Clay house bright with lamps and blazing fire, but its inhabitants deep in melancholy. Mrs. Clay, mournfully pacing the

11

room, whispered, " He sleeps." Stretched full length on the sofa
lay Henry Clay, thin and white, covered from head to foot
with a dark cloak, which looked like "a black pall." Through
the parties of January and February he masked his dejection
under frigid smiles.

Uncertainty about the future increased the official gloom.
Mr. Webster, the distinguished Senator from Massachusetts,
scrawled a memorandum for friends at Boston:—

> Gen. J. will be here abt. 15 Feb.—
> Nobody knows what he will do when he does come. . . .
> My opinion is
> That when he comes he will bring a breeze with him.
> Which way it will blow, I cannot tell. . . .
> My *fear* is stronger than my *hope*.

                    *   *   *

From faraway states the people came to Washington—local
politicians, newspaper editors, war veterans, curiosity seekers,
enthusiasts for Jackson, and just the people. *Their* hope was
stronger than their fear.

They found a scattered, straggling city. The 91,665 feet of
brick pavement, of which the old citizens boasted, was inade-
quate to the mud of February, and the boots of the mob
slogged excitedly, patiently, wearily about the town, to snatch
at the rumors and gawk at the sights and plague the friends of
Jackson. Hospitable taverns served them endless draughts of
gin slings, gin cocktails, sherry cobblers, mint juleps, snakeroot
bitters, timber doodle and eggnog. Local theaters entertained
them with rare divertissement. Some went to the Amphitheatre
to watch George Washington Dixon, "the celebrated Buffo
Singer," first of the great black-face artists, who sang "Push-a-
Long Keep Moving" or "The Hunters of Kentucky" and soon
would delight the land with "Zip Coon" and the haunting
"Coal Black Rose," twanging his banjo and breathing out his
insistent strains. The more "high-toned" preferred bewitching
Clara Fisher at the Theatre, the girl who had won all London
before she was twelve and now, an enchanting seventeen, was
winning America. Steamboats were named after her, and race-
horses, drinks and Negro babies. Soon there would appear the
great Edwin Forrest, mightiest actor of the day, whose swell-
ing muscles and rumbling voice and heroic passion as Brutus
and Virginius thrilled the galleries in dramas of democratic
martyrdom in ancient Rome.

The crowd drifted to inspect Mr. Jefferson's library, on ex-
hibition at the auctioneer's before it went on sale to pay the
debts of his estate. It admired the elegant "Transparent Pan-

oramic View of West Point and the adjacent scenery" at the
Rotundo on the corner of Pennsylvania Avenue and Thir-
teenth Street. It peered through the celebrated solar micro-
scope. It looked with amazement on the cat with the face of
a Greek hero.

Gossip was incessant. Have you heard about Frances Wright,
of Scotland and Nashoba, Tennessee, and her alarming views
on religion and society? New York, Philadelphia and now
neighboring Baltimore quivered with indignation at her presence. And there was always the latest quip about Major Eaton
of Tennessee, and his New Year's Day bride, the notorious
Margaret O'Neale Timberlake. ("There is a vulgar saying of
some vulgar man, I believe Swift, on such unions," the ribald
New York Congressman, C. C. Cambreleng, had written to his
intimate friend Martin Van Buren, " about using a certain
household . . . and then putting it on one's head.")

If other entertainment languished, Congress was inex-
haustible: the Senate, dignified and decorous, and the House,
with members lolling back in armchairs, laughing, coughing,
spitting, rattling newspapers, while some poor speaker tried to
talk above the din. For a few there were the formal banquets,
beginning as late as five-thirty or six, with rich courses served
in quick succession—soup, bass, turkey, beef smothered in
onions, mutton, ham, pheasant, ice cream, jelly, fruit—washed
down by a steady flow of sherry, pale and brown, madeira and
champagne.

But, above all, there were the reports on the progress of
General Jackson. For one terrible day in January, Washington
had trembled at the rumor of his death, till Duff Green printed
an authoritative denial in the *United States Telegraph*, the
Jackson organ; and on February 11 the President-to-be finally
arrived. People noted him as a tall, gaunt man, his face wrin-
kled with pain and age, his thick gray hair turning snow-white.
His eyes were sad and heart empty from the recent death of
his wife, and his right hand ached from the hard grips of ad-
mirers along the way. Through the three weeks before inauguration he quietly consulted with advisers and chose his
cabinet.

The skies were clouded on the fourth of March, but the sun
broke through as General Jackson left for the Capitol, and a
soft southwest wind played over the noisy crowd awaiting him.
The old man, wearing a plain black suit and a black cravat,
stiffly delivered his inaugural address to the excited gathering.
A shrewd Kentucky newspaperman, on from Frankfort for a
job in the new government, reported the mood of the crowd.
"It was a proud day for the people," Amos Kendall wrote his

paper. "General Jackson is *their own* president." But Justice Story, John Marshall's close friend and disciple on the Supreme Court, reported another mood in accents of despair. "The reign of King 'Mob' seemed triumphant."

The friends of Mr. Adams had no monopoly on pessimism. Martin Van Buren, just resigned as Governor of New York to become Jackson's Secretary of State, made his way to the capital amidst discouraging tidings. Levi Woodbury of New Hampshire roused him from bed, late on a March night, in New York, to pour glum prophecies in his ear. At Philadelphia he had a cheerless talk with Edward Livingston and his wife, both old friends of the President. At Newcastle, Louis McLane of Delaware, who had expected a cabinet post, met his steamboat, every line of his face stamped with disappointment. Rushing to take Van Buren's arm, he harangued him over the feebleness of the administration and hinted that he had better get out before becoming involved in its wreck.

It was after dark when Van Buren reached Washington. His coach hardly arrived at the hotel before office-seekers surrounded it. They pursued him inside, flocking relentlessly into the room where he lay on a sofa, weary from the journey. The Secretary of State listened to them patiently for an hour, then dismissed them to go to the White House.

A solitary lamp shone in the vestibule, and a single candle flickered in the President's office, where the old General sat with his intimate from Tennessee, Major Lewis. Jackson was in bad health, tired, uncertain where to turn for loyalty or support. "His friends have no common principle," Daniel Webster had written back to New England, "—they are held together by no common tie." But when Van Buren entered the room, his face brightened and his eye flashed. He rose invincibly to offer his cordial greeting. Van Buren's doubts dropped away in a surge of warmth and confidence in the resolute old man.

The young republic faced its critical test. Could it survive the rule of the people? Or were Webster, Clay, Adams and the friends of Van Buren right in their anticipation of disaster?

John Randolph of Roanoke spoke a prevailing mood with wild intensity. "The country is ruined past redemption," he cried; "it is ruined in the spirit and character of the people."

Was there any hope for the future? "There is an abjectness of spirit that appals and disgusts me," he declared in despair. "Where now could we find leaders of a revolution?"

II *End of Arcadia*

THE AMERICA OF JEFFERSON HAD BEGUN TO DIS-appear before Jefferson himself had retired from the presidential chair. That paradise of small farms, each man secure on his own freehold, resting under his own vine and fig-trees, was already darkened by the shadow of impending change. For Jefferson, Utopia had cast itself in the form of a nation of husbandmen. "Those who labor in the earth," he had said, "are the chosen people of God, if ever He had a chosen people"; and the American dream required that the land be kept free from the corruptions of industrialism. "While we have land to labor then, let us never wish to see our citizens occupied at a work-bench, or twirling a distaff." Far better to send our materials to Europe for manufacture, than to bring working-men to these virgin shores, "and with them their manners and principles." "The mobs of great cities," he concluded ominous-ly, "add just so much to the support of pure government, as sores do to the strength of the human body."

BUT ACTUALITY WAS BETRAYING THE DREAM. THE "Notes on Virginia" furnished imperfect texts for the energies of a bustling nation. Jefferson's own administration became a series of notations on the doom of his Utopia. However wiser it might have been to leave the workshops in Europe, it slowly became more profitable to bring them to the materials. Jefferson himself helped nourish the serpent in his Eden with one of his favorite measures, the Embargo of 1807, which set on firm footing manufacturing establishments started experimentally along the Atlantic coast during the twenty years preceding. The War of 1812 and the British blockade further stimulated domestic manufacturers. A protective tariff followed the war, and behind its wall yet more undertakings sprang up.

The farm remained the statistical center of American life, but business enterprise was exerting stronger and stronger claims on the imagination of the people and the action of the government. The number of persons engaged in manufactures

increased 127 per cent between 1820 and 1840, while agricultural labor increased only 79 per cent. The number of city
dwellers rose similarly. In 1820 less than a twentieth of the
nation lived in communities of eight thousand or over; but two
decades later more than a twelfth lived in such places, and
more than a ninth in towns larger than two thousand.

The new economic life acquired its appropriate institutions.
The private business association was reshaped into an effective
agency of capitalist enterprise; and by its side the chartered
corporation, created by special act of the state legislature, began its rise to dominance, first in banking, then in insurance
and inland transportation, soon in manufacturing.

Paper money underwrote and stimulated the contagion of
enterprise. Banking privileges, jealously guarded in the early
days of the republic and held in deep suspicion by strict Jeffersonians, were extended liberally by state legislatures, especially
in the financial stringency during the War of 1812. Wildcat
paper may not have been the most reliable form of capital, but
the turnover was quick, expansion would take up the slack,
and what merchant, whether bankrupt or wealthy, would not
prefer a ready-flowing supply of money, however imperfect, to
a limited quantity of specie currency? The evident usefulness
and frequent profitability of state banks wiped away many of
the remaining Jeffersonian scruples. So essential did they
speedily become to the new economic fabric that an important
argument in 1816 for establishing a second Bank of the United
States was its indispensability in controlling them. In the
meantime, the nation's thrust to the westward, laying out new
fringes of settlement where money was necessary and specie
scarce, generated further demands for fluid capital.

ALEXANDER HAMILTON, THE BRILLIANT AND AM-
bitious aide of General Washington, gave the new industrialism its political philosophy. The precarious days of the Revolution had convinced him that social stability rested on the firm
alliance of government and business. No society, he believed,
could succeed "which did not unite the interest and credit of
rich individuals with those of the state." As early as 1780, he
was turning over in his mind plans which would "make it the
immediate interest of the moneyed men to co-operate with
government in its support."

To his conviction of the essential wisdom of the wealthy
classes, he added a deep skepticism as to the capacity of the
masses for self-government. "All communities," he told the
men gathered in Philadelphia to ponder a constitution for the

thirteen states, "divide themselves into the few and the many. The first are rich and well-born, the other the mass of the people. . . . The people are turbulent and changing; they seldom judge or determine right." The formula for government was simple. "Give, therefore, to the first class a distinct, permanent share in the government. They will check the unsteadiness of the second, and, as they cannot receive any advantage by a change, they therefore will ever maintain good government."

For Hamilton, then, the problem reduced itself to the invention of means which would secure to the "rich and well-born" their "distinct, permanent share in the government." He first hoped to imbed his scheme in the Constitution; but his failure in the convention taught him that the marriage of the wealthy classes and the state must come after the Constitution, and on grounds which would not shake the loyalty of the masses.

Thus he cheerfully conceded the republican frame of government, and even defended it powerfully in the *Federalist* papers. Then, as Secretary of the Treasury, he saw his chance and proposed a financial program which not only was a statesmanlike solution of pressing financial difficulties, but was brilliantly designed to give the business community its enduring stake in the government. He offered as immediate bait the assumption of the state debts and the funding system. He projected, as the keystone of a durable alliance, the Bank of the United States—a profit-making institution to be privately owned and to enjoy special access to the public funds—which, as he had earlier observed, would link "the interest of the State in an intimate connection with those of the rich individuals belonging to it." And in his celebrated Report on Manufactures he made a classic statement of the long-run possibilities for business in an alliance with the government.

The Report on Manufactures was the first great expression of the industrial vision of the American future. Astutely conceding to the Jeffersonian dream that agriculture has "intrinsically a strong claim to pre-eminence over every other kind of industry," Hamilton proposed to show that its *real* interests "will be advanced, rather than injured, by the due encouragement of manufactures." From this premise the Report marched unconquerably on to its conclusion: the plea for government protection of industry. For all its deference to Jeffersonian sensibilities, for all its silence about the political implications of this scheme to build up the business classes, the drift of the Report was unmistakable, and enterprising capitalists could hardly miss it. Though it caused no immediate action, the Report in the long run was supremely successful,

serving as an arsenal of argument and inspiration for later generations of Hamiltonians. Its progressive enactment became
the index of the rising power of the business community.

The victory of Jefferson in 1800 rebuked the comparative
candor with which Hamilton and the early Federalists had
sought to orient society around the business classes. But the
energies of industrialism were irresistible, and now they began
to work through the Republican party, giving the economic
program of Hamilton a kindlier aspect and a more ingratiating
vocabulary.

Its most persuasive champion after the War of 1812 was
Henry Clay of Kentucky, a former Jeffersonian Republican,
who reshaped it to appeal to the West, from which he had
emerged as the first great political leader. He amplified Hamilton's case for the tariff by expanding the "home market" argument with its assurance that industrialism would buy everything the farmers could raise; and he rounded out the general
program by adding to it the policy of government support of
internal improvements, which further won the West.

The various measures dovetailed neatly in a compact system, based in the large part on the debt created by Hamilton's
funding plan. The dept made the Bank indispensable as a
financial agent, and the tariff indispensable as a source of revenue. The internal-improvements policy promised a future of
steady spending which would save the debt from extinction.
And the debt itself, by its very existence, bound the government to its creditors, the business and financial groups. "A
national debt," Hamilton had written, "if it is not excessive,
will be to us a national blessing."

Henry Clay adorned the Federalist program with all the
fascination of his personality, the fire of his rhetoric and the
daring of his political management. It acquired a broad emotional significance which the colder Hamilton had never suc-
ceeding in giving it. No man in America had a greater gift for
exciting intense personal enthusiasm than Clay. A splendid
orator, with a sure understanding of the crowd, he was endowed with a magnificent and garish imagination, which
caught up and expressed the inarticulate popular feelings in
their vague longing, their vulgarity and their wonder. He made
Federalism a living vision, replacing the dry logical prose of
Hamilton with thrilling pictures of a glorious future. The blaze
of nationalism suggested a new and disarming name—the
American System—and under Clay's solicitous care, this re-
baptized Federalism slowly won its way to the inner councils
of the government.

YET THE ECONOMIC PROGRAM OF HAMILTON, WHICH Clay took over, was but part of a general social philosophy, the object of which was much less to distribute profits than power. Hamilton's distinction between the "rich and well-born" and the "mass of the people" had formulated concisely the problem of government for Federalists. While the spirit of Federalism on the national scene tended increasingly to appropriate the language, the principles and the party of Jefferson, this distinction remained very much alive within the states. The conventions to revise the state constitution provided ample evidence of its vigor in the years after the second war with Britain.

Discontent had welled up with sufficient force in three leading states to compel a scrapping of old constitutions: Massachusetts in 1820, New York in 1821, Virginia in 1829. The delegates included many of the statesmen of the day—John Adams, Daniel Webster, Joseph Story, James Kent, Martin Van Buren, John Marshall, James Madison, James Monroe, John Randolph, Benjamin Watkins Leigh, John Tyler—and their sessions gave a vivid picture of the conflicts which were unsettling the social order. In particular, the debates over property qualifications for suffrage, over religious qualifications for officeholding, and over the judiciary, placed Federalism in the full fire of the democratic attack, eliciting some of the frankest expositions of its underlying principles.

The rock on which Alexander Hamilton built his church was the deep-seated conviction that society would be governed best by an aristocracy, and that an aristocracy was based most properly and enduringly on property. Daniel Webster put the argument in its most massive form in his famous speech in the Massachusetts convention. "Power *naturally* and *necessarily* follows property," he declared; and again, "A republican form of government rests not more on political constitutions than on those laws which regulate the descent and transmission of property." "It would seem, then," he concluded, "to be the part of political wisdom to found government on property; and to establish such distribution of property, by the laws which regulate its transmission and alienation, as to interest the great majority of society in the protection of the government." "Power and property," as Benjamin Watkins Leigh observed in the Virginia convention, "may be separated for a time by force or fraud—but divorced, never. For, so soon as the pang of separation is felt, . . . property will purchase power, or power will take over property. And either way, there must be an end of free Government."

If power and property belonged together, and if they were in fact together by virtue of restricting the franchise to those who could satisfy a property qualification, the task of neo-Federalism was to prevent their separation—that is, to prevent the flight of political power from men of property.

The crucial struggle, then, centered on the extension of the vote to the propertyless masses. "The notion that every man that works a day on the road, or serves an idle hour in the militia," declared the jurist Chancellor Kent with vehemence in the New York convention, "is entitled as of right to an equal participation in the whole power of government, is most unreasonable, and has no foundation in justice." He invoked a favorite image. "Society is an association for the protection of property as well as of life, and the individual who contributes only one cent to the common stock, ought not to have the same power and influence in directing the property concerns of the partnership, as he who contributes his thousands." This was a cherished argument. "It was a principle admitted in all private corporations," another speaker pointed out triumphantly, "that all persons who have a larger share should have a larger vote. So in the community."

The implications of this principle were plain, and the tougher Federalists did not flinch from them. "As the wealth of the commercial and manufacturing classes increases," wrote Jeremiah Mason, whom Daniel Webster considered the best lawyer in the country, "in the same degree ought their political power to increase. . . . I know this aristocracy of wealth is apt to be evil spoken of. But in a country where wealth greatly abounds, I doubt whether any other foundation for a stable free government can be found."

Having justified their political supremacy by expounding the prerogatives of concentrated wealth, they justified concentrated wealth by expounding the virtues of inequality. "The diversity of poverty and riches," in the words of Peter Oxenbridge Thacher, a Boston judge and classical conservative, "is the order of Providence. . . . Why are not all the flowers of the field equally beautiful and fragrant? Why are not all the fruits of the earth equally rich and wholesome? And why," he continued, warming to the subject, "towers the oak in grandeur to heaven, while the shrub at its base is trodden under feet? Will vain regrets, and still vainer discontent change the course of nature?"

The gradation of values was clear, with honor reserved for the towering oak and vice and indolence assigned to the shrub. "The lowest orders of society ordinarily mean the poorest— and the highest, the richest," was the comfortable judgment of the *American Quarterly Review.* "Sensual excess, want of intelligence, and moral debasement, distinguished the former—

knowledge, intellectual superiority, and refined, social, and domestic affections, the latter." Property, in Federalist reflexes, became almost identified with character; and remarks like Nicholas Biddle's petulant complaint about "men with no property to assess and no character to lose" rolled easily off the tongue.

But all the logic of neo-Federalism was in vain. Inexorably, the vote passed on to the propertyless classes. And this divorce of political power from property left Federalist logic itself in a perilous position. For if, as Webster had observed, universal manhood suffrage "could not long exist in a community where there was great inequality of property," and if the states were moving constitutionally toward manhood suffrage, did it not become the obligation of faithful Websterians to strive to reduce economic inequality?

THE FEDERALIST LOGIC OF POWER THUS BECAME A casualty of history, for the neo-Federalists would move neither to redistribute their property nor to reopen the question of manhood suffrage. But they were not at all deflected from their basic purposes; and the American System, already fairly well emancipated by Clay from Hamiltonian premises, was admirably designed to continue the struggle toward Hamiltonian objectives. The aristocracy of property, moreover, attracting whatever in society bestowed prestige, could count on the authority of law and religion to buttress its influence.

At first, the Federalists had drastically underrated the power of the courts. In complete possession of the executive, they had no need of seeking power elsewhere. Even Hamilton dismissed the judiciary as "beyond comparison the weakest of the three departments." Jefferson's victory in 1800 changed the situation. Plunged in despondency, Hamilton now despaired of the Constitution and pronounced it a "frail and worthless fabric." But a more resourceful statesman appeared to take up the standard of conservatism. If the Federalists were expelled from the executive and legislative branches, at least they still had the judiciary, and John Marshall proposed to make it an impregnable fortress. The Federalist party, in Van Buren's phrase, was "conducted to the judicial department of the Government, as to an ark of future safety which the Constitution placed beyond the reach of public opinion."

Marshall proceeded brilliantly to fortify the new battle line. During the next quarter of a century, in spite of the hatred of Jefferson, the indignation of the Virginia school, the occasional raids of men like Richard M. Johnson and Martin Van Buren in the Senate, he invincibly expanded the power of the Supreme Court and indirectly the prestige of the whole judiciary. The courts promised to become a perpetual check on popular government, so long as the judges themselves were safe from the penalties of popular disapproval. A conflict thus arose in the state conventions over what was variously called the "independence" or "irresponsibility" of the judiciary. As Justice Story frankly admitted in the Massachusetts convention, "It is the minority who are interested in the independence of the judges." Backed by British traditions of a free judiciary, the Federalists succeeded pretty well in entrenching themselves in the courts.

In the same spirit they worked to preserve the English common law in all its sanctity and mystery. To their opponents, the common law seemed an infinite morass of judicial precedent which would always result practically in "judge-made" law; and it is true that in the hands of judges like Peter Oxenbridge Thacher the common law became a bottomless reservoir of reasons why no one should do anything. The democratic movement to revise and codify the laws thus produced another heated battle line.

Federalism similarly mobilized religion to support its views of society. At the very start, many conservatives, with the discreet skepticism of eighteenth-century gentlemen, considered religion indispensable to restrain the brute appetites of the lower orders but hardly necessary for the upper classes. As the polite doubts of the eighteenth century passed away, and particularly as the clergy loudly declared Jefferson's deism to be a threat, not only to themselves, but to the foundations of social order, conservatism grew more ardent in its faith. In 1802 Hamilton, seeking desperately to rejuvenate the Federalist party, suggested the formation of a Christian Constitutional Society with the twofold purpose of promoting Christianity and the Constitution.

Though Hamilton's particular scheme never came to anything, the alliance he had in mind was rapidly consummated. Religion, in exchange for protection against Jeffersonian anticlericalism, would hedge the aristocracy of wealth with divinity. To the clergy were assigned the essential functions of reconciling the lower classes to inequality and binding them to absolute obedience to the laws. "Christian morality and piety, in connexion with the intelligence of the common people," declared Calvin Colton, Episcopalian preacher, later Whig pamphleteer, great friend and official biographer of Henry Clay, "are the last hope of the American Republic, and the only adequate means of bridling and holding in salutary check that rampant freedom, which is so characteristic of the American people."

Some clergymen went very far indeed in certifying to the divine origin of Federalism. As Jonathan M. Wainwright, not yet Episcopalian bishop of New York, assured the Massachusetts legislature in 1835, religion "recognizes and sanctions the principle of inequality in the distribution of wealth amongst men . . . to be acquiesced in as a permanent condition of society." Opponents of Federalism were denounced from the pulpit as enemies of the cosmic scheme. "That there should be an inequality in the conditions of men, as there is in all the other works of providence, is clearly a wise and benevolent ordinance of heaven," said the Reverend Hubbard Winslow, who went on to point out ominously that "it was the levelling disposition, that cast down the shining angels from their starry heights"; and Winslow's friend and idol Daniel Webster did his best to read the minister's interpretation of divine intention into the laws of the land.

The support of law and religion strengthened Federalism incalculably by identifying the deepest desires of man—toward social stability and religious salvation—with a particular political order. It guaranteed Federalism, moreover, the loyalty of the only groups in the population with an authority not dependent on property. It meant that whatever there was of an aristocracy of status would surely be on the side of the aristocracy of wealth. The combination of judges, clergymen and men of property seemed invincible.

Only the defection of the Southern planters and the rise of new applicants for the aristocracy of status—generals, editors and literary men—whose claims were resisted by the old Federalism, could provide the great mass with leadership in their struggle for political power.

III *Keepers of the Jeffersonian Conscience*

THE ECONOMIC CHANGES OF THE EARLY YEARS OF THE nineteenth century, blasting the dream of an agricultural Utopia, raised up problems for government hardly contemplated by the Arcadian philosophy of Virginia. Jefferson himself, in whom keen sensitivity to national needs always overcame loyalty to abstractions, steadily revised his views on industrialism during his presidency. "As yet our manufacturers are as much at their ease, as independent and moral as our agricultural inhabitants," he exclaimed in 1805, apparently with surprise. Four years later he conceded that an equilibrium of agriculture, manufacturing and commerce had become essential to American independence. In 1813 he recanted explicitly: events "have settled my doubts." In 1816, at the first serious attempt to enact Hamilton's Report on Manufactures, Jefferson remarked contritely, "Experience has taught me that manufactures are now as necessary to our independence as to our comfort." Eight years of responsibility had made certain the triumph of the statesman over the philosopher.

IF JEFFERSON'S PRESIDENCY WAS A SET OF COMPROmises with necessity, those of his immediate successors took on the aspect almost of surrender. The War of 1812 clearly exposed the inadequacy of simple Jeffersonian solutions for complex questions either of finance or of administration. The postwar economic chaos made the government especially vulnerable to the cogent and specific demands of the business community; and Madison and Monroe, the Virginia Presidents who occupied the White House from 1809 to 1825, lacking either the will or the capacity to work out a program in terms of their own social philosophy, were forced to beat a faltering but unmistakable retreat from the original Jeffersonian positions.

The approval of the Second Bank of the United States in 1816 by the man who twenty-five years before had been the ablest opponent of the First Bank was an appropriate commentary on the breakdown of the Jeffersonian idyl. Madison went on to endorse the tariff of 1816; and then, while refusing to concede the constitutionality of internal improvements, he urged their importance and, like Jefferson himself, advised amending the Constitution in order to sanctify them. Monroe yielded still more ground.

The Federalist party itself had been largely destroyed by its resistance to the War of 1812. With Madison adopting so much of its program, revival was superfluous. Certain local vestiges of the Federalist organization were without much significance in national politics. By 1820, the bitter enmities of 1800 had dissolved into the benign atmosphere of the Era of Good Feelings. The single electoral vote dissenting to Monroe's re-election was occasioned by no more urgent a motive than personal dislike.

Four years later, in 1824, the election was indeed a contest, but it dealt much more in personalities than in issues. Henry Clay was the most outspoken champion of the American System, while John Quincy Adams was suspected of being a Federalist in sheep's clothing; William H. Crawford stood in the strict Jeffersonian school, and Andrew Jackson occupied a vague and intermediate position. But all the candidates were nominally Jeffersonian Republicans, and all were presumed pretty much to accept the drift of the decade preceding.

When no one obtained a majority of electoral votes, the choice fell to the House of Representatives. There, a union of Adams and Clay men elected Adams, and soon after Clay became Secretary of State. The avowed defenders of the American System were now in frank control of the government. The rout of the Jeffersonians was complete.

IV *Background for Revolution*

THE EIGHTEEN-TWENTIES WERE A DECADE OF DIS-content, born in depression, streaked with suffering and panic, shaken by bursts of violence and threats of rebellion. Jefferson's despondency, the intricate anxieties of John Taylor of Caroline, the furious despair of John Randolph, reflected this unrest in the moods of weary elder statesmen. But its main source was the profound frustration of thriving and vigorous classes who felt the central government to be hostile to their needs and interests. The planters of the South, the workingmen of the North, those small farmers of the North and West unconvinced by Henry Clay, could not but have grave misgivings over the workings of the American System. It seemed to them, as it was belatedly seeming to Jefferson, a betrayal of the Jeffersonian promise of equal rights in favor of special benefits for a single class.

This widespread conviction, which would by itself have caused trouble, was aggravated by local grievances. The new Western states felt their development hampered and thwarted by economic and political institutions too much under Eastern control. The new industrial pattern of life in the Northern and Middle states raised painful problems of adjustment for a people habituated to farms, ships and household manufactures. The establishment of the protective tariff exasperated the Southern planters, who regarded it as tribute levied upon them by Northern bankers and manufacturers. And the broadening of the suffrage throughout the nation gave a sense of power to classes which believed themselves denied the benefits of government. Several episodes in this stormy decade, when resentment flared up into conflict, revealed how intensely the Western farmers or Eastern workingmen or the planters felt themselves balked by the existing order, and how far they were prepared to go in transforming it.

IN THE WEST, FINANCIAL CRISES PROVOKED A SERIES of outbursts, of which the most spectacular was the Relief War in Kentucky. Banking on the frontier ran at first into Jeffersonian prejudices against moneyed monopolies. But the scarcity of money during the War of 1812, and the inflationary policies of the Second United States Bank in the first few years after 1816, caused banks to spread fairly indiscriminately through Kentucky, Tennessee and other Western states. Then, with the depression of 1819, the big Bank, reversing its policy, began a peremptory contraction. Specie flowed out of the West, leaving in its wake a trail of bankruptcies and a large debtor population unable to meet obligations.

THE IMPACT OF THE NEW INDUSTRIALISM IN THE Northern and Middle states, and particularly of the capitalist organization of what had been journeyman industries, produced another contagion of discontent. Some workingmen were disquieted by the gradual loss of ownership over their means of production, others by their separation from direct contact with the market, others by the disappearance of any feeling of social or economic equality with the moneyed groups, still others simply by the physiological strain of adjusting to new habits of work and discipline. With a class neither so relatively numerous as the Western debtors nor so intellectually confident as the Southern planters, discontent caused no comparable outbursts, leading rather to a decade of stirrings and mutterings among the laboring men.

Shut off from the rest of society, they began to develop a consciousness of class, which helped them recover a sense of human function in a social order that baffled them by its growing impersonality.

THE SOUTHERN PLANTERS, AS THE RULING CLASS IN their own section, were burdened with responsibilities which prevented them from meddling with government as casually as the poor debtors of Kentucky, or from burning Presidents in effigy, like the workingmen of Washington. Yet, they were no less anxious; and their gestures of defiance, while chiefly on an intellectual plane, would in the end threaten the Union more profoundly than all the noise and violence in the North.

THE VICTORY OF JOHN QUINCY ADAMS GAVE THE business community its last chance. If his administration could solve the urgent problems of discontent, the leadership of the commercial classes would be unchallenged, and the American System with Bank, tariff and internal improvements, remain secure.

The new President had been instructed by John C. Calhoun in the nature of the problem.

The cause of the economic collapse was clear enough— the overexpansion of the paper-money system—but the remedy? "Not discernible," he mused sadly. ". . . Government can do nothing, at least nothing by any measure yet proposed, but transfer discontents, and propitiate one class of people by disgusting another." But if discontent grew intense and fiery, might it not be necessary to "propitiate" the dissatisfied classes, even at the cost of "disgusting" the class in possession?

If Adams's diary was not clear on this point, his administration settled any doubts. When the classes to be propitiated were outside the experience of an Adams, and the class to be disgusted was his own, he could not bring himself to see any advantage in changing the original policy. For all his real abilities, Adams as President showed few evidences of statesmanship. His immobility in the face of crisis allowed the impression to harden through the land "that there was something radically wrong in the administration of the Government." His overthrow in 1828 resulted directly from his failure to meet the problem outlined by Calhoun. In his place, the people thrust forward the man whom they had made their favorite in 1824, and to whom the leaders of the fight against Adams turned after a paralytic stroke eliminated Crawford.

WHO WAS GENERAL ANDREW JACKSON, THE NEW popular favorite? To the nation he was known primarily as a military hero. In the Revolution, an English officer had slashed him with a saber for refusing to clean a pair of boots. In the War of 1812 he had shown great energy and resource in putting down some Indian uprisings, and in 1815, after the treaty of

peace had been signed, he won at New Orleans the greatest
American victory of the war. His nominal profession was the
law, and he had served in the House of Representatives and
Senate of the United States, as well as on the Tennessee Supreme Court. For the decade past, his life had been mainly that
of a Tennessee gentleman, living on a fine plantation near
Nashville, entertaining his friends, racing his horses and heat-
edly talking politics. In 1828 he was sixty-one years old.

His immense popular vote in 1824 came from his military
fame and from the widespread conviction of his integrity. His
actual politics were somewhat vague. In 1808 he had sym-
pathized with the schismatic movement of Randolph and
Macon, but in a letter to President Monroe in 1816 he recommended a policy of reconciliation with the war Federalists
(accompanied by characteristic regrets that the leaders of the
Hartford Convention had escaped hanging). Seven years later
in the Senate, his votes indicated an attitude of at least tolerance toward the American System. He favored what he called
enigmatically a "judicious" tariff in order to end dependence
on foreign nations for war materials, but at the same time he
committed himself definitely against the premises of Federalism. "I am one of those who do not believe that a national debt
is a national blessing," he said, "but rather a curse to a republic; inasmuch as it is calculated to raise around the administration a moneyed aristocracy dangerous to the liberties of the
country."

In Tennessee, he normally acted with the landholding aristocracy both against the financial aristocracy and the cane-
brake democracy. When the depression of 1819 gave Tennessee a relief system similar to Kentucky's, Jackson vainly
opposed it, not in order to protect the banks, but on the correct
conviction that inflation would not solve the problems of the
debtors. Yet he also supported a dubious adventure which
would have despoiled many small farmers of their lands for
the benefit of the speculators. His experience neither in national
nor in state politics afforded any clear indication of what could
be expected from him once in power.

Nor could much be inferred from the nature of his backing
in 1824. Persons of every political faith endorsed him, including even many former Federalists who never forgave John
Quincy Adams for deserting the party; and he was specifically
opposed by the guardians of Virginia orthodoxy. Jefferson
himself is supposed to have told Daniel Webster, "He is one of
the most unfit men I know of for such a place. . . . he is a

dangerous man."* John Taylor (who rather desperately favored Adams) and James Madison shared this mistrust. Martin Van Buren, the chief Crawford manager in 1824, brought the Virginians timidly into the Jackson fold by 1828. There they remained in constant fear of his indiscretion. According to Van Buren, Thomas Ritchie of the *Richmond Enquirer* "scarcely ever went to bed . . . without apprehension that he would wake up to hear of some *coup d'état* by the General."

Jackson did indeed bear the reputation of being intemperate, arbitrary and ambitious for power. As a general he had tended to do necessary things with great expedition and to inquire afterward into their legality. His political opponents, building ardently upon incidents of his military past, managed almost to read into the records of history a legend of his rude violence and uncontrolled irascibility.

In the republic's early years, martial reputation had counted little for future political success. But the broadening of the suffrage, the thrill of surging nationalism and the declining glamour of the old ruling class created a favorable atmosphere for new idols, and the War of 1812 promptly produced the military hero. The old aristocracy resented such vulgar and *parvenu* prestige, and a man with Jackson's credentials was almost forced into the opposition. Moreover, while the newly enfranchised and chauvinistic masses regarded the military hero with wild enthusiasm, to the old aristocracy, raised on classical analogies, no figure could seem more dangerous to the republic. The warnings of Cicero and the example of Caesar supplied ample documentation for their worst misgivings. This background, in addition to Jackson's own record, accounted for the singular consternation which greeted his candidacy.

Yet, in actual fact, virtually all the direct testimony agrees in describing the Jackson of these later years as a man of great urbanity and distinction of manner. His presence in Washington as Senator in the winter of 1823-1824 did much to dispel the impression that he was some kind of border savage. As the elegant wife of the editor of the *National Intelligencer* put it, the General "appears to possess quite as much *suaviter in modo* as *fortiter in re*." Even Daniel Webster, later to become a sedulous promoter of the Jackson legend, commented in

---

*Webster, *Private Correspondence*, Fletcher Webster, ed., I, 371, Cf. also George Ticknor to George Bancroft, December 26, 1824, Bancroft Papers: Mr. Jefferson "expressed his unwillingness to see Genl. Jackson in the chair of state, as decidedly as any New-Englander of us all." When Monroe asked Jefferson whether it would be a good idea to appoint Jackson to the Russian mission, Jefferson burst out, "Why, good God! He would breed you a quarrel before he had been there a month!" Adams, *Memoirs*, IV, 76.

On the other hand, it is fair to state that Webster's original notes of his conversation with Jefferson, which Senator Hoar republished with the flat comment that Webster's record of the talk was "published in full from these *memo-*

1824, "General Jackson's manners are more presidential than those of any of the candidates. . . . My wife is for him decidedly." *

Tall and thin, his white hair pushed straight back from his forehead, his long face reamed with wrinkles, his eyes sharp and commanding, Jackson was a noble and impressive figure. On foot, with firm military step, compressed lips and resolute expression, or on horseback, where his seat was excellent, his hand light and his carriage easy, he had a natural grandeur which few could resist. Many in this bitter day shared the emotions of the conservative Boston merchant who watched out of his window to catch a glimpse of the old General, "regarding him very much as he might have done some dangerous monster which was being led captive past his house." When Jackson finally appeared, his hatred abruptly collapsed. Exclaiming, "Do some one come here and salute the old man!" he thrust his small daughter forward to wave her handkerchief. Jackson, as Josiah Quincy said, "wrought a mysterious charm upon old and young."†

By 1829 he was technically a sick man—many thought dying. His head throbbed with splitting pains apparently produced by years of tobacco chewing, and his lean frame shook with a hacking consumptive cough. Yet, while his face grew whiter and more haggard, his spirit was grim and indomitable.

At White House receptions he remained urbane, though reserved and somewhat formal. Among his intimates he cast off his gravity, becoming sociable and sympathetic. He smoked with fierce energy, usually an old Powhatan bowl pipe with a long stem which rested on his crossed legs, while he puffed out great white clouds until the whole room was "so obfuscated that one could hardly breathe." Or, after the Tennessee cus-

---

randa," do not include any mention of Jefferson's attack on Jackson; and Webster failed to make public his account of the conversation till after Jefferson's death, when it served his political purpose. George F. Hoar, "Daniel Webster," *Scribner's Magazine*, XXVI, 215 (August, 1899). Professor Bassett points out that Webster's statement is hard to reconcile with the tone and content of Jefferson's letter to Jackson of December 18, 1823. Bassett, *Jackson*, 329.

* Letter of Sarah Gales Seaton, December, 1823. She continues, "He is, indeed, a polished and perfect courtier in female society, and polite to all." *William Winston Seaton*, 161. Webster's comment appeared in a letter to Ezekiel Webster, February 22, 1824, Webster, *Private Correspondence*, I, 346. Cf. the remarks of Elijah H. Mills, an old Massachusetts Federalist, in a letter to his wife, January 22, 1824, *Proceedings of the Massachusetts Historical Society*, XIX, 40-41: "He was considered extremely rash and inconsiderate, tyrannical and despotic, in his principles. A personal acquaintance with him has convinced many who held these opinions that they were unfounded. He is very mild and amiable in his disposition, of great benevolence, and his manners, though formed in the wilds of the West, exceedingly polished and polite. Everybody that knows him loves him, and he is exactly the man with whom *you* would be delighted."

† The merchant was Daniel P. Parker; Josiah Quincy, *Figures of the Past*, 363. This essay contains an attractive account of Quincy's own surrender to Jackson's magnetism.

tom, he would chew and spit at regular intervals, while carrying on conversation or even conducting the affairs of state.

He spoke quickly and forcibly, often emphasizing his points
by raising a clenched hand in a brief, sharp gesture. "He obviously had a hidden vein of humor," reported Henry A. Wise,
for many years a bitter foe, "loved aphorism, and could polite-
ly convey a sense of smart travesty. If put upon his mettle, he
was very positive, but gravely respectful." When his mind was
made up, he would draw down the left corner of his mouth,
giving his face, as one observer noted, "a peculiar 'G—d damn
me' expression."

But he was not particularly dogmatic. Though accustomed
to maintain his own position with pertinacity, he yielded gracefully when convinced of his error. No man, as Benton said,
knew better the difference between firmness and obstinacy.
"Of all the Presidents who have done me the honor to listen
to my opinions, there was no one to whom I spoke with more
confidence when I felt myself strongly to be in the right." The
testimony on this point is fairly conclusive. "I never knew a
man," commented Van Buren, "more free from conceit, or one
to whom it was to a greater extent a pleasure, as well as a
recognized duty, to listen patiently to what might be said to
him upon any subject. . . . Akin to his disposition in this
regard was his readiness to acknowledge error."

In fact, far from exacting uniformity of opinion, Jackson so
indulged disagreement that he exasperated his more radical
followers, like Amos Kendall and Roger B. Taney. "If he be
censurable on this score," wrote Kendall, "it is for too much
forbearance." "Frank himself (perhaps almost to a fault in a
public man)," observed Taney, "he loved frankness in others;
and regarded opposition to his opinions, by one who held office
under him, as evidence of firmness as well as of honesty of
purpose."

In his military campaigns he would consult his council of
war, but never submit a question to vote. Similarly as President, he would open up problems to the full discussion of the
cabinet; but when the moment for action came, he always
made up his own mind. "I have accustomed myself to receive
with respect the opinions of others," he explained, "but always
take the responsibility of deciding for myself." Once his mind
was made up, no threats, no warnings of catastrophe, no dic-
tates of prudence, could sway him. "I care nothing about
clamors, sir, mark me! I do precisely what I think just and
right."

So superb a self-sufficiency could be effective only when
matched by an equally superb self-control. Again contrary to

the Jackson myth, there was small basis for the picture of uncontrolled irascibility. Jackson, who knew his reputation, never hesitated to exploit it. "He would sometimes extemporize a fit of passion in order to overwhelm an adversary, when certain of being in the right," said one observer, "but his self-command was always perfect." His towering rages were actually ways of avoiding futile argument. To committees which called on him to protest his financial policy, he would fly into vehement denunciations of the moneyed monopoly. When they left in disgust, he would coolly light his pipe and, chuckling "They thought I was mad," remark blandly on the importance of never compromising vital issues; one always lost friends and never appeased enemies.

Once Van Buren, before he knew Jackson well, watched with disapproval while he stormed before a delegation. As soon as the door was closed behind them, Jackson commented mildly, "I saw that my remarks disturbed you." Van Buren admitted that they had. "No, my friend," his chief replied, "I have great respect for your judgment, but you do not understand these gentlemen as well as I do"; and the sequel vindicated Jackson. "This was but one of numerous instances," Van Buren wrote later, "in which I observed a similar contradiction between his apparent undue excitement and his real coolness and self-possession in which, I may say with truth, he was seldom if ever wanting." Amos Kendall reported flatly, "I never saw him in a passion." N. P. Trist, his private secretary, was equally emphatic: "I never witnessed any thing of the sort."

Jackson's intelligence expressed itself in judgment rather than in analysis. "He had vigorous thoughts," as Benton put it, "but not the faculty of arranging them in a regular composition." "Possessed of a mind that was ever dealing with the substance of things," said Van Buren, "he was not very careful in regard to the precise terms." "He had never studied the niceties of language," said Taney, "—and disliked what he was apt to regard as mere verbal criticisms." He certainly could never have written Benton's erudite discourses, or Van Buren's thoughtful recollections, or the masterly arguments of Taney, or the treatises of Edward Livingston, or the polemics of Amos Kendall. Yet he dominated them all.

In after years, the friends of Jackson wrestled with the problem of what gave his judgment a specific gravity which exposed their facile verbalizations or quick syllogisms and far outran their logical analysis. ("Beware of your metaphysics," Jackson would exclaim. ". . . Hair-splitting is dangerous business.") "The character of his mind," remarked Benton, "was that of judgment, with a rapid and almost intuitive perception, followed by an instant and decisive action." "General Jackson is the most rapid reasoner I have ever met with," declared Louis McLane. "He jumps to a conclusion before I can start on my premises." "He was indeed an extraordinary man," wrote the author James Kirke Paulding; "the only man I ever saw that excited my admiration to the pitch of wonder. To him knowledge seemed entirely unnecessary. He saw intuitively into everything, and reached a conclusion by a short cut while others were beating the bush for the game."

One hot Sunday evening in July of 1858, while the Italian sun lingered over the house tops of Florence, two Americans discovered a mutual reverence for Jackson. Nathaniel Hawthorne had seen him but once, in 1833, when the old General visited Salem. The haunted young recluse had walked to the edge of town to catch a glimpse of the Old Hero. He never forgot the grim, majestic visage. Years later, when he saw Raphael's painting of Pope Julius II, "the best portrait in the whole world," his instant wish was that Raphael could have painted General Jackson.

Hiram Powers, the famous sculptor, had met Jackson and talked to him. "He thinks," Hawthorne reported, "that General Jackson was a man of the keenest and surest intuitions, in respect to men and measures, but with no power of reasoning out his conclusions, or of imparting them intellectually to other persons." Hawthorne mused over what others, Franklin Pierce and James Buchanan, had told him about Jackson. "Men who have known Jackson intimately, and in great affairs, would not agree as to this intellectual and argumentative deficiency, though they would fully allow this intuitive faculty." His conclusion was positive: "Surely he was a great man, and his native strength, as well of intellect as of character, compelled every man to be his tool that came within his reach; and the more cunning the individual might be, it served only to make him the sharper tool." *

Yet, as Jackson paused on the threshold of achievement in 1829, no one could have predicted that crisis would transform him into greatness. The challenge of events, the responsibilities of leadership, the stimulus of popular confidence, the intuitive grasp of the necessities of change: these shaped the man and

* Hawthorne thought that Powers's assertion would be inherently plausible, "were there not such strong evidence to the contrary. The highest, or perhaps any high administrative ability, is intuitive, and precedes argument, and rises above it. It is a revelation of the very thing to be done, and its propriety and necessity are felt so strongly that very likely it cannot be talked about; if the doer can likewise talk, it is an additional and gratuitous faculty, as little to be expected as that a poet should be able to write an explanatory criticism on his own poem." "French and Italian Note-books." *Writings of Nathaniel Hawthorne* (Manse Edition), XXII, 158-160.

drew out his finest possibilities. Like Washington, Lincoln, Wilson, Franklin Roosevelt, he gave small promise in his earlier career of the abilities he was to exhibit as Chief Magistrate. All were educated by the urgencies of the moment.*

Jackson grew visibly from the day of his inauguration. His leadership gained steadily in confidence and imagination. He grew stronger after every contact with the people. In last analysis, there lay the secret of his strength: his deep natural understanding of the people. "They were his blood relations," said Van Buren, "—the only blood relations he had." He believed that "to labour for the good of the masses was a special mission assigned to him by his Creator and no man was ever better disposed to work in his vocation in season and out of season." The people called him, and he came, like the great folk heroes, to lead them out of captivity and bondage.†

* Van Buren perhaps had Jackson in mind when he described the process: "that which similar crises in all countries and times, have brought about, namely, the production of great men by great events, developing and calling into action upon a large scale intellects the power of which, but for their application to great transactions, might have remained unknown alike to their possessors and to the world." Van Buren, *Political Parties,* 171-172.

† Few modern historians hold to the Whig-Republican legend of Jackson in its literal form, but there is a visible tendency to revive it in somewhat more sophisticated version, led especially by Professor T. P. Abernethy in an article, "Andrew Jackson and the Rise of Southwestern Democracy," *American Historical Review,* XXXIII, 64-77, in his excellent book, *From Frontier to Plantation in Tennessee,* and in his sketch of Jackson in the *Dictionary of American Biography,* IX, 526-534.
 Professor Abernethy's thesis seems to be that Jackson, not having been a great democratic leader in Tennessee politics, could not therefore have been a genuine champion of the people, but was an unprincipled opportunist, who happened through a set of accidents to head a democratic movement. Jackson was basically a conservative, Abernethy argues, but he and his backers "had no very strong convictions and were willing to make friends with the times. It is not the greatest men who go to the top in politics." (This aside is typical of the animus against Jackson which runs through Professor Abernethy's work.) "Not only was Jackson not a consistent politican, he was not even a real leader of democracy . . . he always believed in making the public serve the ends of the politicians. Democracy was good talk with which to win the favor of the people and thereby accomplish ulterior objectives. Jackson never really championed the cause of the people." (*From Frontier to Plantation,* 241, 248, 249; *passim,* especially chapter iv.) "No historian has ever accused Jackson, the great Democrat, of having had a political philosophy. It is hard to see that he even had any political principles. . . . He thought he was sincere when he spoke to the people, yet he never really championed their cause. He merely encouraged them to champion his." (*American Historical Review,* XXXIII, 76-77.) "He had little understanding of the democratic movement which bears his name and he came to support it primarily because it supported him." (*Dictionary of American Biography,* IX, 534.)
 The point about Professor Abernethy's thesis is that this conclusion is one to be established by evidence, not by deductive logic. A judgment on the character of Jackson's democracy must be founded on an examination of what Jackson did as President, and on nothing else; certainly not on an extrapolation made on the basis of his career before he became President.
 No amount of inference based on what Jackson was like before 1828 can be a substitute for the facts after 1828. Yet Abernethy's own published work was concerned almost exclusively with Jackson in Tennessee. His bias is sufficiently betrayed by the odd and otherwise baffling proportions of his article in the *Dictionary of American Biography,* which devotes over two thirds of its space to Jackson before he became President. If Abernethy were to use the same method on Lincoln, or Wilson, or Franklin Roosevelt—that is, to dogmatize on their presidencies on the basis of their pre-presidential records—his results would be self-evidently absurd.

V The First Year

THE SHOUTING CROWD ON INAUGURATION DAY, DANIEL Webster noted sarcastically, really seemed to think "the country is rescued from some dreadful danger." Yet where was this danger? It was clear that Jackson had an impressive mandate, but it was not so clear what the mandate was for. Through the land, an excitement for change had welled up from profound frustration. But its concrete expressions were only slogans, epithets, meaningless phrases, the shout of crowds—not issues, programs, policies.

THE NEW PRESIDENT'S SUPPORTERS IN CONGRESS HAD conspicuously failed to develop measures to meet the discontents which had toppled the previous administration. The campaign had reflected its shallowness. Hardly an issue of policy figured in the canvass, and, when Jackson triumphed, no one could be certain that his administration would not duplicate that of Madison or Monroe or even of Adams.

As for the new President, he was not only tired, sick and depressed by grief, but politically inexperienced. The problems he faced were new to him; and for a man who learned by dealing with actualities rather than by intellectual analysis this was a serious handicap. He had to feel his way and let things seep in before he could move with decision. In the meantime the demand for "reform" had to be met. The common man, too long thwarted by official indifference, had to be given a sense that the government was in truth the people's government. Jackson's answer was shrewd and swift: a redistribution of federal offices.

This measure served obvious political needs. It adapted to national purposes methods of political reward, long employed in some of the states, and became an invaluable means of unifying administration support.

But, while helping to build the party, the spoils system also contributed to the main objective of helping restore faith in the government. In the eyes of the people, the bureaucracy had been corrupted by its vested interests in its own power.

The doctrine of rotation-in-office was thus in large part conceived as a sincere measure of reform. The spoils system, whatever its faults, at least destroyed peaceably the monopoly of offices by a class which could not govern, and brought to power a fresh and alert group which had the energy to meet the needs of the day.

Until recent years, the study of the spoils system has been marred by a tendency to substitute moral disapproval for an understanding of causes and necessities. There can be small doubt today that, whatever evils it brought into American life, its historical function was to narrow the gap between the people and the government—to expand popular participation in the workings of democracy. For Jackson it was an essential step in the gradual formulation of a program for democratic America.

As THE JACKSON ADMINISTRATION MOVED THROUGH its first year, two hostile factions began to emerge within the party, one pressing Vice-President John C. Calhoun's claims for the presidency in 1832, the other supporting Martin Van Buren, the Secretary of State.

Van Buren had been born forty-six years before at Kinderhook, a small village of old New York, the son of a farmer and tavern-keeper of Dutch stock. After scant schooling, he entered a law office at the age of fourteen. For six years, in between sweeping the floor, lighting fires in winter and copying legal papers, he pored over law books and prepared himself for a career at the bar. Successful in practice, he soon went into politics, where his talents for intrigue and leadership won him rapid promotion. He played a dominant role in the state constitutional convention of 1821 and the same year he was sent to the Senate. There he remained until elected Governor in 1828, from which office Jackson called him to the State Department.

In public office Van Buren pursued a steady Jeffersonian policy. He was one of the first in the nation to introduce bills against imprisonment for debt. He marshaled the liberal forces in the New York constitutional convention and delivered the most crushing reply to the neo-Federalist arguments of Chancellor Kent on the question of the suffrage. In the United States Senate he continued his fight against debt imprisonment, opposed federal expenditures for internal improvements, favored settlement of the Western lands and led the assault on the Supreme Court.

He spent his brief term as Governor mainly in an attack on the banking problem, proposing to protect the public "and more particularly the laboring classes" from losses through the reckless issue of paper money and, at the same time, to move toward the abolition of the state banking monopoly. As early as 1817, he had recommended a law to end the system of special charters and throw banking open to general competition, but this measure was ahead of its time even in 1829. The chief result of his three-month term was the so-called safety-fund plan. Since the chartered banks enjoyed the exclusive and highly profitable privilege of issuing paper money, the statute sought to guarantee the soundness of their currency by requiring each institution to contribute a proportion of its capital to a general fund, which could be drawn upon to redeem the notes of any bank becoming insolvent. A board of commissioners was to supervise banking operations. Though essentially a stopgap system, the safety-fund plan brought banks much more under state control and distinctly improved the condition of the currency.

Yet the fact remains that, in spite of his known convictions and his record of forceful leadership, Van Buren enjoyed a name for noncommittalism that survived when most other things about him were forgotten. His nicknames—the Little Magician, the American Talleyrand, the Red Fox of Kinderhook—suggest his popular reputation. They were certainly confirmed by the almost systematic obscurity of some of his public utterances. Once he had reached a decision, his stand would probably be unequivocal and aggressive; but in the course of a long political career he encountered many questions on which he had not yet made up his mind. For these contingencies he became the master of an enormously complicated and diffuse style, which enabled him to say many intelligent things for and against a policy without conveying a very clear idea of his own sentiments. "Mr. Knower! that was a very able speech!" an Albany wool buyer exclaimed to a friend after hearing Van Buren explain his views on the tariff in 1827. "Yes, very able!" was the answer. "Mr. Knower!" said the wool buyer, after a considerable pause, "on what side of the Tariff question was it?"

Intellectually he suffered from a surprising sense of inferiority. His writings reveal an acute and reflective mind, shrewd in judging men and analyzing events. William Cullen Bryant was much impressed that Van Buren could "so steadily command resources beyond the occupations in which so large a part of his life had been engaged." His legal ability prompted John Quincy Adams to urge his appointment to the Supreme Court; and the veteran Federalist, Rufus King, agreed that no man was "better qualified for a high and difficult judicial station." Yet, Van Buren always felt the lack of college training "to sustain me in my conflicts with able and better educated men." "My mind might have lost a portion of its vivacity, in

the plodding habits formed by such a course," he wrote, "but
it could not have failed to acquire in the elements of strength
supplied by a good education much more than it lost."

He sought reassurance in many ways. He carefully prac-
tised intellectual humility. "Whatever weaknesses I may be
subject to,—and doubtless they are numerous,—dogmatism,
I am very sure, is not one of them." He cultivated the com-
panionship of intellectuals and men of letters. Bryant was for
some years a close friend, Washington Irving another. He
numbered Frances Wright and Robert Dale Owen among his
acquaintances. As President he gave government posts to
Hawthorne, George Bancroft, J. K. Paulding, Orestes A.
Brownson and William Leggett.

His lack of intellectual confidence made him tame and un-
original as a political thinker. A pious Jeffersonian, he rarely
ventured to do more than annotate the gospel. His posthumous
work on political parties is a classic of Virginia fundamental-
ism. He took the strict-construction dogma much more seriously than Jackson himself, or most others of the inner
circle. He more than once counseled new kinds of governmental action, but he justified them always in terms of the
sacred texts.

    YET, FOR ALL HIS RELUCTANCE TO ABANDON DOGMA,
Van Buren was fertile in introducing new methods. Endowed
with practical political intuitions of the highest order, he was
the first national leader really to take advantage of the growing
demand of the people for more active participation in the decisions of government. Political bosses had existed before Van
Buren, and he invented no important technical device of party
organization. Yet his management of the Albany Regency, as
his own group was called, raised the methods of Aaron Burr
in New York, the Essex Junto in Massachusetts, the Richmond
Junto in Virginia, to a new efficiency; and his own career,
especially after the lessons taught him by the outcry against the
caucus system in 1824, was based on a thorough understanding of the importance of the press, city machines, county committees, nominating conventions, stump speaking, monster
mass meetings and all other expedients reaching out to the
people.

The growing importance of the common man was accompanied by a declining importance of Congress. The function of
the legislature was now rather to elicit, register and influence
public opinion than to assert its independent will. The great
party leader was no longer the eloquent parliamentary orator,

whose fine periods could sweep his colleagues into supporting his measures, but the popular hero, capable of bidding directly for the confidence of the masses. Van Buren thought Voltairean conceptions of politics fatally underestimated the power of public opinion. "Those who have wrought great changes in the world," he wrote, "never succeeded by gaining over chiefs; but always by exciting the multitude. The first is the resource of intrigue and produces only secondary results, the second is the resort of genius and transforms the face of the universe."*

Van Buren's point was fully borne out by the party struggles of the thirties. The two greatest orators of the day, Webster and Clay, were almost invariably on the losing side.

Van Buren's understanding of the new functions of public opinion, as well as of Congress, furnished the practical mechanisms which transformed Jackson's extraordinary popularity into the instruments of power. Most of the devices he developed to increase governmental responsiveness to the popular will could become devices for frustrating the popular will. Yet without them the gains of Jacksonian democracy would have been impossible.

VI *The Men Around the President*

THE BATTLE AGAINST THE AMERICAN SYSTEM WAS RELYing increasingly on the political and intellectual resources of the Jeffersonian tradition; the break with Calhoun in 1830-31 made certain that Jackson's interpretation of the Jeffersonian heritage would not stem from men for whom Jeffersonianism was hardening into a sectional philosophy. In the later writings of Virginia, deep solicitude for slavery had diluted the old republican faith in liberty and equality; and, with Calhoun, the State-rights strain was growing to a degree that threatened to smother the democratic strain. While this Southern version opposed the American System with all vigor, it hardly did so for the benefit of the common man. Now it had lost its power in the administration. The men who remained stood for a different reading of the Jeffersonian creed. Inspired by the democratic, rather than by the sectional, utterances of Taylor, Ran-

---

* The new leader, Van Buren went on, would never make "overtures to leaders to gain over parties," but would win over "the mass of the parties that he might be in a situation to displace the leaders." Notebook, Van Buren Papers.

dolph and Macon, they conceived of Jeffersonianism in terms of equality rather than of provincial security.

IF THE JACKSONIAN DRIVE WERE TO CONTINUE, THE President required followers who would keep fighting on the economic front.

The President needed men who shared fully his deepening belief that the economic problem, the balance of class power, overshadowed all other questions of the day. There were such men. In the Senate, he could rely on Thomas Hart Benton of Missouri. A native of North Carolina, Benton had moved West as a young man, first to Tennessee, where he and Jackson had mixed in an angry frontier brawl, then to Missouri. In 1820 he entered the Senate, and four years later he and Jackson were reconciled.

IN THE HOUSE, JACKSON COULD COUNT ON THE UN-faltering support of a young friend from Tennessee, James K. Polk. Like Benton, a native of North Carolina, Polk had attended the University of North Carolina, moved West and in 1820 settled as a lawyer in Columbia, Tennessee. Five years later he was elected to Congress. Only thirty-four years old in 1830, he was already a leading figure in the House.

C. C. Cambreleng, the crony of Van Buren and Representative from the city of New York, gave Polk active support. Another North Carolinian, now in his early forties, Cambreleng had left school at the age of twelve, gone to New York at sixteen and entered a highly successful business career. In 1821 he drifted into politics, probably with the encouragement of Van Buren, and won a seat in Congress.

Cambreleng had great influence in the House. A small man, inclining toward portliness, alert in expression, friendly in manner, he would be in his seat early, deep in perusal of a huge mass of documents, or tirelessly answering letters from constituents. When the Speaker called the House to order, he would apply a double quizzing glass to his eye, gaze around the hall and then return to work. Though always seemingly immersed in his papers, he was ever ready to leap to his feet for the heated exchanges which frequently enlivened the House. He excelled on economic questions—his Report from the Commerce and Navigation Committee in 1830 was an early classic of American free-trade literature—but he spoke on all issues of human liberty. His rebuke of Edward Everett's gratuitous defense of slavery in 1826—the handsome New Englander, ex-minister, ex-college professor, had announced,

"There is no cause in which I would sooner buckle a knapsack on my back and put a musket on my shoulder than that of putting down a servile insurrection at the South"—was not soon forgotten.

THE CABINET AS REORGANIZED IN 1831 SHOULD HAVE provided further aid for the common cause, but political necessities and Jackson's own amiability intervened. The new set of ministers turned out to be only slightly more concerned with executing the presidential policy than the old.

The Secretary of State, Jackson's old friend, Edward Livingston, of Louisiana, was a charming, scholarly gentleman, devoted to literature, historical research, legal reform and his lovely wife, but without much interest in broad social questions or much zest for controversy.

Louis McLane, the Secretary of the Treasury, was a bold, ambitious man of Federalist antecedents who was aiming systematically for the presidency.

Lewis Cass, Secretary of War, a lazy, dark-faced man, almost fifty years old, had been Governor of the Michigan Territory. Jackson and Taney provided almost identical testimony on his main weakness. "It is hard for him to say no," remarked the President, "and he thinks all men honest."

Levi Woodbury, Secretary of the Navy, was a truly noncommittal man beside whom even Van Buren might seem a chatterbox. A person of strong and shrewd mind, he undoubtedly held definite ideas of his own; but he was singularly wary, never committing himself to a position upon which he was not immediately obliged to act, and then never further than that action required.

Roger D. Taney, Attorney General, was the spearhead of radicalism in the new cabinet. A Maryland lawyer, fifty-four years old in 1831, he had once, like McLane, been a Federalist; but he left the party during the War of 1812 and by 1824 was a Jackson leader in Maryland. A tall, sharp-faced man, with nearsighted eyes, a large mouth and irregular yellow teeth, generally clamped on a long black cigar, he made a bad first impression. He was ordinarily dressed in ill-fitting black clothes; and his voice, still bearing traces of an impediment, was flat and hollow. But people soon forgot his appearance. He would speak in low tones, sincerely and without gestures, relying on the lucidity of the argument and his own quiet conviction. His performances before the Supreme Court impressed both Marshall and Story, and his appointment as Attorney General was widely applauded.

While not a dominating personality, like McLane, Taney was a man of unshakable determination. His experience as a lawyer had deepened his feelings against the unnecessary concentration of power in the hands of the business community; and from the first, the radicals, somewhat to their surprise, found him their spokesman in the inner council. Cambreleng wrote to Van Buren early in 1832 that Taney was "the only efficient man of sound principles in the Cabinet."

William T. Barry, Postmaster General, alone survived the reorganization, largely because neither he nor his position was considered important. He had shown his radical leanings in the Kentucky Relief War; but he lacked both firmness and intellectual conviction.

The cabinet, then, promised Jackson highly uncertain support for a radical program. Far from being an effective instrument of the executive, it was a group of squabbling men, some in basic disagreement with the President, and one at least intent on defeating his policy.

It should be remembered, too, that the conception of the function of the cabinet was in process of change. Washington, thinking of the cabinet as a council for reconciling antagonistic interests, had appointed a Jefferson to one post and a Hamilton to another. John Quincy Adams retained somewhat this conception as late as 1825, when he considered inviting his defeated opponents into his official family. Under Jackson the cabinet was in transition, and the debate over the dismissal of Duane in 1833 would show the confusion of ideas; but the imperatives of the party system were slowly requiring the cabinet to be an efficient arm of the executive.

THE DRIVING ENERGY OF JACKSONIAN DEMOCRACY, like that of any aggressive reform movement, came from a small group of men, joined together by essential sympathies in a concerted attempt to transform the existing order. Communion among these men was frank and free, and the men themselves were utterly loyal to the cause. Few nationally known politicians, available for cabinet posts, could meet the necessary standards of selflessness and candor. As a result, Jackson had to turn away from his cabinet for his most confidential counsel to men more basically dissatisfied with the existing order. There thus sprang into existence the celebrated Kitchen Cabinet, "an influence, at Washington," as one member of the official cabinet ominously described it, "unknown to the constitution and to the country."

Such an influence naturally drew to a considerable degree on rising social groups as yet denied the prestige to which they felt their power and energies entitled them. One such class was, of course, that of the military hero, of which Jackson himself was the outstanding example. Another consisted of the literary man in general and of the newspaperman in particular. The journalist had hitherto been indulgently accepted as the friend or servant of the governing class, but never as an equal. William Cullen Bryant wryly described the attitude toward his profession: "Contempt is too harsh a word for it, perhaps, but it is far below respect."

The two leading members of the Kitchen Cabinet, both ex-newspapermen, were Amos Kendall and Francis Preston Blair. Kendall was born in 1789 on a barren farm at Dunstable, Massachusetts.

After Dartmouth Kendall went to Groton where he taught in the Academy and studied law. At the age of twenty-five he emigrated to Kentucky. Kendall plunged into Kentucky journalism with celerity, quickly adapting himself to its rugged ways. At one period, as editor of the *Argus of Western America* at Frankfort, he had to carry a dirk, at another a pistol, and he always made his pen do the service of both. His trenchant intelligence, his honesty and pertinacity, his facility both at lofty exhortation and at coarse invective, quickly made the *Argus* the best paper in the state and soon one of the most influential in the West.

In the Kentucky struggle over banking, Kendall at first opposed the relief measures, considering that salvation for the lower classes lay in the direction of hard money rather than inflation. But with Richard M. Johnson and W. T. Barry, another of his patrons, leading the Relief party, and the issue so formulated as to make an alliance with the aristocracy the only alternative, Kendall had small choice but to support their program. Eventually he became a director of the Commonwealth Bank and later claimed to have been responsible for restraining its policy of note issue.

Jackson's election gave Kendall his great opportunity to leave Kentucky. Van Buren remarked, "Kendall is to be an influential man. I wish the President would invite him to dinner." Kendall was not only invited, but soon received appointment as fourth auditor of the Treasury. There he went conscientiously to work and discovered large frauds in the accounts of his predecessor, Tobias Watkins, a close friend of John Quincy Adams. This feat, which gave the spoils system a temporary odor of sanctity, especially endeared him to the President.

Blair, a native-born Virginian taken to Kentucky as a child, was thirty-nine years old in 1830. Like Kendall, Blair supported Clay in 1824, but the Relief War drove a wedge between them, and Blair drifted to his more natural alliance with the Jackson party. "I never deserted your banner," he told Clay, "until the questions on which you and I so frequently differed in private discussion—(State rights, the Bank, the power of the Judiciary, &c.)—became the criterions to distinguish the parties." He was a fiery pamphleteer during the Relief War, entering the lists with much more enthusiasm than Kendall, becoming Clerk of the New Court and later president of the Commonwealth Bank. After Kendall's departure he was the logical man to edit the *Argus*.

Though Van Buren's friends had been suspicious of Duff Green since 1828, the initiative toward a new press was taken mainly by the Kentucky group. Kendall seems to have broached the subject to Blair in July, 1830. Blair, who was $40,000 in debt, required certain preliminary financial arrangements, which Kendall took care of, and late in the year Blair was called to Washington. The inner circle anxiously awaited this new champion, who was to chastise Duff Green, whittle down Calhoun and defend the administration.

The first number of the *Washington Globe,* as it was called, came out in December.

Blair was profoundly impressed with the President. "I can tell you that he is as much superior here as he was with our generals during the war," he wrote after a few months. Jackson on his part warmed to Blair as he had to Van Buren and Kendall. "Give it to Blair," he would say when he wanted to reach the public (he pronounced it *Blar*), and Blair would convert the President's suggestions into fighting editorials, ordinarily penciled on scraps of paper held on his knee, sometimes at such furious speed that two boys were kept busy carrying copy to the typesetters.

Like Kendall, Blair went to Washington with predilections for Calhoun; but, as he participated in the conferences about the President, he came to see that Van Buren, Benton and Taney had the welfare of the common man much more at heart. His affectionate nature led him to warm personal attachments with all three, and particularly with Van Buren.

VII *Beginnings of the Bank War*

IN 1836 THE CHARTER OF THE SECOND BANK OF THE
United States was to expire. This institution was not in the
later sense a national bank. It was a banking corporation, lo-
cated in Philadelphia, privately controlled, but possessing
unique and profitable relations with the government. To its
capital of thirty-five million dollars, the government had subscribed one fifth. It served as repository of the public funds,
which it could use for its own banking purposes without payment of interest. It could issue bank notes up to the physical
ability of the president and cashier to sign them; after 1827 it
evaded this limitation by the invention of "branch drafts,"
which looked and circulated like notes but were actually bills
of exchange. The Bank was not to be taxed by the states and
no similar institution was to be chartered by Congress. In return for these privileges the Bank paid a bonus of one and a
half million dollars, transferred public funds and made public
payments without charge, and allowed the government to appoint five out of the twenty-five directors. The Secretary of the
Treasury could remove the government deposits provided he
laid the reasons before Congress.

EVEN ADVOCATES OF THE BANK CONCEDED THAT THIS
charter bestowed too much power.

There could be no question either about the Bank's pretensions to complete independence of popular control. Biddle
brooked no opposition from within, and the government representatives sat through the directors' meetings baffled and indignant.

Biddle not only suppressed all internal dissent but insisted
flatly that the Bank was not accountable to the government or
the people.

In Biddle's eyes the Bank was thus an independent corporation, on a level with the state, and not responsible to it except
as the narrowest interpretation of the charter compelled.
Biddle tried to strengthen this position by flourishing a theory
that the Bank was beyond political good or evil, but Alexander Hamilton had written with far more candor that "such a
bank is not a mere matter of private property, but a political
machine of the greatest importance to the State." The Second

Bank of the United States was, in fact, as Hamilton had intended such a bank should be, the keystone in the alliance between the government and the business community.

THE ORDINARY FOLLOWER OF JACKSON IN THE WEST also regarded the Bank with strong latent antagonism, but for very different reasons. Its policy in 1819 of recalling specie and checking the note issue of state banks had gained it few friends in any class, and, in Kentucky especially, the Relief War kept resentments alive. But this anti-Bank feeling owed little to reasoned distrust of paper money or to a Jeffersonian desire for specie. As a debtor section the West naturally preferred cheap money; and Kentucky, for example, which most vociferously opposed the United States Bank, also resorted most ardently to wildcat banking of its own. The crux of the Kentucky fight against the Bank was not the paper system, but outside control: the Bank's sin lay not in circulating paper money itself, but in restraining its circulation by Kentucky banks. Almost nowhere, apart from doctrinaires like Jackson and Benton, did Westerners object to state banks under local control.

Similar objections to control from Philadelphia ranged many Easterners against the Bank. State institutions hoped, by falling heir to the government deposits, to enlarge their banking capital, at no expense to themselves. Special grievances multiplied the motives. The state banks of New York, for example, envied the United States Bank because its loan operations were not restricted by Van Buren's safety-fund system. New York City had long resented the choice of Philadelphia as the nation's financial capital. Thus in a fight against the Bank Jackson could expect the backing of a decent minority of the local banking interests.

But there was still another and more reliable source of support. In March, 1829, after the grim depression winter, a group of Philadelphia workingmen, under the very shadow of the Bank, called a meeting "opposed to the chartering of any more new banks." The hard times were blamed upon the "too great extensions of paper credit," and the gathering concluded by appointing a committee, "without confining ourselves to the working classes," to draw up a report on the banking system. A week later the committee pronounced its verdict on the paper system:—

That banks are useful as offices of deposit and transfer, we readily admit; but we cannot see that the benefits they confer in this way are so great as to compensate for the evils they produce, in . . . laying the foundation of *artificial* inequality of wealth, and, thereby, of *artificial* inequality of power. . . . If the present system of banking and paper money be extended and perpetuated, the great body of the working people must give over all hopes of ever acquiring any property.

This view was spreading rapidly through the Middle and Northern states of the East in the late eighteen-twenties. The working class was no more affected by an instinctive antipathy toward banking than the backwoodsmen beyond the Alleghenies; but they never enjoyed the Western opportunity of having banks under their own control. Their opposition, instead of remaining fitful and capricious, began slowly to harden into formal anti-banking principle. Their bitter collective experience with paper money brought them to the same doctrines which Jackson and Benton gained from the Jeffersonian inheritance.

THE WAR AGAINST THE BANK THUS ENLISTED THE ENthusiastic support of two basically antagonistic groups: on the one hand, debtor interests of the West and local banking interests of the East; on the other, Eastern workingmen and champions of the radical Jeffersonian tradition. The essential incompatibility between cheap money and hard could be somewhat concealed in the clamor of the crusade. Yet that incompatibility remained, and it came to represent increasingly a difference between the Western and Eastern wings of the party, as the state banking group gradually abandoned the Jackson ranks. It was, indeed, a new form of the distinction between Western and Eastern readings of "equality." The West, in its quest for political democracy and home rule, did not object to paper money under local control, while the submerged classes of the East, seeking economic democracy, fought the whole banking swindle, as it seemed to them, root and branch.

The administration took care not to offend its cheap-money adherents by openly avowing hard-money ideas. Yet, the drift was unmistakable, and it rendered ineffective some of Jackson's Western followers for whom the battle was being pressed on lines they could not understand. In general, the Western politicians, torn between the hard-money leanings of the White House and the cheap-money preferences of the folks back home, tended to pursue an erratic course.

Only the intellectuals, who did not have to think about re-election, effected a quick adjustment. Amos Kendall, who had been originally a hard-money man, perhaps from his Eastern upbringing, found no difficulty in reverting to his earlier opinions. Frank Blair also rapidly shifted his ground after coming to Washington. These were not basic reversals of position. Their allegiance, after all, had been primarily to a social class, not to a set of financial theories. Kendall and Blair, liberated from their local obligations, naturally turned to hard-money ideas as affording the only permanent solutions for the financial problems in favor of the non-business classes.

Thomas Hart Benton had long awaited the opportunity to fight for this solution.

He tried several times to get the floor in the Senate, but the friends of the Bank succeeded always in silencing him by parliamentary technicalities. Finally, on February 2, 1831, he out-maneuvered the opposition and launched his comprehensive indictment:—

First: Mr. President, I object to the renewal of the charter . . . because I look upon the bank as an institution too great and powerful to be tolerated in a Government of free and equal laws. . . .
Secondly, I object . . . because its tendencies are dangerous and pernicious to the Government and the people. . . . It tends to aggravate the inequality of fortunes; to make the rich richer, and the poor poorer; to multiply nabobs and paupers. . . .
Thirdly, I object . . . on account of the exclusive privileges, and anti-republican monopoly, which it gives to the stockholders.

And his own policy? "Gold and silver is the best currency for a republic," he thundered; "it suits the men of middle property and the working people best; and if I was going to establish a working man's party, it should be on the basis of hard money; a hard money party against a paper party." The words reverberated through the hall—"a hard money party against a paper party"—as Mr. Webster of Massachusetts hastily rose to call for a vote which defeated Benton's resolution against recharter.

But the words also reverberated through the country.

NICHOLAS BIDDLE, IN HIS FINE OFFICES ON CHESTNUT Street, was disturbed. This able, suave and cosmopolitan Philadelphian was only thirty-seven when he became president of the Bank in 1823. He had been known mainly as a literary man—an early training which instilled a weakness for writing public letters that would often prove embarrassing. One English traveler pronounced him "the most perfect specimen of an American gentleman that I had yet seen" and commended his "exemption from national characteristics."

As head of the Bank, he inclined to pursue an active policy; but up to 1830 all his ventures had succeeded, he had taken no unnecessary risks (except perhaps for the "branch draft" device), and his judgment was universally respected. Yet, for all his ability, he suffered from a fatal self-confidence, a disposition to underrate his opponents and a lack of political imagination. He sought now to make a deal with the administration, while working on public opinion by newspaper articles, loans to editors and personal contacts. But his ultimate reliance was on two of the nation's giants, Henry Clay and Daniel Webster.

Henry Clay was the most beloved politician of the day.

Brilliant, reckless, fascinating, indolent, Clay was irresistibly attractive. Exhilarated by his sense of personal power, he loved to dominate his human environment everywhere, in Congress and at party councils, at dinner and in conversation; but he was not meanly ambitious. If he possessed few settled principles and small analytical curiosity, he had broad and exciting visions, which took the place of ideas.

Daniel Webster lacked precisely that talent for stirring the popular imagination. He was an awe-inspiring figure, solid as granite, with strong shoulders and an iron frame. He loved his comfort too much: liquor and rest, duck-shooting at Marshfield and adulation in Boston. His intellectual ability was great, but he used it only under the spur of crisis. In his great speeches inspiration would take charge of his deep booming voice, and he would shake the world. Then he was, as Emerson remembered him, "the great cannon loaded to the lips." But when inspiration lagged he became simply pompous.

The nation never gave its heart to Webster. The merchants of Boston did, along with a share of their purses, and also the speculators of Wall Street and rich men everywhere. But the plain man did not much respond to him, except for a few Yankee farmers in New Hampshire, who liked to hobnob with statesmen.

Clay fought for Biddle and his Bank because it fitted in with his superb vision of America, but Webster fought for it in great part because it was a dependable source of private revenue. "I believe my retainer has not been renewed or *refreshed* as usual," he wrote at one point when the Bank had its back to the wall. "If it be wished that my relation to the Bank should be continued, it may be well to send me the usual retainers." How could Daniel Webster expect the American people to follow him through hell and high water when he would not lead unless someone made up a purse for him? *

IN THE SPRING OF 1830 A HOUSE COMMITTEE, directed by George McDuffie, had brought in a report clearing the Bank of the charges made by Jackson in his first message to Congress. Jackson returned to the subject in more detail in his second message, and Benton's speech in 1831 thrust the question vigorously to the fore.

Biddle would have much preferred to keep the Bank out of politics altogether. His one interest was in renewing the charter. This he would do with Jackson's help, if possible; with Clay's, if necessary. Thus, during 1830 and 1831 he carefully explored the chances of winning over the President. The active co-operation of McLane and Livingston and the evident division in Jackson's party raised Biddle's hopes. The President, in the meantime, while saying quietly that his view had not changed, allowed McLane to recommend recharter in his Treasury report and barely mentioned the Bank question in his message of 1831.

But for all his amiability Jackson remained unyielding, while the Van Buren group seemed irrevocably hostile. Henry Clay, fearful lest so good an issue slip through his fingers, kept pressing Biddle to let him make recharter a party question. Biddle hesitated, considered, stalled, watched the National Republican convention nominate Clay, with John Sergeant, a lawyer for the Bank, as running mate, read the party address denouncing Jackson's views on the Bank—and on January 9, 1832, petitions for recharter were presented in each House of Congress.

Benton, certain that the Bank could carry Congress, realized that the administration's only hope lay in postponement. Accordingly he had a good many obstructionist amendments pre-

* Stephen Vincent Benét's recent skillful attempt to make Webster a hero of myth would have surprised many of Webster's contemporaries. The real Webster lacked the generosity and warm humanity of Mr. Benét's hero, and would have opposed many of the things which Mr. Benét himself has stood for today. In fact, the least plausible part of Mr. Benét's charming tale is not that a New Hampshire man should sell his soul to the devil, or that Benedict Arnold and Simon Girty should be on tap for jury service, but that Daniel Webster should be found arguing against the sanctity of contract.

pared for the Senate, and in the House he set in motion plans for an investigating committee.

The Bank forces could hardly refuse this request without raising strange suspicions. Yet, they first resisted it, then tried to keep it in their own hands, then tried to restrict its scope—overruling McDuffie, who understood perfectly the futility of these tactics—with the result that by the time the committee was appointed the Bank had lost considerable prestige through the country. After six weeks in Philadelphia, examining records and questioning witnesses, it issued three reports: a majority report against the Bank, and two minority dissents, one by Adams.*

In May the fight began in earnest. Biddle had already sent an advance guard of crack lobbyists, but, with the crucial struggle about to start, he took personal command. By now he was growing drunk with power. When Nathan Appleton, Massachusetts mill owner and member of the House, proposed the charter be modified, Biddle scorned the suggestion, and Clay interceded with Appleton, begging him to vote for the measure as it stood. "Should Jackson veto it," exclaimed Clay with an oath, "I shall veto him!"

On June 11 the bill passed the Senate, 28-20, and on July 3 it passed the House, 107-85. When Biddle made a smiling appearance on the floor after the passage, members crowded round to shake his hand. A riotous party in his lodgings celebrated the victory late into the night.

* The operations of this committee confound naïve theories of economic determinism. All the opponents of the Bank were in debt to it (Clayton, $400; Johnson, $650; Thomas, $650; Cambreleng, $400), while the friends of the Bank owed it much less (McDuffie, $500; Watmough, $300; Adams, nothing). Though the Jacksonians made a good deal of the Bank's loans to Congressmen, there was not much correlation between the size of the loans and the intensity of the devotion to the Bank; see *House Report*, 22 Congress 1 Session, no. 460, "Bank of the United States," especially 569-570.

This statement does not apply at all, however, to loans to newspaper editors; and Taney's analysis of one Congressman's change of opinion after a large loan was certainly true for a small number of individual cases. "Now I do not mean to say," wrote Taney, "that he was directly bribed to give this vote. From the character he sustained and from what I knew of him I think he would have resented any thing that he regarded as an attempt to corrupt him. But he wanted the money—and felt grateful for the favor: and perhaps he thought that an institution which was so useful to him, and had behaved with so much kindness, could not be injurious or dangerous to the public, and that it would be as well to continue it. Men under the influence of interest or passion . . . do not always acknowledge even to themselves the motives upon which they really act. They sometimes persuade themselves that they are acting, on a motive consistent with their own self-respect, and sense of right, and shut their eyes to the one which in fact governs their conduct." Bank War Manuscript, 113-114.

VIII *Veto*

JACKSON'S GRIM CALM DURING 1831 CLOAKED NO BASIC
wavering of purpose. With characteristic political tact he presented an irresolute and amenable face to the world in order
to hold the party together. Benton and Kendall were in his confidence, but very few others. His apparent moderation deceived not only Biddle but many of the Bank's enemies.

In particular, Jackson's cabinet misinterpreted his pose.
McLane, Livingston and Taney were all convinced that compromise was possible, greatly to the relief of the two and the
despair of the third. Taney was coming to believe that he stood
alone in the cabinet and almost in the country in opposing recharter. In the meantime, the Bank's alacrity in opening new
offices and making long-term loans, though its charter was
soon to expire, seemed "conclusive evidence of its determination to fasten itself by means of its money so firmly on the
country that it will be impossible . . . to shake it off without
producing the most severe and extensive public suffering.—
And this very attempt," he cried, "calls for prompt resistance
—for future resistance will be in vain if the charter is renewed."

But who would lead the resistance? He watched the debates
drag on and the votes pile up through the spring of 1832 with
mounting apprehension. In the late spring, having to attend
the Maryland Court of Appeals, he decided to prepare a
memorandum setting forth his conviction that recharter should
be vetoed. He finished it the night before his departure and
notified the President that the opinion would be delivered as
soon as the bill was passed.

On July 3 Jackson received the bill. Hearing the news, Martin Van Buren, just back from England, went straight on to
Washington, arriving at midnight. The General, still awake,
stretched on a sickbed, pale and haggard and propped up by
pillows, grasped his friend's hand. Passing his other hand
through his snow-white hair, he said firmly but without passion, "The bank, Mr. Van Buren, is trying to kill me, *but I will
kill it!*"

A day or two later, Taney, busy in Annapolis, received
word to hurry back to Washington. He found the President
out of bed and eager for action. He had read Taney's memorandum with emphatic agreement and then had heard the
arguments of the rest of the cabinet. While disapproving the

bill, they wanted him to place his rejection on grounds which would allow the question to be reopened in the future. Jackson, unwilling to compromise, then turned to Amos Kendall for a first draft of the veto message. Andrew J. Donelson was now revising Kendall's draft in the room across the hall. Would Taney help? The lean, determined face of the Attorney General expressed no reservations.

It took three days to finish the document. The first day Taney and Donelson worked alone, except for Jackson and Ralph Earl, an artist who lived at the White House and used this room as a studio, painting away, oblivious of the tense consultations, the hasty scribbles, the words crossed out, the phrases laboriously worked over, the notes torn up and discarded. On the second day Levi Woodbury, having decided to change his stand, made an unabashed appearance and assisted till the job was done. Jackson meanwhile passed in and out of the room, listening to the different parts, weighing the various suggestions and directing what should be inserted or altered.

THE MESSAGE, DATED JULY 10, BURST LIKE A THUN-derclap over the nation. Its core was a ringing statement of Jackson's belief in the essential rights of the common man. "But when the laws undertake to add to these natural and just advantages artificial distinctions . . . to make the rich richer and the potent more powerful, the humble members of society —the farmers, mechanics, and laborers—who have neither the time nor the means of securing like favors to themselves, have a right to complain of the injustice of their Government."

But the case against the Bank could not rest simply on generalities. Jackson's real opposition, of course, and that of Benton, Taney and Kendall, arose from their hard-money views. Yet, a great part of their backing came from cheap-money men. Thus powerful hard-money arguments—the economic argument that the paper system caused periodic depressions, and the social argument that it built up an aristocracy—were unavailable because they were as fatal to the debtor and state banking positions as to the Bank itself.

The veto message was brilliantly successful in meeting this dilemma.

The distinction between "the humble members of society" and "the rich and powerful" drew quick reactions from both classes. The common man through the land responded enthusiastically to his leader's appeal.

But men who believed that the political power of the business community should increase with its wealth were deeply alarmed. When Jackson said, "It is not conceivable how the present stockholders can have any claim to the special favor of the Government," did he mean that the common man had the same rights as the rich and wellborn to control of the state?

No wonder Nicholas Biddle roared to Henry Clay, "It has all the fury of a chained panther, biting the bars of his cage. It is really a manifesto of anarchy, such as Marat or Robespierre might have issued to the mob of the Faubourg St. Antoine." Webster, rising gravely in the Senate, summed up the indictment: "It manifestly seeks to influence the poor against the rich. It wantonly attacks whole classes of the people, for the purpose of turning against them the prejudices and resentments of other classes. It is a State paper which finds no topic too exciting for its use, no passion too inflammable for its address and its solicitation." For Webster, as for Jackson, it was becoming a battle between antagonistic philosophies of government: one declaring, like Webster at the Massachusetts convention, that property should control the state; the other denying that property had a superior claim to governmental privileges and benefits.

THE VETO STRUCK CONSTERNATION THROUGH SOME parts of the Democratic party. The summer and fall of 1832 saw a hasty recasting of party lines.

Two thirds of the press, largely perhaps because of advertising pressure, supported the Bank.*

A part of the business community stuck by Jackson. Some merchants opposed the concentration of power in the Bank. Some distrusted Biddle. Some hoped the Bank would be replaced by a Democratic Bank of the United States in which they might hold stock. Some were investors or officers in state banks with an eye on the government deposits. But they made up a small part of the whole.

As the day of election drew near, the universal debate went

* Two thirds was the estimate of W. M. Holland in 1835, *Life and Political Opinions of Martin Van Buren*, 365; Van Buren's own estimate was three fourths, *Autobiography*, 746. As for the cause, as a discerning English traveler pointed out, "Relying chiefly, if not entirely, on their advertisements for support, and these being furnished by persons engaged in the mercantile and trading operations, they can hardly dare offend those on whom they are so dependent. . . . Hence they are almost all Whigs." Buckingham, *America*, III, 332. The report of the Philadelphia workingmen's committee of 1829, largely the work of two editors, W. M. Gouge and Condy Raguet, charged: "Even now it is impossible to obtain entrance into many papers for free disquisitions of the [banking] system. The conductor of a public journal who ventures on so bold a step, risks his means of subsistence." *Free Trade Advocate*, May 9, 16, 1829. Biddle's newspaper loans were notorious. The most celebrated example was the reversal of the policy of the *New York Courier and Enquirer*, formerly a strong Jackson paper, on receiving loans which aggregated to nearly $53,000 and were very risky business ventures.

on with increasing acrimony, from the shacks of Maine fisher-men to the parlors of Philadelphia and the plantations of Ala-bama.

August gave way to September, September to October, and the clamor grew increasingly furious. Jackson men paraded the streets in the glare of torches, singing campaign songs, car-rying hickory poles, gathering around huge bonfires blazing high into the night. Late in October, Horace Binney solemnly told a Philadelphia audience that "the preservation of the Con-stitution itself" depended on the defeat of Jackson, congratu-lating them that the right of a free election could still be exer-cised with safety. "How long it will continue so, or how long the enjoyment of it will be of any value to you, are questions upon which the short remainder of the present year will prob-ably furnish materials for a decisive judgment." Fanny Kem-ble, resting in Philadelphia after her successes in Washington (where she had dazzled Chief Justice Marshall and Justice Story as well as Frank Blair of the *Globe*), was assured by her friends that Henry Clay, "the leader of the aristocratic party," was already certain of election.

But the people had not spoken. Soon their time came: "The news from the voting States," Rufus Choate wrote to Edward Everett, "blows over us like a great cold storm." The results rolled in: Jackson, 219, Clay 49, John Floyd, 11, William Wirt, 7. *

IN JULY, 1832, JACKSON HAD SIGNED A NEW TARIFF bill, lowering the duties but leaving them still clearly protec-tive. South Carolina, unsatisfied, prepared to object. Late in November, a state convention declared the tariffs of 1828 and 1832 void within the state after February 1, 1833.

Jackson met the South Carolina ordinance with a ringing proclamation on the nature of the Union, drawn up in large part by Edward Livingston. As the crisis approached, a "force bill," authorizing the President to use force to execute the laws, was introduced in the Senate. At the same time, however, the President acted to abate the actual grievance by furthering a compromise on the tariff. Late in December friends of Van Buren sponsored a much lower tariff bill in the House. Henry

* A later President's judgment on Jackson's opposition has bearing on both their experiences. "An overwhelming proportion of the material power of the Nation was against him. The great media for the dissemination of information and the molding of public opinion fought him. Haughty and sterile intellectual-ism opposed him. Musty reaction disapproved him. Hollow and outworn tradi-tionalism shook a trembling finger at him. It seemed sometimes that all were against him—all but the people of the United States." Franklin D. Roosevelt, Jackson Day Address, January 8, 1936, *Public Papers and Addresses of Frank-lin D. Roosevelt*, Samuel I. Rosenman, ed., V. 40.

Clay, aware of the nation's peril but reluctant to enhance Van Buren's prestige or to reduce rates unduly, countered with a somewhat more protectionist compromise. By some parliamentary sleight-of-hand the Clay bill replaced the first bill in the House; and it also quickly passed the Senate with the support of Calhoun, who thought higher duties a small price to pay for the pleasure of thwarting Van Buren and the administration.

With compromise achieved, South Carolina now rescinded the ordinance nullifying the tariff, but, to score a final victory for its logic, it passed another, nullifying the now unnecessary force bill. This was a hollow triumph, for the episode had shown that in practice nullification was indistinguishable from rebellion and would call down the force of the government. Though nullification had paid its way this time, everyone knew it never would again.

By his masterly statesmanship Jackson had maintained the supremacy of the Union. But, in so doing, he had committed himself to doctrines on the nature of the Union which frightened the State-rights fundamentalists among his supporters. The spectacle of Daniel Webster and John Quincy Adams defending Jackson in Congress, and of Justice Story remarking that he and Marshall had become the President's "warmest supporters," deepened Jeffersonian misgivings. Van Buren, ever cautious, was gravely concerned. C. C. Cambreleng objected to "the metaphysics of the Montesquieu of the Cabinet," as he labeled Livingston, but consoled himself that "happily the mass of the people sleep over such parts of it and dwell only on those which make them think and feel like men." Benton was without enthusiasm. Many years later, after guns had boomed over Sumter, Taney declared that he had not seen the proclamation until it was in print and that he disapproved some of its principles. Young Theodore Sedgwick, Jr., of Massachusetts, asked the essential question: could Jeffersonians "endure from any other man the profession of the same sentiments which they received with acclamation from General Jackson? Would these Doctrines be as safe in any other hands as they are in his?"

Yet, only a few politicians and intellectuals worried about constitutional hairsplitting. The mass of the people, as Cambreleng observed, slept over such passages while responding unreservedly to the central appeal—the preservation of the Union. Party lines faded as men who had cursed Jackson a few months before now rushed to praise him. "It is amusing to witness the unanimity of public opinion at this moment," commented the popular novelist, Catharine Maria Sedgwick,

"—to hear the old sober standard anti Jackson men, who tho't the republic was lost if he were reëlected say 'well: I really believe it is all for the best that Jackson is president.'" It would not be the last time that conservatism, scared by national crisis, would shelter itself gratefully behind the vigorous leadership of a Democratic President it had previously denounced.

Jackson became for the moment the country's hero. It was whispered that even Daniel Webster, dissatisfied with a junior partnership in the opposition, would join the administration. Webster himself was reported to regard Jackson's anti-Bank attitude as the only obstacle—which led Louis McLane to remark, "I consider this only the last qualm of a frail lady, who notwithstanding, finally falls into the arms of the seducer." But why, in any case, should Jackson not forget the Bank? As McLane added, "If he devote the remainder of his term to tranquilize the public mind, he will go into retirement with greater fame than any other man in our history."

But these calculations omitted General Jackson, who cared less for his popularity than for his program. Early in December, Amos Kendall made one of his rare public speeches to the Central Hickory Club. "In all civilized as well as barbarous countries," he declared, "a few rich and intelligent men have built up *Nobility Systems;* by which, under some name, and by some contrivance, the few are enabled to live upon the labor of the many." These ruling classes, he said, have had many names—kings, lords, priests, fundholders, but all "are founded on deception, and maintained by power. The people are persuaded to permit their introduction, under the plea of public good and public necessity. As soon as they are firmly established, they turn upon the people, tax and control them by the influence of monopolies, the declamation of priestcraft and government-craft, and in the last resort by military force." Was America immune from this universal pattern? "The United States," said Kendall ominously, "have their young *Nobility System.* Its head is the Bank of the United States; its right arm, a protecting Tariff and Manufacturing Monopolies; its left, growing State debts and State incorporations." The friends of Daniel Webster might well ponder these quiet words.

JACKSON'S RE-ELECTION AND THE POPULAR ACCLAIM following the nullification crisis only reinforced the administration's resolve to press the offensive against the American "Nobility System." The first necessity was to destroy its "head," the Bank. But the charter still had well over three years to run. The Bank was still backed by the National Republican party, most of the press and many leading citizens.

The solution lay in withdrawing the deposits. This would cripple the Bank's attempt to convulse the money market and probably provoke it into an all-out fight against the only man who could whip it, thus foreclosing the issue once and for all. Jackson seems to have decided on this course shortly after his re-election.

McLane and Biddle, indeed, went quickly to work to forestall the President. A special Treasury investigator reported early in 1833 that the Bank was sound, and in March the House upheld a majority report of the Ways and Means Committee declaring the funds perfectly safe in the Bank's custody. These incidents only confirmed the radicals' conviction of the extent of Biddle's power.

The campaign for removal slowed down in May and June, during the President's trip to New York and New England.

In the meantime the transfer of Livingston to the French ministry and of McLane to the State Department had created a vacancy in the Treasury for which McLane proposed William J. Duane, the Philadelphia lawyer who had signed the anti-Bank report of the workingmen's meeting in March, 1829. Jackson approved, and Duane took office on June 1. This appointment raised fresh difficulties. Though Duane could hardly have been much surprised on learning Jackson's sentiments about removal, he played an equivocal part, neither accepting nor opposing the President's views, but stalling and obstructing.

July, as usual, was unbearable in Washington. Jackson, sick and weary, prepared to go to Rip-raps in Virginia for a rest. Where, in this moment of loneliness, stood the Vice-President? Van Buren at first had opposed immediate removal. The imminence of 1836, and his role as heir-apparent, had probably intensified his natural caution. Sometime in the spring, during a heated discussion with Van Buren, Amos Kendall, rising from his seat in excitement, warned that a Bank victory in 1836 was certain unless it were stripped of the power it gained from managing the public money: "I can live under a corrupt despotism, as well as any other man, by keeping out of its way, which I shall certainly do." Impressed by Kendall's vehemence, Van Buren changed his attitude, though he never allowed himself to become identified with the measure.

Frank Blair accompanied Jackson to the seaside, where the two households spent a pleasant month, the invigorating salt air restoring Jackson's appetite and improving his health. Letters bombarded the President, pleading with him not to disturb the deposits. What seemed an organized campaign only strengthened his purpose: "Mr. Blair, Providence may change me but it is not in the power of man to do it." In spare moments, he shaped his notes into a militant and uncompromising document. Returned to the White House late in August, he resolved to end the matter before Congress convened.

On September 10 he presented Kendall's report on the state banks to the cabinet, Taney and Woodbury backed the proposal to discontinue placing funds with the Bank on October 1, while McLane, Cass and Duane vigorously opposed it. Duane's assent as Secretary of the Treasury was necessary for the action. By September 14 Jackson, having tortuously overcome his scruples against discharging persons who disagreed with him, suggested to Duane that he resign; perhaps he might be named Minister to Russia. Duane refused. The next day Jackson handed Taney for revision the fiery paper he had dictated at Ripraps. On the eighteenth he read this paper to the cabinet. Two days later the *Globe* announced the plan to cease deposits in the Bank after October 1. Duane continued in frightened obstinacy, agreeing to the removal of neither the deposits nor himself. "He is either the weakest mortal, or the most strange composition I have ever met with," Jackson wrote in exasperation. The next five days exhausted even the President's patience. He dismissed Duane and appointed Taney to the place.

The radical Jacksonians exulted at the removal. "This is the crowning glory of A. J.'s life and the most important service he has ever rendered his country," cried Nicholas P. Trist, the intelligent young Virginian who served as the President's secretary. "Independently of its misdeeds, the mere *power*,—the bare existence of such a power,—is a thing irreconcilable with the nature and spirit of our institutions." Benton pronounced it "the most masterly movement in politics which the age had witnessed." The *Boston Post* put it in the same class as Christ's expelling the money-changers from the Temple. The sturdy and rebellious William Cobbett, in England, called it "one of the greatest acts of his whole wonderful life." Jovial Charles Gordon Greene, editor of the *Boston Post,* even composed an epitaph for the bank: "BIDDLED, DIDDLED, and UNDONE."

But Biddle was not yet convinced that it was the Bank which needed the epitaph.

IX *Counterattack*

THE NEW STORM OF DENUNCIATION MADE THE attack on the veto seem a model of good temper. Biddle, convinced by midsummer that the deposits were doomed, began in August to fight back. Employing to the full his power over the state banks, he commenced to present their notes for redemption, reduce discounts and call in loans. While claiming to be simply winding up business in preparation for the expiration of the charter, he was in fact embarked on the campaign the radicals above all had feared: the deliberate creation of a panic in order to blackmail the government into rechartering the Bank. "Nothing but the evidence of suffering abroad will produce any effect in Congress," he wrote privately to a friend. ". . . if . . . the Bank permits itself to be frightened or coaxed into any relaxation of its present measures, the relief will itself be cited as evidence that the measures of the Govt. are not injurious, or oppressive, and the Bank will inevitably be prostrated." "My own course is decided," he informed another, "—all the other Banks and all the merchants may break, but the Bank of the United States shall not break."

THE STRATEGY WAS AT FIRST BRILLIANTLY SUCCESSful. The business community, already incensed by Jackson's measures, was easily persuaded that deflation was the inevitable consequence of removal. The contraction of loans by the Bank tightened credit all long the line. Businesses failed, men were thrown out of work, money was unobtainable. Memorials, petitions, letters, delegations and protests of every kind deluged Congress.

The friends of the administration now needed all their skill.

ROGER B. TANEY SET FORTH THE ISSUE IN THE REPORT he rendered to the House early in the session. "It is a fixed principle of our political institutions," he declared, "to guard against the unnecessary accumulation of power over persons and property in any hands. And no hands are less worthy to be trusted with it than those of a moneyed corporation." What would be the future of American democracy if the course of the government was to be regulated by fear of the Bank?

"They may now demand the possession of the public money, or the renewal of the charter; and if these objects are yielded to them from apprehensions of their power, or from the suffering which rapid curtailments on their part are inflicting on the community, what may they not next require? Will submission render such a corporation more forbearing in its course?"

This was indeed the question: if Mr. Biddle's panic could coerce the Congress into restoring the deposits, would not the bank, strengthened by the deposits, in the same manner coerce the Congress into recharter; and as its power grew, would not its demands become more exigent, until democracy was dead?

The Bank forces were now reinforced by the support, under complex and tenuous conditions, of John C. Calhoun. The philosopher from South Carolina proved helpful in lifting the issue to more elevated planes of discussion. He sharply denied that the struggle was over the question of Bank or no Bank. If it were, "if it involved the existence of the banking system, . . . I would hesitate, long hesitate, before I would be found under the banner of the system." What then was it all about? "I answer, it is a struggle between the executive and legislative departments of the Government; a struggle, not in relation to the existence of the bank, but which, Congress or the President, should have the power to create a bank, and the consequent control over the currency of the country. This is the real question."

While this was hardly the real question, it was certainly a far nobler question than the discredited plea for recharter. It fitted neatly into the ancient picture of Jackson as a backwoods Caesar, bent on establishing a military dictatorship; and it supplied an issue on which the friends of the Bank and the friends of nullification could unite in an anti-Jackson front.

On February 5 a resolution passed declaring Taney's reasons for removal unsatisfactory, and on March 28 came another charging Jackson with having acted in derogation of the Constitution. When Jackson replied by a long protest, the Senate refused to enter it in its records, and the session came to a bitter end.

Events moved more favorably in the House. The quiet, remorseless leadership of James K. Polk kept the discussion to the point. "The Bank of the United States has set itself up as a great irresponsible rival power of the Government," he declared; and if it won this fight, no man thereafter could expect "to arrive at the first station in this great republic, without first making terms with the despot." He assailed the attempt to divert the debate into quibbles about constitutionality. "The present is, in substance and in fact, the question of recharter or no recharter. The question is, in fact, whether we shall have the republic without the bank, or the bank without the republic."

Horace Binney replied in a three-day attack on the removal. Cambreleng responded to Binney, and Samuel Beardsley added, in words which seemed to unveil the secret purposes of Jackson and Amos Kendall, that, if the credit and commerce of the country depended upon the Bank, "I, for one, say perish credit; perish commerce; . . . give us a broken, a deranged, and a worthless currency, rather than the ignoble and corrupting tyranny of an irresponsible corporation."

Perish credit; perish commerce: these chilling words struck terror in the hearts of the more apprehensive conservatives. Was not this the whole drift of the administration policy? First, the Maysville veto, then the Bank veto, then the removal of the deposits—who knew what would follow? "How far this Catilinarian conspiracy has been carried, who but the miscreants concerned in the plot can now disclose to the nation?" snarled fiery Tristram Burges, of Rhode Island. "Have they already parcelled out our cities and villages, and appointed some Lentulus to superintend their conflagration?" But Polk steered straight to his objectives, through all these furious gales, carrying through the House forthright resolutions against recharter, against restoration of the deposits, and in favor of a new deposit system employing state banks.

The President meanwhile remained unshaken by all the uproar. James Fenimore Cooper began to believe that "hickory will prove to be stronger than gold," and he need never have doubted. One day it was reported in Washington that a Baltimore mob was threatening to camp on Capitol Hill till the deposits were restored. A group of quaking administration Congressmen beseeched Jackson to say what was to be done. "Gentlemen," the old General reassured them with grim humor, "I shall be glad to see this federal mob on Capitol Hill. I will fix their heads on the iron palisades around the square to assist your deliberations. The leaders I will hang as high as Haman to deter forever all attempts to control the legislation of the Congress by intimidation and design."

Delegations of businessmen, from New York, Baltimore and Philadelphia, also beset the President. Jackson, disliking to argue with people who were either fools enough to believe Nicholas Biddle or knaves enough to work for him, would make his unshakable determination clear by launching into fearful tirades against the Bank. A deputation from New York found him writing at his desk, smoking fiercely away at his long pipe. He excused himself, finished the paper and rose.

"Now gentlemen, what is your pleasure with me?" James G. King, son of Rufus King, had hardly spoken a few sentences of a prepared address asking for relief when Jackson interrupted angrily: "Go to Nicholas Biddle. We have no money here, gentlemen. Biddle has all the money. He has millions of specie in his vaults, at this moment, lying idle, and yet you come to *me* to save you from breaking." And so on, with mounting vehemence, until the visitors departed. The man who had introduced them was overtaken by a messenger on the White House stairs and asked to return to the President's office. He found Jackson chuckling over the interview: "Didn't I manage them well?"

A Philadelphia delegation barely announced its mission when Jackson broke in with an excited speech. *"Andrew Jackson* never would restore the deposits to the bank—*Andrew Jackson* would never recharter that monster of corruption . . . . sooner than live in a country where such a power prevailed, he would seek an asylum in the wilds of Arabia." (Biddle, on hearing this, observed that he might "as well send at once and engage lodgings.") A Baltimore deputation, waiting on Taney, declared that, unless the government changed its policy, a large part of the business community would fail, and understood Taney to reply, "If *all* did fail, the policy of the government would not be changed." Jackson provided little more sympathy. "The failures that are now taking place," he told them, "are amongst the stock-jobbers, brokers, and gamblers, and would to God, they were all swept from the land!" *Go to Nicholas Biddle* was Jackson's refrain, until he felt that his interviews had been so deliberately misquoted that he would receive no more committees.

"THE NATION STANDS ON THE VERY BRINK OF A HORRIBLE PRECIPICE," exclaimed Hezekiah Niles, in March, on behalf of the business community.

The "natural aristocracy" was everywhere shocked into fantasies of collapse. Chancellor Kent departed from judicial calm to proclaim comprehensively: "I look upon Jackson as a detestable, ignorant, reckless, vain & malignant tyrant." Justice Story was sufficiently under the influence of Clay's rhetoric to observe, "Though we live under the form of a republic we are in fact under the absolute rule of a single man." He felt himself called back as in a dream to the last days of the Roman republic, when the mob shouted for Caesar, and liberty expired with the dark and prophetic words of Cicero. "It has been remarked with much justice and truth," a Missouri businessman wrote Frank Blair, "that the merchants through the

United States, as a class, are opposed to our present Administration."

On the very day that Story was delivering himself of his classical vision, Edward Everett told an English banker, "The present contest is nothing less than a war of Numbers against Property." He reported the rise of the mob with horror. "In Philadelphia, after the powerful expression of sentiment proceeding from the merchants and men of business, [Congressman] Southerland coolly observed that this was only the view of Chestnut Street and Market Street; that he went to the lanes and alleys, where they held a different language." Appalling—and only one man, Daniel Webster, could save the nation, though this, of course, required certain preliminaries! Everett was candid: "If our friends in Boston mean that their houses, their lands, their stocks shall really be their own much longer, they must make the effort; they must make it at once. It is but $1000 each for one hundred gentlemen."

BUT BIDDLE COULD NOT HOPE TO FOOL THE BUSINESS community indefinitely. More and more merchants were coming to believe that he was carrying the money pressure farther than necessary, and few would agree that it was worth breaking "all the other Banks and all the merchants" to restore Nicholas Biddle to power. Late in February, Governor George Wolf of Pennsylvania, hitherto a leading Bank Democrat, came out against the Bank. Clay probably sensed the reaction in March when Van Buren offered to bet him a suit of clothes on the elections in Virginia and New York City. The Senator responded gallantly that if the people did support the administration, he would fear self-government had failed; but it is noticeable that he did not take up the Vice-President's wager.

In the same month, the leading merchants of Boston gathered at Faneuil Hall to appoint a committee to go to Washington with another petition. When Nathan Appleton, the chairman, reached New York, he discovered his old suspicion of Biddle's motives confirmed by James G. King and Albert Gallatin. King, as chairman of a New York committee, had already threatened the Bank with exposure if it did not change its policy. (*Go to Nicholas Biddle*, the old General had said; James G. King was quick to get the point.) Though Biddle had ignored earlier attempts at persuasion, this threat spoke in another tone, and he hurried to New York for personal consultations. Appleton and others of the Boston committee backed up King and Gallatin, informing Biddle that he knew very well the contraction was not necessary for the safety of the Bank, and that his whole object was to extort a charter from the government. Biddle could not talk himself out of the hole, and he knew that repudiation by Gallatin, an honored champion of the Bank, would be fatal. "Hence the Bank had to do something," as he explained to Watmough, the Bank lackey, "for the evil of such an announcement would have been enormous." So during April the pressure relaxed, but in May it resumed with greater violence than before, though even Webster now counseled prudence.

On returning to Boston, Appleton found that, though the politicians proposed to support Biddle at any cost, the business community had lost all patience. When the contraction continued into June, he wrote a long letter to the directors of the Boston branch for transmission to Biddle. Signed by many of the solidest and most conservative merchants—such men as George Bond, Henry Lee, Warren Dutton, Amos Lawrence, G. W. Lyman, W. P. Eustis—and also approved by Abbott Lawrence and William Appleton, it abundantly documented the Jacksonian indictment from a quarter whose every predilection was on the side of Nicholas Biddle.

Biddle responded evasively and desperately, apparently even denying that there was any systematic curtailment of discounts. In a second letter Appleton blasted Biddle's claims with a grim array of evidence, mostly taken from the Bank's own statements, concluding with the harsh but essential question: "what is the policy of the Bank? why is it pursuing a course of policy so utterly irreconcilable with the ordinary principles of Banking?" *

BIDDLE ACKNOWLEDGED THE ANSWER HIMSELF ON September 16 when he gave the lie direct to the case for curtailment by suddenly entering on a policy of expansion. After reducing its loans by well over eighteen million dollars from August 1, 1833, to November 1, 1834, under the plea of winding up its affairs, the Bank in the next five months *increased* its loans by almost fourteen and a half million. On June 1, 1835, the loans were almost what they were when Biddle's campaign began in August, 1833, and the note cir-

* Appleton, *et al.*, to the Board of Directors of the United States Branch Bank at Boston (draft), June 21, 1834, Appleton to Biddle (draft), July, 1834, Appleton Papers. Appleton's opinion of Biddle did not improve with time. "The case of the U. States Bank," he wrote in 1853, ". . . was the result of Mr. Biddle's wanton abuse of the power intrusted to him. He pursued a course of unnecessary contraction under the pretence that it was necessary to the winding up of the Bank, until after the rising of Congress, when finding that he could not coerce them into a renewal of the charter he most wantonly and recklessly increased his discounts." Appleton to Samuel Hooper, February 21, 1853, Appleton Papers; cf. Appleton, *Remarks on Currency*, 38-39.

culation was actually greater than ever before. The panic was over, and the Bank had not recovered the deposits.

Somewhere along the way, Biddle had lost his grip on reality. Ambition, vanity and love of power had crossed the thin line of megalomania. So little had he understood the American people that he ordered the circulation of thirty thousand copies of the Bank veto as a campaign document for Henry Clay. He completely misconceived the grounds of the Jacksonian attack; and, when the President stated them, Biddle brushed the explanation aside as mere demagogy. As late as the summer of 1833, he still believed that Jackson's secret purpose was to found a new national bank of his own.

Senator Theodore Frelinghuysen of New Jersey, his friend and defender, found the exact image for such a man. "There," Frelinghuysen observed with satisfaction, speaking on the effects of the panic, "sits Mr. Biddle, in the presidency of the Bank, as calm as a summer's morning, with his directors around him, receiving his salary, with everything moving on harmoniously: and has this stroke reached him? No, sir. The blow has fallen on the friends of the President [Jackson] and the country." What a touching picture of innocent virtue! (Roger B. Taney muttered ungraciously, "Nero is said to have fiddled while Rome was burning, but I have not learned from history that even his courtiers praised him for doing so.")

Biddle continued to console himself by fantasy. "My theory in regard to the present condition of the country is in a few words this," he wrote in 1835. "For the last few years the Executive power of the Govt. has been wielded by a mere gang of banditti. I know these people perfectly—keep the police on them constantly—and in my deliberate judgment, there is not on the face of the earth a more profligate crew." He warned the alumni of Princeton of the insolent ambitions of "some frontier Cataline." "It cannot be," he concluded with a flash of bravado, "that our free nation can long endure the vulgar dominion of ignorance and profligacy. You will live to see the laws re-established—these banditti will be scourged back to their caverns—the penitentiary will reclaim its fugitives in office, and the only remembrance which history will preserve of them, is the energy with which you resisted and defeated them."

X Hard Money

THE DETERMINATION WHICH ENABLED JACKSON TO resist the hysteria of panic came basically from the possession of an alternative policy of his own. Madison had surrendered to a corresponding, though less intense, pressure in 1816 because he had no constructive program to offer. But, for Jackson, the emotions and ideas which underlay the hard-money case against the Bank were crystallizing into a coherent and concrete set of measures, designed to capture the government for "the humble members of society," as Hamilton's system had captured it for "the rich and powerful."

THE JEFFERSONIAN TRADITION PROVIDED THE MAIN inspiration for this program. The Virginia condemnation of paper money, pronounced by Jefferson, formulated profoundly by Taylor, kept pure and uncompromising by Macon and Randolph, had passed on as a vital ideological legacy to Jackson, Benton, Van Buren, Polk, Cambreleng. Yet it was handed down as a series of keen but despairing criticisms delivered in the shadow of an invincible industrialism. The creative statesmen of the Jackson administration now proposed to transform it into a positive governmental policy.

The Bank War played an indispensable role in the precipitation of hard-money ideas. It dramatized currency questions in a way which captured the imagination of the people and excited their desire for further action on the financial front. It enlisted the enthusiasm of intellectuals, stimulating them to further analysis, widening the range and competence of economic theory. It tightened class lines, and the new bitterness of feeling sharpened the intellectual weapons.

Above all, the Bank War triumphantly established Jackson in the confidence of the people. Their faith in him had survived ordeals and won vindication: thereafter, when faced by a choice between Jackson and a cherished policy, most of them would choose Jackson. The effect of this mandate was particularly to sell the West on an intricate economic program, which many Westerners did not understand and which ran counter to their preconceptions.

The uncertainty about the West had postponed the avowal of the hard-money system.* The veto message, written by

* Orestes A. Brownson later declared that he had been urged in 1831 by "men high in the confidence of the party . . . to support the administration of

67

three men of known hard-money convictions, Jackson, Taney and Kendall, suppressed mention of the doctrine, as if by main force. But the election of 1832 increased Jackson's confidence. He could have lost the entire West and still have broken even with Clay, but he carried the whole West except for Kentucky.† He now felt certain of vigorous national support, and also of probable Western support, even for his economic ideas.

He thus was emboldened to come out publicly for the hard-money policy, expressing himself first in his interview with the Philadelphia delegation a few days before his second inaugural. His objective, he said, was gradually to reduce the circulation of paper, by forbidding deposit banks to issue small notes and by refusing such notes in payment for taxes, until all notes under twenty dollars would be eliminated and "thus a metallic currency be ensured for all the common purposes of life, while the use of bank notes would be confined to those engaged in commerce."

Soon after, he reorganized his cabinet, turning it for the first time into an effective unit. The administration was now streamlined for action.

THE HARD-MONEY SYSTEM OWED MANY OF ITS MAX-ims and dogmas to the Jeffersonians, and much of its vitality to the Northern workingmen who backed it so warmly; but the man to whom, after Jackson, Benton and Taney, it perhaps owed most for its emergence as a constructive policy was William M. Gouge, the Philadelphia editor and economist. Gouge put the hard-money doctrines in the clearest form, furnished the most cogent indictment of the paper system, stated the general problems in a way (unlike the Jeffersonian) relevant to a society where finance capitalism was well entrenched, and proved unfailingly resourceful in working out the practical measures to realize his policy. Thirty-seven years old in 1833, he had been from 1823 to 1831 editor and part proprietor of the *Philadelphia Gazette.* For the next two years, he busied himself with a treatise on the banking system, published in Philadelphia in February, 1833, under the title *A Short History of Paper Money and Banking in the United States.*

The work consisted of an analysis of the social consequences of the paper system, followed by a detailed account of the

---

that day, on the ground that it was opposed to all corporate banking, whether state or national." This was, of course, long before any such purpose was avowed as party policy. *Boston Reformer,* August 4, 1837.

† The "West" here includes Alabama, Mississippi, Lousiana, Kentucky, Tennessee, Ohio, Indiana, Illinois and Missouri. Jackson had only to carry one Western state to get a majority of the electoral votes.

history of paper money in America. The first section set forth the broad theoretical case, while the second provided the crushing documentation. Facts were Gouge's most powerful weapons; and in a plain, circumstantial way, occasionally flavored by irony, constantly buttressed by names, dates and citations, he supplied a crisp and comprehensive statement of the hard-money position.

The book became an instant success. Probably no work in economics had ever circulated so widely in the United States. The first edition was nearly exhausted by the fall of 1834, and, in 1835, it was reprinted in cheap stereotyped form to sell for twenty-five cents. By 1837 it had gone into a third edition. It was serialized in the *New York Evening Post* in 1834, and later in the *Washington Globe* and many other papers.

The book's success was deserved. Its historical sections went unchallenged, even by the most ardent defenders of the system; and Gouge's keenness of analysis, as well as his accuracy, has won the approval of our ablest historians of banking.

THE HARD-MONEY POLICY WAS CONCEIVED BY GOUGE and its other champions as a total alternative to the Hamiltonian system. Its central point was the exclusion of banks from control over the currency. It was not, as its opponents persisted in describing it, a demand for the annihilation of the banking system and the establishment of an exclusively metallic currency. It proposed merely to limit bank paper to commercial transactions, and to confine banks to the functions of deposit and discount, slowly withdrawing from them the privilege of note issue.

The main purposes were three. One was essentially economic: to prevent periodic depressions, another essentially political: to prevent the rise within the state of independent powers, not responsible to the people and able to defy the government; and the third essentially social: to prevent the rule of a moneyed aristocracy systematically exploiting the "humble members of society."

On the most obvious level, the working classes believed that they were regularly cheated by paper money. A good portion of the small notes they received in wages were depreciated, worthless or counterfeit. Unscrupulous employers even bought up depreciated notes and palmed them off on their workingmen at face value. And, in the larger economic picture, all the stable-income classes had to stand by helpless and impotent during the unpredictable rise and fall of prices or ebb and flow of credit.

The administration proposed to rescue the working classes from this treacherous economic order.

Prompted by these aims, the Jacksonians began to sketch out fairly coherent theories of self-generating business cycles.

In its simplest outline the theory was this: Banks incline to overissue their notes. Prices then rise, and a speculative fever begins to spread. Excited by the appearance of prosperity that accompanies boom, people spend freely. The general expansion of credit leads to overtrading and inflation. Every new business operation on credit creates more promissory notes, and these increase the demand for discounts, till finally the currency depreciates so greatly that specie is required for export in order to pay foreign debts. With specie at a premium, contraction sets in. Banks call in their loans, timid people start runs on banks, contraction turns to panic, and panic to collapse. "One man is unable to pay his debts," wrote Gouge. "His creditor depended on him for the means of paying a third person to whom he is himself indebted. The circle extends through society. Multitudes become bankrupt, and a few successful speculators get possession of the earnings and savings of many of their frugal and industrious neighbors."

The more careful analysts pointed out the complex interdependence of bank credit and general business activity, but political pamphleteers skipped the subtleties and blamed depressions on the paper-money system alone.

THE POLITICAL ARGUMENT—OPPOSITION TO THE RISE of independent powers within the state—had general premises deeply entrenched in the national consciousness. Everyone, from right to left, believed, with more or fewer qualifications, that sovereignty belonged to the people. It was but one step from this to declare that the people's government, therefore, should not be defied by private institutions; and it was easy to extend this proposition to economic institutions, as well as political.

In their nature as corporations, banks gave rise to one set of objections, springing from their monopoly of financial prerogative through special charter. Indeed, they provided so much the most flagrant instances of abuse of corporate privilege that they were mainly responsible for fixing national attention on the problem.

The behavior of banks in practice, moreover, violated the national faith in popular rule. The most powerful argument against Biddle's Bank was always its calm assumption of independence. "The Bank of the United States," Jackson charged, "is in itself a Government which has gradually increased in strength from the day of its establishment. The question between it and the people has become one of power." Biddle's conduct, in 1834, in refusing to allow a House committee to investigate the Bank records or examine the Bank officers, was simply the climax of his oft-expressed theory of the Bank's independence. "This powerful corporation, and those who defend it," as Taney said, without much exaggeration, "seem to regard it as an independent sovereignty, and to have forgotten that it owes any duties to the People, or is bound by any laws but its own will."

THE SOCIAL ARGUMENT—THE BATTLE AGAINST DOMination by "the rich and powerful"—represented the culmination of the hard-money doctrine. The economic and political arguments, though capable of standing by themselves, were ultimately directed at conditions preliminary to the question: who shall rule in the state? The recurrent economic crises were evil, not only in themselves, but because they facilitated a redistribution of wealth that built up the moneyed aristocracy. The irresponsible political sovereignties were evil, not only in themselves, but because they provided the aristocracy with instruments of power and places of refuge.

The Bank War compelled people to speculate once again about the conflict of classes. "There are but two parties," exclaimed Thomas Hart Benton, giving the period its keynote; "there never has been but two parties . . . founded in the radical question, whether PEOPLE, or PROPERTY, shall govern? Democracy implies a government by the people. . . . Aristocracy implies a government of the rich. . . . and in these words are contained the sum of party distinction."

The paper banking system was considered to play a leading role in this everlasting struggle. Men living by the issue and circulation of paper money produced nothing; they added nothing to the national income; yet, they flourished and grew wealthy.

The hard-money policy attacked both the techniques of plunder and the general strategy of warfare. By doing away with paper money, it proposed to restrict the steady transfer of wealth from the farmer and laborer to the business community. By limiting banks to commercial credit and denying them control over the currency, it proposed to lessen their influence and power.

By origin and interest, it was a policy which appealed mainly to the submerged classes of the East and to the farmers of the

South rather than to the frontier. Historians have too long been misled by the tableau of Jackson, the wild backwoodsman, erupting into the White House. In fact, the hard-money doctrine, which was not at all a frontier doctrine, was the controlling policy of the administration from the winter of 1833 on; and for some time it had been the secret goal of a small group, led by Jackson, Taney, Benton and Kendall, and passively encouraged by Van Buren.

Andrew Jackson ably summed up its broad aims. "The planter, the farmer, the mechanic, and the laborer," he wrote, "all know that their success depends upon their own industry and economy, and that they must not expect to become suddenly rich by the fruits of their toil." These classes "form the great body of the people of the United States; they are the bone and sinew of the country." Yet "they are in constant danger of losing their fair influence in the Government." Why? "The mischief springs from the power which the moneyed interest derives from a paper currency, which they are able to control, from the multitude of corporations with exclusive privileges which they have succeeded in obtaining in the different States." His warning to his people was solemn. "Unless you become more watchful . . . you will in the end find that the most important powers of Government have been given or bartered away, and the control over your dearest interests has passed into the hands of these corporations."

TANEY AND BENTON WORKED OUT THE DETAILS OF THE immediate hard-money measures. They proposed to increase the metallic basis of the currency in two directions: by the restoration of gold to circulation, and by the suppression of small notes.

The change in the coinage ratio was one of Benton's greatest triumphs.

The effects of revaluation were immediate. Levi Woodbury reported in December, 1836, that more gold had been coined in the twelve months preceding than in the first sixteen years of the mint's existence, and more in the two and a half years since revaluation than in the thirty-one before. In October, 1833, there had been only thirty million dollars of specie in the country, of which twenty-six million was in banks. In December, 1836, there was seventy-three million dollars, of which only forty-five million was in banks.

BUT THE ADMINISTRATION'S CAMPAIGN CAME TOO late. The wise counsels of the hard-money advocates were drowned out by the roar of the nation's greatest boom in years. The Bank of the United States alone enlarged its loans an average of two and a half million dollars a month and its paper circulation by a total of ten million dollars between December, 1834, and July, 1835. Smaller banks rushed to follow, increasing the amount of paper money from eighty-two million dollars on January 1, 1835, to one hundred and eight million, a year later, and one hundred and twenty million by December 1, 1836.

Wages climbed, opportunity seemed limitless and riches appeared to lie everywhere.

The administration watched the speculative mania with profound alarm.

Jackson, in the early months of 1836, lifted his voice in consternation against "the mad career" in which the nation was rushing to ruin.

A basic cause of the inflation was land speculation, and the administration had already moved to plug up this great hole in the national economy. The receivability of bank notes in payment for the public lands had practically converted the national domain into a fund for the redemption of the notes, providing in effect a capital for seven or eight hundred institutions to bank on, and filling the Treasury with more or less worthless paper. Benton had pointed out in detail how land sales passed on to the government the job of underwriting the whole banking system. Speculators would borrow five, ten, twenty, fifty thousand dollars in paper from banks on the condition of using it on the frontier. They would then pay the notes to government land offices in exchange for land, which served as security for additional loans; meanwhile, the notes circulated freely as land-office money, some never returning to the original bank for redemption, the rest only after a long interval. This racket not only subsidized the banking interest— land sales had risen from four million dollars a year to five million a quarter—but it also, in Benton's words, irretrievably entangled "the federal Government with the ups and downs of the whole paper system, and all the fluctuations, convulsions, and disasters, to which it was subject."

Benton introduced a resolution requiring that the public lands be paid for in specie. Webster, with his usual policy of supporting sound money except when concrete measures were proposed which might secure it, led the attack on this measure, and a combination of Whigs and conservative Democrats killed it in the Senate. But after adjournment Jackson had Benton draw up an executive order embodying his idea, and the famous "Specie Circular" was issued.

The business community grew furious over this latest evidence of executive despotism. When Congress reassembled in December, the Whigs demanded the repeal of the Circular and the reopening of the land offices to wildcat money, and the Democrats split wide under the pressure. One wing, led by William Cabell Rives of Virginia and N. P. Tallmadge of New York, emerged as defenders of the state banks. Benton vainly urged the imminence of a financial explosion which would leave the Treasury holding the bag; but his efforts won him little more than denunciation as "that most miserable Jacobin of the woods of Missouri, who, with an impudence and insolence unparalleled, has attempted to overthrow the commercial and financial relations and institutions of this country." The final vote disclosed a tiny group of five men, led by Benton and Silas Wright, upholding the hard-money position. The bill passed the House and went to the President on the day before adjournment. Firm to the end, the old General returned it with his veto.

Jackson thus had to overrule Congress to sustain the hard-money policy. But the Specie Circular furnished the only tense financial issue in the last years of his administration. After the panic session the great scenes of battle began to shift to the states. Here, in places inaccessible to the long arm and grim energy of General Jackson, little bands of devoted Jacksonians fought to stem the rush for bank and corporate charters, unfolding the potentialities of the Jacksonian program, enriching the techniques and amplifying the intellectual resources.

Above all, these local battles called forth the common people in cities, towns and country—the poor day laborer, the industrious mechanic, the hard-handed farmer—the "humble members of society" everywhere. They listened for hours on hot summer days to dry expositions of financial policy. They crowded in bare and unheated halls on cold winter nights to hear about the evils of banking. They read, and thumbed, and passed along tracts and speeches attacking the paper system. They saw the dizzy climb of prices, wages lagging behind, raged silently at discounted bank notes, and wondered at the behavior of Democratic politicians pledged against voting for incorporations. They talked among themselves, with shrewdness and good sense and alarm. . . . Their discontent was real and widespread. It found its leaders, and the experience of these years prepared them for one great final drive on the national scene.

XI *Credo of the Workingmen*

DURING THE EIGHTEEN-TWENTIES, THE NEW INDUS-
trial order had stirred deep currents of discontent through the
laboring classes of the North and East. The tensions of adjustment to new modes of employment and production created
pervasive anxieties, and evidence of actual suffering under the
new system led humble working people to fear for their very
self-respect and status in society. An inexorable destiny seemed
to be pressing them into a separate estate as the dispossessed of
the nation, and they were struggling frantically to escape.

SOME BENEFICIARIES OF THE NEW ORDER SOUGHT TO
explain away industrial poverty by proclaiming its inevitability,
when they did not proclaim its nonexistence. Such men as
Mathew Carey supplied a valuable corrective. Carey was no
radical—rather, a rich Philadelphia businessman of conservative political views; but the lower classes seemed to him no
more naturally depraved than any other class, and he proposed
that the main cause of their discontent was wages too low for
subsistence.

Carey set forth this view in indignant pamphlets, fortified by
statistics and by the reports of competent observers, detailing
the plight of those who supported themselves by their hands.
Carey estimated there to be eight or nine million of them, and
sought to tell their story.

His list of "erroneous opinions" about the poor is an apt
comment on the folklore of the possessing classes to this day.

1. That every man, woman, and grown child able and
willing to work may find employment.

2. That the poor, by industry, prudence, and economy,
may at all times support themselves comfortably, without
depending on eleemosynary aid—and, as a corollary from
these positions.

3. That their sufferings and distresses chiefly, if not
wholly, arise from their idleness, their dissipation, and their
extravagance.

4. That taxes for the support of the poor, and aid
afforded them by charitable individuals, or benevolent so-
cieties, are pernicious, as by encouraging the poor to depend

on them, they foster their idleness and improvidence, and thus produce, or at least increase, the poverty and distress they are intended to relieve.

The remedy? Carey despaired of finding any, so long as the supply of labor exceeded the demand, and suggested only palliatives, chiefly charity and self-restraint.

Though mechanics and small shopkeepers in the towns and men on the farms did not themselves ordinarily experience this direct physical distress, such reports as those of Carey produced among them a grim determination to resist the extension of this misery. Active opposition thus first arose among these still fairly prosperous groups, not yet injured by the new industrialism, but frightened by the desolation it spread elsewhere.

Their demands accordingly had little to do with specific economic grievances. For them the central concern was, in the words of a Workingmen's leader from western Massachusetts, "that the laboring classes in our country, in consequence of the inroads and usurpations of the wealthy and powerful, have for years been gradually sinking in the scale of public estimation." The main source of this growing sense of inequality, as another Workingmen's orator put it, lay in the "continued prevalence of irrational, anti-republican and unchristian opinions in relation to the worth and respectability of *manual labor*."

The first necessity in combating this assault on the dignity of labor was the unity of the working classes; and after this came a series of special demands, intended to improve labor morale rather than its economic position. These made regular appearances, with slight variations, on the mastheads of nearly all the Workingmen's papers:—

Equal Universal Education.
Abolition of Imprisonment for Debt.
Abolition of all Licensed Monopolies.
An entire Revision, or Abolition of the present Militia System.
A Less Expensive Law System.
Equal Taxation on Property.
An Effective Lien Law for Laborers.
All Officers to be Elected by the People.
No Legislation on Religion.

THE MOST IMPORTANT OF THE PLANKS WERE THE DEmands for education and for the abolition of imprisonment for debt. Education would diffuse knowledge, and knowledge, the early labor leaders believed, was power. In these United

States, said Dr. Charles Douglas, an ardent New England radical, "knowledge and union will always insure reform." Labor agitation played an important part in the rise of education in these years.

But the main specific grievance came to be the question of imprisonment for debt. In 1830 five sixths of the persons in the jails of New England and the Middle states were debtors, most of them owing less than twenty dollars. The law was thus, in effect, a class law, applying chiefly to the poor. It was an irrational law, for, by withdrawing debtors from the economic world, it prevented their saving up and paying off. It was, moreover, insulting, for in last analysis it assumed that debtors would never meet their obligations unless prompted by terror of punishment. General fears about loss of status thus began to focus on imprisonment for debt as a peculiarly cruel and wanton agency of degradation.*

The first bill calling for a complete repeal of the system, except in instances of fraud, was introduced in the New York Senate in 1817 by Martin Van Buren, who had sponsored a bill for the relief of small debtors as early as 1813. Colonel Richard M. Johnson, a debtor himself in 1819 and many other years, soon began a similar campaign, in Kentucky.

The chief opposition came from the business community with its vague but deep conviction that imprisonment for debt was bound up with sanctity of contracts.

When Jackson became President, he added his prestige to Johnson's perseverance ("it should be the care of a republic not to exert a grinding power over misfortune and poverty"), and finally, in 1832, the bill passed both Houses and became a law. In another decade the penalty had disappeared from the statute books of nearly all the states.

COLONEL JOHNSON'S TIRELESS WORK ON BEHALF OF the poor debtors gave him the special confidence of the working class. His role in another controversy was now to establish him more than ever as their faithful champion.

Social radicalism in America had long been tinged with anticlericalism. The old alliances of church establishments with local aristocracies, and the widespread assumption of the clergy that God was a disciple of Alexander Hamilton, had antagonized men of liberal inclination; and European deism

---

* This was more true in the city than in the country. Agricultural debtors, confronted with the surrender of their land as the normal alternative to imprisonment, were consequently less enthusiastic about the reform, preferring to suffer imprisonment themselves while leaving their families to run the farm. For an admirable account and analysis of the agitation, see G. P. Bauer, "The Movement Against Imprisonment for Debt in the United States," unpublished doctoral thesis, Harvard University.

obligingly provided plausible arguments from history and philosophy for detesting the clergy and spurning revealed religion. The French Revolution sharpened the issue when its antireligious excesses provoked preachers through the country to warn against too much democracy.

This revival of anticlericalism answered oddly well to certain perplexities of the working classes. The discontent stirred up by industrial change needed intensely an object on which it could release its aggressions, and it settled upon this alleged conspiracy to reunite Church and State.

The final event, which came as a striking confirmation of Jeffersonian suspicions was a Fourth of July sermon delivered in Philadelphia in 1827 by the Reverend Ezra Stiles Ely of the Presbyterian church. Ely was an old friend of Jackson's, and his address was actually a concealed attack on Adams as a Unitarian. Yet it contained passages which seemed to disclose the most secret intentions of the evangelical sects. "I propose, fellow-citizens," said Ely, "a new sort of union, or, if you please, *a Christian party in politics.*" If the Presbyterians, Baptists, Methodists, Congregationalists and Episcopalians would only unite on voting day, Ely declared, they "could govern every public election in our country."

A Christian party in politics: THE PHRASE RANG OMInously in the ears of the leaders of the workingmen. Then, in the next May, a convention of ministers and laymen met in New York to form the General Union for Promoting the Observance of the Christian Sabbath.

The chief danger of the purity of the Sabbath, according to the General Union, lay in the transportation of mail on that day. In 1810 postmasters had been ordered to keep their offices open for one hour on Sunday after the arrival of mail. Remonstrances against this practice drifted into Congress during the next few years but to no effect. In 1825 post offices which received mail on Sunday were required to be kept open all day. It was this deed of profanation which the Sabbatarians now determined to undo.

Most of the leaders in the campaign were conservative businessmen, disturbed by the rumblings of the people and longing for the restoration of moral authority.

The flow of petitions to Congress was meanwhile diverted to a Senate committee headed by Colonel Johnson, which rejected them with a resounding statement of religious liberty. "It is not the legitimate province of the Legislature to determine what religion is true, or what false," Johnson declared in his first report. "Our Government is a civil, and not a religious institution."*

Richard M. Johnson, the opponent of imprisonment for debt, now became in addition the great champion of religious liberty.

JOHNSON HAD STRUCK FIRE WITH THE WORKING classes because his embodiment of political democracy in the Western manner coincided in good part with the Eastern workingmen's fears of loss of status: this natural classlessness of the frontier was precisely what they felt was vanishing from their lives. But the Bank War raised new questions. How much, in fact, had the standard Workingmen's program to do with the causes of labor discontent?

Measured in terms of the antagonisms which Jackson was beginning to uncover, their platform seemed increasingly irrelevant. It was, in fact, a humanitarian program, formulated out of a sympathy for distress rather than out of the experience of exploitation, thus appealing to almost anyone of humane and generous disposition. Most conservatives were actually as much in favor of education as the laboring classes, if only because it seemed the way to make the best of universal suffrage. Many conservatives were as much opposed to imprisonment for debt. Many conservatives favored Sunday mails; and few people in any case took the question very seriously. In fact, the whole Sunday-mail controversy evaporated with great rapidity. There was not a shred of evidence for the great Church and State conspiracy, and in the second year of its existence the General Union for Promoting the Observance of the Christian Sabbath had only twenty-six local chapters and

---

* R. M. Johnson, *Report on the Transportation of the Mail on Sunday*, 5-6. Johnson's second report, when reprinted in London in 1053, was declared to be "probably the ablest state document on record on the non-interference of government with the observance of the Sabbath, and the noblest political plea for the rights of conscience produced in modern times." *The Parliamentary Observance of the Sabbath an Infringement of Public Right and Liberty of Conscience*, 3.

The actual authorship of the report is a matter of some question. It was produced in the home of the Reverend O. B. Brown, for some years the center of the Kentucky influence in Washington. Johnson boarded there, Amos Kendall put up there when he first came to Washington, and Brown himself was chief clerk of the Post Office Department under William T. Barry on week days, in addition to being a Baptist preacher on Sundays. The reports are written in a loose rhetorical style, at which Johnson, Barry, Brown and Kendall were all adept. Probably Brown did most of the actual writing, in consultation with Johnson. Kendall later revised the report. Johnson took the responsibility and never refused the credit. Brown later came to grief when a Senate committee accused him of using his position to borrow from mail contractors and invest in mail contracts. See Meyer, *Johnson*, 256-263; Kendall, *Autobiography*, 288, 307; *Washington Globe*, February 10, 1835; Ben: Perley Poore, *Reminiscences*, I, 96, 218. The report was also attributed, without any perceptible reason, to Calhoun; A. Mazyck to R. K. Crallé, September 13, 1854 (1844), F. W. Moore, ed., "Calhoun by His Political Friends," *Publications of Southern History Association*, VII, 420.

less than $230 in its treasury. The main Workingmen's issues thus hardly touched the economic grounds of their dilemma.

The Jacksonian movement brought the decisive reminder that this dilemma was a problem, not of clericalism or of education, but the wealth. Politicians and middle-class intellectuals, enlightened by Jeffersonian insights into the economic basis of democracy, began to bring the working classes nearer the actual causes of their discontent. During the Bank War, laboring men began slowly to turn to Jackson as their leader, and his party as their party. Their own parties, engaged in kindhearted activity on the periphery of the problem, disappeared.

This conversion of the working classes to the hard-money policy injected new strength and determination into the hard-money party. It took place mainly in the states, mainly in terms of local issues, mainly out of local experiences. From it would come the impetus to carry through the second stage in the national struggles of Jacksonian democracy.

XII *Stirrings in the Bay State*

IF THE IMPACT OF THE INDUSTRIAL REVOLUTION WAS responsible for the particular direction which the Jacksonians gave to the philosophy of Jefferson, then the most serious discussion of Jacksonian issues was to be looked for in the states most dominated by the new industrialism. These states were Massachusetts and New York. In them, the banking system was firmly entrenched. Manufacturing had gained a strong foothold. Financial, industrial and commercial groups were active in politics. The working classes were becoming conscious of a common plight which required unity for defense. When the Jacksonian effort shifted in the middle thirties to the states, it was thus in Massachusetts and New York that the crucial problems of Jacksonian democracy received most urgent attention.

MASSACHUSETTS SUCCUMBED TO THE INDUSTRIAL REVolution in the first three decades of the nineteenth century. Slowly, mills, factories and banks displaced shipbuilding and seafaring as the focus of business activity. The curve of this change could be traced in the permutations of Daniel Webster's

views on the tariff, as his thunderous briefs for the merchant
and free trade began to hesitate and quaver, till they gave way
to equally thunderous briefs for the mill owner and protection.

Massachusetts leaders like John Quincy Adams, Justice
Story, Governor Levi Lincoln and Alexander H. Everett, editor of the *North American Review,* had already assisted at the
transformation of right-wing Jeffersonianism into the National
Republican party; and most of the former Federalists, like
Webster, eventually joined them there in defense of the American System.

With Webster, Adams and Lincoln at their head, the National Republicans ran the state politically. Among the younger
group, the most promising in 1830 was perhaps Edward
Everett, that pale, courteous and polished man, tall and erect,
with his handsome, conventional face and his fatal flow of
rhetoric, who was nearly smothered by the adulation which
surrounded him. Barely turned twenty, he had been a brilliant
minister whose sermons moved John Quincy Adams to tears.
Soon he left the pulpit for a chair at Harvard where his golden
periods re-created Greece for Ralph Waldo Emerson. Now he
shone in politics, a leading member of the House and the white
hope of the clubs of Boston. In John Davis of Worcester, the
conservatives had a good lawyer, reliable legislator and enormously successful vote-getter; he was known as "Honest John
Davis," which is supposed to have provoked Henry Clay to
exclaim, *"Honest John Davis, I say, Cunning John Fox!"*
From the bar conservatism recruited such talented younger
men as Rufus Choate and Caleb Cushing, and from the business community itself came the independent and conscientious
Nathan Appleton and able Abbott Lawrence.

The sanction of Culture was reinforced by the immutable
prescriptions of Justice and Law, as interpreted by such judges
as Peter Oxenbridge Thacher and such lawyers as Jeremiah
Mason. The clergy hastened to add Religion. Some preachers,
like James Walker and Hubbard Winslow, openly advocated
conservatism, while others, like William Ellery Channing, accomplished much the same end by urging reform, but only in
ways in which it could not practically be achieved. The work
of Channing in sabotaging the liberal impulses of his day by his
theory of "internal" reform, with its indifference to external
social change, has never been properly appreciated.

Thus on all fronts the "natural aristocracy" of Massachusetts wheeled into action. Richard Hildreth, associate editor of
the furious Whig sheet, the *Boston Atlas,* frankly described the
result:—

The truth is, that so stern, severe, active and influential was the authority which the allied hierarchy exercised, that few men who had property, standing, character, friends, to lose, cared to risk the consequences of those bulls of excommunication which were fulminated from the pulpit and the press, and those torrents of calumny, denunciation, and abuse, poured forth by a thousand fluent tongues, against whomsoever deserted the ark of the covenant, and allied himself to the uncircumcised Philistines.

AND WHAT OF THE PHILISTINES? "THIS DAY ASSEMBLE in State convention the Jackson party," the librarian of the American Antiquarian Society noted in his diary on September 1, 1831. ". . . It is rather a miserable concern and is composed of such as want office and the disaffected of all parties."*

Who else would be a Democrat? In 1828 two factions had supported Jackson: the diehard Federalists, led by Theodore Lyman, and a group of small businessmen and politicans, refused social and political acceptance by the governing class, led by David Henshaw. Jackson's victory made Henshaw collector of the Port of Boston, with control over the federal patronage, and thus boss of the party in the state. Gruff, candid and confident, Henshaw aimed straight at his objectives and accomplished them with a minimum of moral scruple. His health was bad, and in later years the gout ruined an already unstable temper.

Though a wealthy man, Henshaw had many of the prejudices of his humble origin. His personal rancor toward the aristocracy which had snubbed him was not unlike that of his good friend Isaac Hill. He took a forthright progressive stand on issues like imprisonment for debt and ballot reform; and he led the fight for a free bridge across the Charles River, a project bitterly opposed by conservatives because it threatened the profits of a neighboring toll-bridge, owned by Harvard and by prominent Bostonians.

FOR MANY YEARS MASSACHUSETTS HAD REQUIRED little more than these minor differences between a Henshaw and a Webster. But industrialism was stirring up new politi-

* C. C. Baldwin, *Diary*, 139. Cf. Hildreth's account of the Democrats: "The mass of the party seemed made up like the band of David, when he rose in rebellion against the Lord's anointed;—all who were in debt, all who were in distress, all who were discontented, enlisted beneath this banner; and to believe the account of their opponents, not the tatterdemalions of Falstaff's enlistment were more idle, vicious, dishonest and dangerous." *Despotism in America*, 13.

cal demands which a straight line drawn between Webster and
Henshaw failed to hold in check. The factory system, appear-
ing at a time when both farmers and independent journeymen
found the going increasingly hard, seemed to prefigure the
gloomy end to which the laboring class was descending. The
mill owners inadvertently intensified these anxieties by insist-
ing on reprinting grim tales of English factory conditions as
part of their campaign for a protective tariff.

During 1830, in the towns of eastern Massachusetts, small
mechanics and workers, similarly apprehensive over their role
in an industrialized future, began to form urban chapters of the
Workingmen's party. The movement spread. A meeting at Boston, in February, 1832, was followed in September by a general convention of what was now called the "New England
Association of Farmers, Mechanics and other Workingmen."

A more colorful champion of the New England Association
was the *Artisan's* "Travelling Agent," Seth Luther. In 1832
Luther was nearly forty, tall and lanky, tending toward bald-
ness, with a cud of tobacco generally in his mouth, and cherishing a bitter passion for the working classes. He had knocked
a good deal around the country, East and West, town and
frontier, even taking long trips through the wilderness.

When he returned to New England about 1830, he found
the independent Yankee yeoman confronted by the menace of
the new industrialism. His ready sympathies seized on the situation, spurred on by the writings of Douglas and of Theophilus Fisk (who had now left *Priestcraft Unmasked* to make
a hard hitting radical sheet out of the *New Haven Examiner*).
In 1832 Luther, conspicuous in his famous green jacket,
traveled through the mill towns, haranguing the operatives,
checking on conditions and agitating for the New England
Association, though few of its members were themselves factory workers. The intense interest excited by his reports of mill
life reflected the deep concern with which the submerged
classes were contemplating their future.

SUCH INTIMATIONS FROM WASHINGTON, JACKSON'S
triumphant tour of New England and the example of the New
York Workingmen helped break down labor neutrality. Late
in 1833 Samuel Clesson Allen rejected overtures to become the
National Republican nominee for Governor with an able
statement of his grounds for backing Jackson:

There are two great classes in the community founded in
the relation they respectively bear to the subject of its

wealth. The one is the *producer,* and the other the *accumulator.* The whole products are divided between them. Has not one an interest to retain as much as it can, and the other an interest to *get* as much as it can? . . .

The administration of every government, whether it is seen or not, will be guided and controlled by one or the other of these interests. . . .

It is in the nature of things that government will always adapt its policy, be the theory of its constitution what it may, to the interests and aims of the predominating class. . . .

I ask if labor has ever had a predominating influence in any government? . . .

I should be glad to see an experiment of *one* administration, of which the interests of this class should be the guiding star. . . .

I am encouraged in my hopes of an economical reform by the course which the President has taken in regard to the United States Bank. . . .

What government in these days has been able to stand against the power of *associated wealth?* It is the *real dynasty* of modern states.

The New England Association promptly endorsed Allen's letter, and a few days later a committee of Charlestown Workingmen invited him to be their candidate for Governor.

XIII *George Bancroft and Radicalism in Massachusetts*

IN 1834 A THIRD LEADER EMERGED IN WESTERN MASSachusetts, younger and more aggressive than Allen or Sedgwick. George Bancroft of Northampton, like the others, sharply repudiated his past in assuming his new role. He was the son of the Reverend Aaron Bancroft of Worcester, president of the American Unitarian Association and a staunch conservative. He was the son-in-law of Jonathan Dwight, a wealthy capitalist of Springfield. He was, moreover, the brother-in-law of Honest John Davis, soon to succeed Levi Lincoln as Governor, and Edward Everett had been one of his closest friends since Harvard days. He was a consultant contributor to the *North American Review,* and till 1831 was co-proprietor of the Round Hill School at Northampton, which drew its students from some of the richest families in the country. All Bancroft's normal allegiances, in short, were with the "natural aristocracy."

YET BANCROFT WAS TOO CLEVER AND TOO SKEPTICAL to accept the values of Boston with the piety of an Everett, or to tailor his talents according to specifications laid down by Harvard and State Street. He went to Europe after finishing college in 1817; and when he returned the Athens of America seemed flat and disappointing. He appeared in a few pulpits, tutored a little at Harvard, published a book of poems and finally in 1823 helped establish a progressive school at Northampton. Though the Round Hill School flourished in the twenties, Bancroft was no great teacher, and Northampton too restricted a stage. More and more his writings won him attention as a rising young literary man.

Politics, too, vaguely attracted him. In 1826, in a Fourth of July speech at Northampton, he declared bravely in favor of "a democracy, a determined, uncompromising democracy," at a time when the word still sounded in some Massachusetts ears with the horrors of the French Revolution. But when actually elected to the state legislature in 1830 by the Workingmen's party, he declined to serve. In the fall of 1830 he ignored the plea of the Jackson paper in Springfield that he stand for Congress. Early in 1831 he declined the nomination of the Workingmen for the state Senate. A few months later he even incorporated in an essay for the *North American Review* a passage discouraging young men of talent and education from entering politics.

In the meantime, however, he wrote, also for the *North American,* an article on the United States Bank so unfriendly as to shock the Everetts and delight Martin Van Buren. Warning the Everetts that they might find his remarks on the McDuffie report "a little heretical," Bancroft still allowed them to believe that he ultimately favored recharter. Edward Everett confessed himself "embarrassed" over what should be done with the somewhat irreverent manuscript, and A. H. Everett tried to fix it up by tacking on a final sentence which explicitly advocated recharter. "I thought it on the whole more politic in the interest of the Review that this point should be quite clear," he explained to Bancroft in words which perhaps lend color to the charge that the *North American* was in the pay of the Bank. But Everett's conclusion hardly followed from Bancroft's argument. "There is very little reason to doubt,"

Bancroft had blandly declared, "that the sun would still rise and set, and the day be spent in its usual business, and merchandise be bought and sold, and bills of exchange be negotiated, even without . . . the Bank of the United States." This was more than a "little heretical," and Everett found a follow-up article "so decidedly hostile" to the Bank that he saw no choice but to refuse it.

Bancroft, who knew what he was about, took care that Van Buren should see the *North American* piece, confiding to him that he considered the Bank contrary to the principles of equal rights. Actually, his case in the article rested much more on state-banking prejudices than on broad principle. "The undoubted merits of the National Bank are urged too exclusively," he suavely observed, "as though other sound establishments of the country were not just as wisely, moderately, and efficiently conducted." The display of technical knowledge suggests that he consulted with Jonathan Dwight, his father-in-law and a heavy investor in state banks.

Bancroft was still not ready to make the break. When he attended a presidential reception in 1831, he was still the supercilious Harvardian, conceding Jackson's good manners and warm heart, "but touching his qualifications for President, avast there—Sparta hath many a wiser son than he." The next year at the National Republican State Convention at Worcester he served, along with Edward Everett, Abbott Lawrence and others, on the committee which issued a ringing anti-Jackson address to the people.

Sometime after the election of 1832, he decided to abandon his class and cast his lot with the despised Democrats and Workingmen. Political apostasy is too complex a problem to be ascribed simply to ambition or treachery. Bancroft's whole life had been a series of minor revolts against the "natural aristocracy," and occasional outbursts like his speech of 1826 betrayed a profound sympathy with the idea of democracy. But his whole upbringing proscribed these liberal impulses. Thus a precarious balance of loyalties developed, producing a vacillation which was by no means evidence of insincerity.

What precipitated the final decision? Bancroft had already begun work on his great history of the United States, the first volume of which would come out in 1834. This determination to devote his life to such a history, which he conceived as the story of the invincible progress of human liberty, undoubtedly released his democratic prepossessions in full flood.

He finally took the step, not as an item in political opportunism, but as an act of faith. Though he often in later life ignored his views of 1834, he never recanted them. And, in expressing them in 1834, joining a minority group in a solidly conservative state, he clearly had little to gain. "I have never made disclaimers or apologies," he said rather sadly a decade later. "To advocate Democracy in Massachusetts, is no holiday pastime. . . . Our course is not too often enlivened by success; we are wounded sometimes even by our friends. We tread a thorny path, but it leads upwards to the home of freedom, of justice, of truth."

THE CONGRESSIONAL TICKET FOR 1836 SHOWED THE strength of the radicals. The list was headed by Bancroft, Samuel Clesson Allen, Theodore Sedgwick, Alexander H. Everett and Amasa Walker. Able Marcus Morton was the candidate for governor. The platform was unequivocally radical. As one paper remarked, the Workingmen's measures had now been "adopted in all the addresses and at all the conventions of the Democratic party, and are, in fact, part and parcel of their cause."

The transformation from the philosophy of David Henshaw to the philosophy of Andrew Jackson was nearly complete. It paid both in men and in votes. The Democrats presented strong candidates in 1836 for a party which had been a despised minority a few years before; and, though the Whigs still carried the state, Morton's vote reached a new high of nearly thirty-six thousand, an increase of almost eleven thousand over 1835 and of thirty-one and a half thousand over 1828.

XIV *Radicalism in New York*

IN NEW YORK, THE OLD JEFFERSONIAN PARTY WAS dominant rather than the party of the business community, and the crucial Jacksonian struggles thus began within the Democratic organization. The powerful commercial groups which had inevitably clustered round the governing party fought grimly with the men of labor and the radical democrats, each faction vying with the other in bringing pressure on the people who controlled the party machine—above all, on Martin Van Buren and the Albany Regency.

VAN BUREN'S POWER WITHIN THE STATE RESTED IN great part on this informal organization. The Regency directed policy, distributed offices, ran campaigns and made the important party decisions. Its political unity was cemented by close personal relations. The members dined and drank together, talked, joked and argued till late in the night. Their families were friendly, and their wives kissed when they met. They took care that no one who served the Regency should suffer as a consequence, and young men of talent and Jeffersonian principle were certain of rapid promotion. Their ideal of public service was high.

Other things being equal, the Regency favored reform. Van Buren, a veteran of bitter fights against imprisonment for debt and for the extension of the suffrage, pushed through the safety-fund act of 1829, which, for all its weaknesses, at least forced the banks to yield for the first time to conditions prescribed by the legislature.

IN THE MEANTIME DEEPER URGENCIES WERE AT WORK among the laboring classes. New York was affected no less than Massachusetts by sudden fears of dispossession sweeping among the wage earners like chill ocean winds. But the New York movement was much more an urban affair because of the comparative prosperity of the farmers upstate. The struggles over debt imprisonment and the Sunday mails were intense, especially in New York City, and through the decade of the twenties there was an insistent demand for action on most of the items in the familiar platform of Workingmen's grievances.

The most ambitious attempt to provide a new platform for labor unrest had been made by Robert Owen, the Scotch philanthropist, in the middle twenties. Though many of his remarks on property and some on religion appealed to the wage earners, his general solution—a co-operative commonwealth along the lines of New Harmony—was essentially unreal, both for people whose habits and obligations bound them to existing society, and for an economy whose greatest potentialities, for production and for profit, lay in the direction of increased industrialization.

The Owenite theories had a greater impact through the influence of Frances Wright. A young Scotswoman, who had come to America in 1818 and again with Lafayette in 1824, she had undertaken in 1826 the famous Nashoba experiment in an attempt to mitigate the slavery problem. Failure at Nashoba settled her conviction that the basic obstacle to reform was the corruption of the American people by a false system of education maintained by the clergy. Her belief in the omnipotence of the environment in forming character, as well as her anticlericalism, inclined her to a sympathy with Owen. On visits to New Harmony, she won an enthusiastic follower in Robert Dale Owen. In 1828 she became co-editor of the *New Harmony Gazette* with young Owen, and in 1829 they moved the journal to New York, renaming it the *Free Enquirer*.

Thirty-five years old in 1830, Fanny Wright had an attractive, unclouded face, with chestnut hair falling in natural curls, large blue eyes, clear and serious, and a tall, slender, graceful figure. She spoke in a rich, musical voice, disarming the most bitter by her radiant enthusiasm. Her mind was courageous, logical and independent, and she wrote militant and vivid prose. Her followers adored her. Hard-handed mechanics and workers crowded the halls when she lectured, and pored over copies of the *Free Enquirer* in flickering light late into the evening.

A carpenter named Walter Whitman, staunch radical Democrat and admirer of Tom Paine, listened raptly to Miss Wright and subscribed to the *Free Enquirer*. He named one son after Thomas Jefferson and another after Andrew Jackson; a third, whom he called simply Walter, after himself, used to muse in later years on lovely Fanny Wright. "She has always been to me one of the sweetest of sweet memories," he said: "we all loved her: fell down before her: her very appearance seemed to enthrall us . . . graceful, deer-like . . . she was beautiful in bodily shape and gifts of soul." Old Walt Whitman was deep in recollection. "I never felt so glowingly towards any other woman," he finally said. ". . . she possessed herself of my body and soul."

This was Fanny Wright—this was "the great Red Harlot of Infidelity." Around her gathered the live spirits of the Workingmen's movement. Robert Dale Owen, her closest associate, was six years younger, a short, blue-eyed, sandy-haired man.

They discovered a useful ally in George H. Evans, an English printer who had come to America some years before. Like the others, Evans was an agnostic and an anticlerical. Late in 1829 he founded the *Working Man's Advocate*, perhaps the most influential of the labor papers.

On the outskirts of the group, more interested in the anticlerical than the anticapitalist side of the *Free Enquirer*, was another Englishman, Dr. Gilbert Vale, who had come to New York in 1823. A man of some learning in the sciences, especially astronomy and navigation, he edited a free-thinking journal called *The Beacon* and wrote a biography of Tom Paine.

BUT FANNY WRIGHT DOMINATED THE GROUP. HER thrilling perceptions of the social crisis inflamed everyone dissatisfied with the existing order. "The most dull can perceive that a moral excitement, new in its nature and rapid in its progress, pervades the world," she would say in her fine contralto voice. ". . . The priest trembles for his craft, the rich man for his hoard, the politician for his influence. . . . From the people—ay! from the people, arise the hum and stir of awakening intelligence, enquiry, and preparation."

What were the causes of the crisis? First, the stimulus given to business enterprise by technological improvements, and even more by competition, which would continue "until it results in the ruin of small capitalists, and in the oppression of the whole laboring class of the community"; second, the banking system and paper money, "one of the deepest sources of industrial oppression and national demoralization"; third, the "professional aristocracy" of priests, lawyers and politicians, using their power to cheat the people; and fourth and most fundamental, "a false system of education, stolen from aristocratic Europe."

THE *New York Evening Post* HAD COME FAR FOR A paper founded by Alexander Hamilton. When William Coleman, the original editor, died in 1829, it passed into the hands of William Cullen Bryant, a literary man from Massachusetts. As a child Bryant had delighted his Federalist father by writing a poetical satire against Jefferson; but Theodore Sedgwick, a friend of the family, assisted in his political emancipation, and he came to New York in 1826 already a confirmed free trader. There he met James Fenimore Cooper, G. C. Verplanck and Benjamin F. Butler, all ardent Democrats. In the election of 1828 he contributed a vote and an ode to Jackson's victory. By 1830 Edward Everett had to report him regretfully as "poisoned with the gall of Jacksonism."

A man of middle height, thirty-six years old in 1830, Bryant had a large, sallow face, piercing gray eyes and heavy eyebrows which gave him an almost saturnine cast of countenance, too often verified by his coldness of manner, though intimates sometimes found him chatty and even gay. He worked painfully at a small space, cleared by main force, on a desk piled two feet high with books, pamphlets, political documents, opened letters and forgotten manuscripts, scrawling his editorials on the back of pieces of waste paper and objecting to all proposals for improvement.

Though his free-trade convictions first inclined him toward

Jackson, they were not the cause of his continued support. When other free traders, like J. G. King and Verplanck, turned against the administration because of the Bank War, Bryant stoutly backed the old General, to the horror of the business community which the *Evening Post* primarily served. Like Sedgwick and Foster, Bryant was genuinely a humanitarian radical. And, for all his austerity, he was capable of direct action. When he got into a quarrel in 1831, with Colonel William L. Stone, editor of the conservative *Commercial Advertiser,* he tried to horsewhip Stone on the streets of New York. Stone in response splintered a bamboo cane on Bryant's arm, revealing a dagger inside. For a moment the atmosphere was charged; then spectators swept in and separated them.

Early in 1829 Bryant hired a literary man-about-town named William Leggett as his assistant.

The Bank War led Leggett to define his economic ideas, and he quickly advanced, through sheer passion for logic, to extreme radical positions. He was most interested, as he constantly reiterated, in general principles of government. His body of editorials constituted an education in political philosophy for the New York Democrats.

In 1835 they were joined by Theodore Sedgwick, Jr., the bright twenty-four-year-old son of Bryant's old friend in Stockbridge. When he went to New York to work in his uncle's law office, he found Leggett, short-handed with Bryant away in Europe, pleased to accept contributions on the Bank War in the *Post.* The occasional pithy articles signed by "Veto" became a valuable addition to the *Post's* influence.

THE BANK WAR STIMULATED THE BRETHREN OF THE *Post* to launch into the questions of currency and incorporation. Leggett had an edition of Gouge's *Paper Money* stereotyped at his own expense, and Sedgwick set forth the position on monopoly in a series of articles, beginning in the *Post* late in 1834, afterwards expanded into a responsible and reasoned pamphlet entitled *What Is a Monopoly?*

His main object of attack was the system of special charters, which made, as he said, each act of incorporation "a grant of exclusive privilege, and every grant of exclusive privilege," he went on, "strictly speaking, creates a monopoly." That is, every such grant carried on its face that the corporators had received special advantages from which the mass of the people were excluded. "This is the very substance of monopoly. . . . Every corporate grant is directly in the teeth of the doctrine of equal rights." Since our nation has been founded on that doctrine, exceptions to it should be permitted only when the objects attained were of "paramount public necessity," and obtainable no other way. Was this the case with corporations? Sedgwick thought not, and proposed to show that the commercial advantages could be more equitably secured under another system.

What should be done? "Enact a general law," Sedgwick answered, under which any group of individuals might form a corporation without application to the legislature. Let all businesses, and banking among them, be thrown open to universal competition (except for railroads and turnpikes, where the object could not be attained without monopoly rights, but here the charters should have reservations of revocability). The antimonopoly party must smash the system of special charters, with its by-products of graft, log-rolling, lobbying and political dishonesty, and open the field to genuine free enterprise.

Sedgwick's unimpassioned manner, the force of his documentation and the good sense of his solution aroused wide attention; and when these arguments were transmuted by Leggett's flaming pen into editorials for the *Evening Post*, they caused a sensation. Bryant, Leggett and Sedgwick were saved from traveling the conservative path of most free traders by their vivid sense of class conflict. Basic to their use of the laissez-faire arsenal was a perception of what Sedgwick called "the social division of parties"—a division which, he pointed out, had run through our history. The upper classes, distinguished socially by exclusiveness, economically by wealth, and politically by mistrust of the people, had always grasped after all the power in the state. Jackson had revived the democratic tradition, and "the *upper classes* are now perhaps more universally arrayed against us than they have ever yet been." Leggett characteristically rejoiced in the situation. "It may be said that this open and direct array of one class of the community against the other, is dangerous to the future peace and happiness of our city. . . . Well, so it is. But who has drawn the line? Who has beat the alarm?" "We venture to predict," said Bryant, "that so long as our legislative bodies continue to deal out with unsparing hand, bank charters . . . this feeling of the poor towards the rich will become every day more aggravated."

XV *Rise of the Locofocos*

THE BEGINNINGS OF INFLATION IN 1834 SHARPENED the interest with which the common people of New York and their mentors watched the banking situation. Early in August, Leggett declared that the *Post* would support only those candidates committed unequivocally against bills under $5 and against further bank charters. Following his lead, the Workingmen's party secured pledges from the Democratic nominees in exchange for labor endorsement. When the Democrats swept the fall elections, Leggett continued his pressure on Governor Marcy and the new legislature. ("Marcy, as usual, got so frightened whilst the Post was at him," John Van Buren wrote to his father, "that before the Message came out, he was a pretty thorough radical.") With the opening of the session, the issue was posed. Would the New York Democrats oppose all irresponsible paper money, or only paper put out by Whig banks?

A FEW DAYS SUPPLIED THE ANSWER. THE CONSERVAtive Democrats, developing a theory of "judicious" opposition to monopoly (i.e., opposition to Whig monopoly), proceeded to churn out bank charters for deserving Democrats.

In October, 1835, the Democrats of the city, now aroused, met at Tammany Hall to pass on the nominations for the impending election. Preliminary mutterings indicated that the proceedings would be less perfunctory than usual. By six-thirty, a throng of determined men had gathered outside the hall, and when the doors were opened, they rushed in, taking the seats nearest the platform. The atmosphere grew quickly tense, with the conservative Democrats alarmed about their slate, and the radicals waiting impatiently to bring their own list forward.

The organization ticket was finally announced to a chorus of hisses, hoots and catcalls. In the midst of the tumult the committee declared their nominations carried and hastily retired. The crowd roared that Joel Curtis, a veteran of the early Workingmen's party, be made chairman, raised banners with radical mottoes and booed the Bank Democrats. Alexander Ming, Jr., son of the agrarian of a few years back, a printer and officeholder, climbed up on a table and motioned for silence. The hubbub quieted down; but, before he could speak, the gas light went out, throwing the hall into darkness—an ancient and honorable formula for quelling mutiny at Tammany. This time the insurgents were prepared. Taking from their pockets the new friction matches, popularly known as "locofocos," they lined the platform with fifty lighted candles. The people said, "let there be light," as one orator put it, and there was light. The meeting then named its own candidates and eventually dissolved into boisterous torchlight procession.

The conservative Democrats stuck to their candidate, Gideon Lee, who won, probably with Whig support. But Charles G. Ferris, the radical nominee, polled over 3500 votes, and the Locofocos, as they were called, first sarcastically by their enemies, then proudly by themselves, took heart for the future. If Tammany Hall would not heed them, they could always strike out for the balance of power.

THE MILITARY AND CIVIC HOTEL WAS A DINGY, YELLOW frame building, not quite two stories high, on the corner of Broome Street and the Bowery. Many nights in 1836 and 1837 groups of men would descend the two or three steps from the street, pass the bar to the shabby staircase, faintly lit by a dark japanned lamp, and climb the half story to the meeting room. There, under the low ceiling, the walls smoked up by candle black, with a platform barely large enough for a small table and three or four chairs, the Locofocos gathered.

Some who climbed the well-worn stairs—John Windt, Gilbert Vale, Joel Curtis, George H. Evans (in poor health and soon to retire to a New Jersey farm)—had been Workingmen in the days of Fanny Wright. Others, like Alexander Ming, Jr., were steadfast Democrats fed up with Tammany dictatorship. Still others were ordinary men turning to politics because they felt the issues reached down to themselves. The Hecker brothers, hard-working German bakers, set up a hand press in the garret of their shop and printed hard-money sentiments on the back of paper currency they received from their customers.

And still others were vagrant intellectuals, to whom the Jackson administration had given a sense of the urgency of politics—Clinton Roosevelt, for example, a man of great good will and ingenuity, equally adept at inventing machines or systems of government, whose early pamphlet, *The Mode of Protecting Domestic Industries*, had assailed the high tariff and paper money, and broached a new currency plan guaranteed to solve the problems of the day. Roosevelt's own nostrum attracted no following, but he caught on with the Locofocos, out of his benevolent desire for human betterment, though in a few years he would be a forcible critic of the laissez-faire philosophy they espoused.

From the trade-union movement the Locofocos gained three leaders: John Commerford of the Chair-makers and Gilders, an honest and outspoken radical; the redheaded, ambitious and unreliable Levi D. Slamm of the Journeymen Locksmiths; and Robert Townsend, Jr., of the House Carpenters. Thus when the courts struck down the unions early in 1836, the Locofocos stood ready to redirect labor energy into political channels and become the receivers of the union movement.

They had already set up an independent organization, which had run Ming for Mayor in the spring elections of 1836, and they had a paper, the *Democrat,* printed by John Windt and edited by Clinton Roosevelt. The great meeting in the Park to protest the conviction of the tailors took up the Locofoco call for a state convention. In September ninety-three delegates met at Utica, nominating Isaac S. Smith, a veteran of the old Workingmen's party, for Governor, and Moses Jaques for Lieutenant Governor. The city organization filled out the ticket, combining with the Whigs on several nominations.

The elections showed that the Locofocos had the balance of power. Cambreleng and Ely Moore, the only successful Tammany congressional candidates, both had Locofoco support. Townsend and Roosevelt were sent to the assembly in the deal with the Whigs, and in exchange the Locofocos helped elect one Whig to Congress and another to the state Senate, both of whom promptly forgot the antimonopoly pledges they had signed before election. The Democratic organization thus suffered deep inroads, because it refused to follow the policy of the national administration.

THE NATIONAL ADMINISTRATION IN THE MEANTIME had been watching the New York Democratic organization with a disgust hardly less than that of the Locofocos. As early as February, 1835, Cambreleng had set forth what many believed to be Van Buren's views in a plain-spoken speech in the House. The period of reform, he said, had begun, and the most vital field for action lay outside the power of Washington. "Our State Governments, some at least, if not all, have outstripped even this Government in a rapid career of vicious and corrupt legislation." Corporations have multiplied, speculation flourishes, but "the greatest and most alarming abuse now existing in this country is the incorporation of near 600 banks of circulation." Such sentiments hardly raised the roof in Albany.

Dissatisfaction grew among the radical wing of the Regency as the conservative Democrats succumbed comfortably to the temptations of boom. "I have long since ceased to watch the proceedings of our Legislature," Silas Wright exclaimed bitterly, "for any other purpose than to see when they would adjourn." For the first time in his political life he stopped reading the *Albany Argus,* which Edwin Croswell had transformed into the mouthpiece of the state-banking Democrats. "If we cannot get a different class of men into the legislature," John A. Dix told Van Buren, "the sooner we go into a minority the better. . . . We must have less strength or more virtue if we would administer the affairs of the State either for our own honor or the public good."

The split in New York State reflected the split in the New York delegation at Washington, first over the distribution of the surplus revenue, then over the specie circular, with Silas Wright heading one group and N. P. Tallmadge the other. In June, 1836, Tallmadge made a bid for national recognition as leader of the conservative Democrats by defending the inflation against the slurs of "political economists," who were "frightened at this prosperity" and blind to "the cause which makes us, above all others, a happy, great, and prosperous people." What could that be? "Sir, it is contained in two words: it is our CREDIT SYSTEM." The lines within the party were drawing tight.

XVI *The Pattern of Locofocoism*

PENNSYLVANIA HAD TO ORIENT ITS POLITICAL CONflicts about the problems of industrialism nearly to the same extent as Massachusetts and New York. Philadelphia, the home of Nicholas Biddle and the United States Bank, was also the home of America's first city central labor union, in 1827, and of the first Workingmen's party the next year. The contrast between the Greek temple on Chestnut Street and the slums which so appalled Mathew Carey provided a background against which the Bank War raged with unusual intensity.

BUT THE BANK WAS RESOURCEFUL AND HAD MANY ways of circumventing opposition. The leading spokesman of the Philadelphia Workingmen's party of 1828-1831 was Stephen Simpson, a political careerist in his early forties, formerly a cashier in Stephen Girard's bank and for many years a journalist. An "original" Jackson man as early as 1822, he failed of his expected reward in 1829 and turned against the administration, emerging in the fall of 1830 as nominee for Congress on the Federal ticket. (Federalism still lingered in Philadelphia, even then a main backwater of American politics.) He also obtained the Workingmen's endorsement. He was beaten; but his political intuitions were aroused, as when a pointer lifts his nose at the whiff of game, and he turned to writing a book which would insinuate himself into the confidence of the growing labor movement.

HENRY D. GILPIN WAS ANOTHER INTELLECTUAL CON-verted to the Jacksonian cause. A slender man, wearing gold-rimmed spectacles, thirty-two years old in 1833, he was a good lawyer with a cultivated background and literary inclinations. For six years he edited the *Atlantic Souvenir,* an annual, and he was later to become president of the Pennsylvania Academy of Fine Arts. As government director of the Bank, he learned its character at first hand, becoming profoundly convinced that corporations were the "great question of the time in morals as much as politics."

The boom of 1834-1835 caused the same split in the Pennsylvania Democratic party as in New York and Massachusetts. The progressive wing favored Henry A. Muhlenberg, the leading radical in the Pennsylvania delegation in Congress, over George Wolf, the conservative Democratic Governor. In Philadelphia the Muhlenberg ticket, supported by the *Pennsylvanian* and by the labor leaders, included William English as nominee for the state Senate, and Thomas Hogan, another union man, for the Assembly. As in New York and Massachusetts, the progressives were fighting to force their views on the whole state party.

THIS WAS THE PATTERN OF LOCOFOCOISM. THERE were leaders in the West dedicated to the principles of democracy—men like Moses Dawson, Thomas Morris, Benjamin Tappan and William Allen in Ohio, Robert Dale Owen now serving as a Democrat in the legislature of Indiana, Kingsley Bingham in Michigan, Polk and William Carroll in Tennessee, Benton in Missouri—but even their ideas and solutions were largely borrowed from the East. In the thirties this radical group was strongest in Ohio, which most approximated the economic conditions of the East and actually underwent its own version of the Locofoco schism in 1836. In the forties, as the dominion of the new finance crept westward, the radical Democrats grew stronger, and Locofoco ideas played a vital and sometimes dominating role in the state constitutional conventions of that and the next decade.

But the East remained the source of the effective expression of Jacksonian radicalism, and Eastern ideas rose to supremacy in Washington as Jacksonianism changed from an agitation into a program. (The test of this would come when Jacksonian measures were presented to the West without the magic of Andrew Jackson.) The East simply had the consistent and bitter experience which alone could serve as a crucible of radicalism.

The great illusion of historians of the frontier has been that social equality produces economic equalitarianism. In fact, the demand for economic equality is generally born out of conditions of social inequality, and becomes the more passionate, deeply felt and specific as the inequality becomes more rigid. The actual existence of equal opportunities is likely to diminish the vigilance with which they are guarded, and to stimulate the race for power and privilege. The fur capitalists of St. Louis and the land speculators of Mississippi were as characteristic of the West as Andrew Jackson.

XVII *The Third Term*

HENRY CLAY HAD DESCRIBED THE REVOLUTION AS "hitherto bloodless," but how long would the qualification hold true? Calhoun opened 1835 with premonitions of catastrophe; the government was so corrupt, he said, that "the time had arrived when reformation or revolution must go on." Many agreed, and for a time feeling ran so high that Van Buren took to wearing a brace of pistols, even when presiding over the Senate.

Hezekiah Niles meanwhile kept conscientious account of the upsurge of popular violence. "The time predicted seems rapidly approaching when the mob shall rule." In the first week of September alone, he clipped over five hundred items from the press of the country. "*Society seems everywhere un-*

hinged," he said, "and the demon of 'blood and slaughter' has been let loose upon us." What had happened? "The character of our countrymen seems suddenly changed." Niles grew increasingly melancholy and ended with a quotation from Gouverneur Morris.

Disorder afflicted foreign travelers with misgivings, even some who had come to admire the great democratic experiment. The Saint-Simonian Michel Chevalier, deciding that the reign of terror had begun, devoted a chapter in his book on America to "Symptomes de Révolution." Thomas Brothers, the Philadelphia radical, shocked altogether out of his passion for change, snarled his farewell to Utopia in *The United States of North America as They Are; Not as They Are Generally Described: Being a Cure for Radicalism,* devoting a neat appendix to "Miscellaneous Murders, Riots, and other Outrages, in 1834, 1835, 1836, 1837, and 1838."

BUT THE IMPENDING ELECTION GAVE STABILITY A fresh chance to reassert itself. Unable to unite on a candidate, the Whigs decided to run popular local favorites, in the hope of throwing the election to the House. They made their major challenge in the Southwest, where they bid for the conservative Democratic vote by backing an old friend of Jackson's, Hugh Lawson White, Senator from Tennessee. Just over sixty, White was a lean, sinewy man, with a long, emaciated face and flowing gray hair, thrown back from his forehead and curling on his shoulders. His plain manners, firm conscience and sturdy sense of honor had won him wide respect.

As one of Jackson's first supporters, White had watched the dwindling of Western influence and the rise of Van Buren and Locofocoism with alarm. White himself had been for many years president of the State Bank of Tennessee, and Samuel Jaudon, the cashier of the United States Bank and an influential figure in Bank activities, was his son-in-law. The open adoption of the hard-money policy thus increased his anxiety. When Jackson consulted him in the summer of 1833 about removing the deposits, White strongly opposed the idea, though party fidelity led him to defend it in the Senate.

Meanwhile he had married a divorcée who kept the Washington boardinghouse in which he had lived for twelve years. Her ambitions for him, and his own misgivings and disappointments, made him particularly receptive to suggestions for 1836. John Bell took the lead in persuading White, and Daniel Webster used his massive presence to inflame the hopes of Mrs.

White. *"Judge White is on the track,"* a Kentucky Whig soon wrote back to a friend, *"running gayly, and won't come off; and if he would, his wife won't let him."*

For the Northwest, the Whigs dug up the Clerk of the Court of Common Pleas in Cincinnati, a genial antiquity still vaguely remembered as the hero of the battle of Tippecanoe almost a quarter of a century before. Nicholas Biddle delivered in memorable language the instructions for William Henry Harrison's campaign:—

> Let him say not a single word about his principles, or his creed—let him say nothing—promise nothing. Let no Committee, no convention—no town meeting ever extract from him a single word, about what he thinks now, or what he will do hereafter. Let the use of pen and ink be wholly forbidden as if he were a mad poet in Bedlam.

In the Northeast, Webster would stand where General Harrison did not; and in the Southeast, John C. Calhoun could be relied upon to regard the election with an indifference which would not benefit Van Buren.

FOR THE DEMOCRATS THE FIRST PROBLEM WAS TO DIS-pose of Colonel Johnson. Both his own ambition and his popularity among the workingmen were as strong as ever. As early as January, 1833, George H. Evans had put forward Johnson's name for 1836, and in August of that year flaming handbills to the same effect, supposedly issued by the Workingmen of Boston, were posted on grocery doors in the remotest backwoods towns of Indiana.

The Johnson campaign was under way. Soon William Emmons contributed a biography, someone else turned out a ballad entitled "The Warrior Sage, a National Song," and Richard Emmons was delivered of *Tecumseh; or, the Battle of the Thames, a National Drama, in Five Acts*. This last opened in Baltimore in January, 1834, under the direction of a good press agent, who endowed the cast with the "identical dress" worn by Tecumseh at his death and the *"same pistols* with which the hero slew his savage foe." The Secretary of War also co-operated by allowing the actual British standard captured by Johnson to be displayed in the course of the evening. When the play came to Washington, the warrior sage himself sat in a box and acknowledged the salutes of the audience.

Van Buren's managers, impressed by Johnson's activity, decided to silence him by offering the vice-presidency. Sentiment was not, however, unanimous. John Catron, an old friend of Jackson's from Tennessee, soon to be elevated to the Supreme Court, rejected the view that "a lucky random shot, even if it did hit Tecumseh, qualifies a man for Vice President." The South in general opposed Johnson because of his domestic arrangements. He had two daughters by his housekeeper, a mulatto named Julia Chinn. The girls were well educated and attractive, eventually marrying white men and inheriting part of their father's estate. After Julia's death Johnson took up with another high-yellow girl, who ran off with an Indian in 1835. When he recaptured the fugitives, gossip whispered, he sold the girl down the river and moved on to her sister. The facts themselves could hardly have been shocking to a plantation society, but Johnson's failure to conceal them was, and the South did not propose to reward such misplaced candor by the vice-presidency. In the convention, Johnson finally won out with Van Buren's support over William Cabell Rives of Virginia, but the Virginia delegation broke into hisses and refused to support the Kentuckian at the election.

Van Buren himself, overcoming the fears which undid him during the removal of the deposits, had decided to advance the revolution. "The ground, that this is in truth a question between Aristocracy and Democracy," he declared in 1834, "cannot be too often or too forcibly impressed upon the minds of the people." In 1835 there appeared Professor William M. Holland's semi-authorized campaign biography, written by a former contributor to the *Free Enquirer* with the endorsement of Benjamin F. Butler, and inspired by the author's belief, as he put it, "in the most ultra democratic doctrines, and his partiality towards the subject of this narrative as the champion of those doctrines."

Except for the Locofoco party in New York, nearly all the radicals were rallying around Van Buren: Bancroft and Allen in Massachusetts, Robert Dale Owen in Indiana, Ely Moore and William Leggett in New York. Fanny Wright began a long lecture tour in May, 1836, to explain the urgency of the election. In New York she tried to end the Locofoco schism, feeling that the menace of Whiggery left no time for petulance over doctrine. In Boston, attended by Abner Kneeland of the local Society of Free Enquirers, she spoke to an audience of two hundred, including thirty-two women. Her interests, reporters noted, seemed now exclusively political; her speech "did not contain a single allusion, direct or indirect, to any theological topic."

BUT THE WHIGS WERE EQUALLY ACTIVE, CONCENTRAT-
ing their energies on a brilliant smear campaign from which
Van Buren's reputation has never quite recovered. It had long
been a favorite tactic to denounce the administration by fixing
on sinister advisers in the background rather than affronting
directly the national enthusiasm for the Hero of New Orleans.
Amos Kendall was a leading nominee for scapegoat-in-chief.
"For the last eight years," cried a Whig politician in 1837,
"Amos Kendall (who before he was driven from Kentucky by
public indignation, had reduced this state to almost utter ruin),
has been emphatically the president of the United States . . .
he has for eight years, through an infatuated and imbecile old
man, ruled and ruined this nation."

On the while, however, Van Buren nosed out Kendall for
this distinction. In the words of William H. Seward, the rising
young Whig leader in New York, Van Buren was "a crawling
reptile, whose only claim was that he had inveigled the confidence of a credulous, blind, dotard, old man." Webster and
Calhoun had developed this theme in thundering denunciations
in the Senate. Davy Crockett, the ex-frontier hero, lent his
name to a so-called biography of Van Buren which reproduced
the pattern in its crudest form. Another version was to be
found in the most famous series of Jack Downing papers, written by Charles A. Davis, a director of the New York branch of
the United States Bank and close friend of Nicholas Biddle's.
Beverley Tucker's novel, *The Partisan Leader*, published by
Duff Green in 1836, set forth the Van Buren stereotype in
somewhat more literate terms and from the point of view of
an admirer of Calhoun. A thousand Whig jokes and cartoons
and broadsides depicted the smooth and sly Van Buren manip-
ulating his foolish chief for diabolical ends.

Yet all the caterwauling could not compete against the confidence in Jackson in the West, and the solid respect with
which Van Buren was regarded in the East by people who
knew him other than by reputation. White ran as a "true"
Jacksonian, and not insincerely; he certainly stood for what a
good deal of the West thought Jackson had stood for in 1828
and 1832. To Jackson's disgust, he carried Tennessee, and
young Westerners like Andrew Johnson and Abraham Lincoln
voted for him. Webster won only Massachusetts, and barely
polled 55 per cent of the votes there. The surprise was Harrison's strong showing—seven states in his pocket and good results wherever he was on the ticket. But Van Buren ran far too
well, amassing 170 electoral votes to the aggregate 124 of his
opponents. The Jacksonian revolution was going into its third
term.

PARTING GIFTS FLOODED THE WHITE HOUSE AS THE old General labored with Roger B. Taney on his Farewell Address and preparations began for the final removal. March 4, 1837, was clear and tranquil. Jackson, pale, composed and happy, rode by Van Buren's side to the Capitol. At noon the two men appeared on the eastern portico. Chief Justice Taney, rejected by the Senate for the offices of Secretary of the Treasury and Associate Justice of the Supreme Court, now administered the oath to Martin Van Buren, rejected as Minister to England, and Jackson, plain and contented as a private citizen, watched with deep satisfaction.

The crowd which packed the East Lawn, their faces upturned in the noon sun, were profoundly silent. After the inaugural address the old General started slowly down the broad steps toward the carriage below. As he descended the people yielded to their feelings; the pent-up flood of cheers and shouts broke forth; and they paid their long, last, irresistible tribute to the man they loved. . . . Thomas Hart Benton, watching from a side window, felt himself stirred as never before. In later years he would recall many inaugurations, but compared to this they all seemed as pageants, "empty and soulless, brief to the view, unreal to the touch, and soon to vanish." This was reality, the living relation between a man and his people, distilled for a pause in the rhythm of events, rising for a moment of wild and soaring enthusiasm, then dying away into the chambers of memory.

Philip Hone scribbled a vengeful farewell to the "terrible old man." "This is the end of Gen. Jackson's administration—the most disastrous in the annals of the country." But who was Philip Hone to speak for the people? "This day," wrote William Leggett, "completes a period that will shine in American history with more inherent and undying lustre, than any other which the chronicler has yet recorded, or which perhaps will ever form a portion of our country's annals."

"This day," wrote a patriarchal New England preacher, "closes the administration of Andrew Jackson, who has spent the greater part of his life in public services. . . . I know of nothing, that a people may reasonably expect from good government, but that the United States have enjoyed under his administration."

XVIII *Panic*

THE MONEY BOOM ROARED ON THROUGH 1836, TO the increasing alarm of hard-money men. "When will the bubble burst?" asked William Cullen Bryant in the spring. "When will the great catastrophe which the banks have been preparing for us actually come?" Robert Rantoul predicted collapse within a year, and in the fall John A. Dix wrote glumly, "We are on the eve of one of the severest reactions in business of almost every description with which we have been visited for years. . . . Do not set me down for a croaker."

BUT WHO WOULD NOT SET HIM DOWN FOR A CROAKER? Even nominal hard-money men were not convinced by exercises in extrapolation. Some months after the first rumblings, in February, 1837, Benton, beckoning the President-elect into the finance committee room of the Senate, told him that the nation was on the verge of a financial explosion. Van Buren smilingly chaffed Old Bullion: "Your friends think you a little exalted in the head on that subject"; and Benton, stopping short in his economic exposition, only muttered to himself, *"You will soon feel the thunderbolt."* ("I should not mention this," Benton said in the Senate three years later, "if it was not that the President himself well remembers it, and often mentions it.")

Croakers soon had their evidence. The proportion of paper to specie lengthened, gambling in banks, internal improvements and public lands grew more frenzied, and the economic structure became increasingly speculative and unsound. Crop failures in 1835 toppled the first domino. Farmers could not pay merchants and speculators, who in turn could not pay banks; and the decline of agricultural exports, making the international balance of trade unusually heavy against the United States, caused an unexpected demand abroad for payment in specie. Meanwhile, the Specie Circular called the bluff of banks issuing their notes on the public land.

In destroying the Bank, Jackson had removed a valuable brake on credit expansion; and in sponsoring the system of deposit in state banks, he had accelerated the tendencies toward inflation. Yet the hard-money Democrats at least understood the danger and tried vainly, by the example of the federal government and by pressure within the states, to halt the dizzy pyramiding of paper credits. The business community, however, fascinated by the illusion of quick returns, fought the hard-money program all along the line.* Now they were reaping the whirlwind.

THE CRASH BROUGHT SUFFERING AND DISTRESS. PRICES of essential foods shot out of the reach of the poor. Flour, which had sold at $5.62 a barrel in March, 1835, rose to $7.75 in March, 1836, and $12 in March, 1837. Pork climbed from $10 in March, 1835, to $16.25 a year later and to $18.25 in March, 1837. The wholesale price of coal mounted from $6 a ton in January, 1835, to $10.50 in January, 1837, and rents increased proportionately.

THE CRASH WAS GIVING NEW COURAGE TO THE CONservative Democrats, now emerging as a distinct faction under the leadership of Tallmadge and W. C. Rives. They proposed to control Van Buren as they never dared try to control his predecessor, and their immediate plans centered on repealing the Specie Circular as the first step in dismantling the whole hard-money program.

The new President pondered their hot arguments for repeal, and then turned to a memorandum, drawn up by Gouge, on the "Probable Consequences" of such an action. The weakness of the Specie Circular, the memorandum urged, was "not that it is too powerful, but that it is not powerful enough." "The disease under which the country is at this moment suffering," Gouge declared, "is overtrading, produced by over-banking. The true remedy . . . is to bank less and trade less. The Treasury Order has in no way contributed to the disease. On the contrary, it has checked it." This seemed good sense, as well as good hard-money doctrine, and Van Buren quietly endorsed a list of questions he had thought to put to his cabinet: "Not submitted as I decided to take the entire responsibility and had moreover reason to believe that the Cabinet would be divided upon the subject. *MVB*." The example of Jackson had not been wasted, and the circular was for the moment preserved.

But so small a setback only increased the pressure. Nicholas

* Even so determined a conservative as Philip Hone could not avoid occasional inadvertent expressions of disgust. "This is another evidence of the reckless manner in which business has been conducted," he allowed himself to say of one failure—though he quickly caught himself and returned to the party line, "or rather, to speak more charitably, of the straits to which men have been driven by the wicked interference of the government with the currency of the country." Hone, *Diary*, I, 248-249.

Biddle, complete with delusions of grandeur, now presented himself at the White House. (Biddle's hold on actuality had long since disappeared. "As to mere power," he boasted, "I have been for years in the daily exercise of more personal authority than any President habitually enjoys." When old Thomas Cooper, of South Carolina, a man of no political consequence, proposed the White House to him, Biddle answered modestly that he stood ready for the country's service. Ever confident that the Bank was about to be restored, he kept writing letters to Forsyth or J. K. Poinsett of Van Buren's cabinet offering compromises.) When Van Buren received him with imperturbable good manners but asked no advice about public affairs, Biddle had a hurt paragraph inserted in the papers animadverting on the President's unaccountable failure to take advantage of his opportunity.

In April a Committee of Fifty, chosen by New York merchants to "remonstrate" with the President, brought a somewhat more serious expression of business sentiment. One merchant had refused to serve, saying bitterly that he would "never consent, under any circumstances, to 'remonstrate' with Martin Van Buren. . . . When some *other* and more summary course is proposed, and the pursuing it placed in the hands of a committee of *ten thousand*, I, for one, hold myself ready to discharge my duty to my country."

Others were found, however, and Van Buren received the delegation with his usual politeness. But he gave no satisfaction; the Committee reported itself compelled to surrender all hope that "either the justice of our claims or the severity of our sufferings, will induce the Executive to abandon or relax the policy which has produced such desolating effects." The meeting which convened to hear the report was more violent than the original one, even after Philip Hone succeeded in softening some of the resolutions. Van Buren was declared to have "uniformly acted, and uniformly succeeded," on the principle that "the poor naturally hate the rich." "In a great majority of cases," it was comfortably asserted, "the possession of property is the proof of merit." While foregoing rebellion, the assembled merchants allowed that "the pages of history record, and the opinions of mankind justify, numerous instances of popular insurrection, the provocation to which was less severe than the evils of which we complain."

THE LAST OBSERVATION CONTAINED A THREAT OFTEN sounded in these days of tension (and coming perhaps with ill grace from men who disapproved of flour riots). In May, for example, a group of Boston businessmen, meeting at Faneuil Hall to protest against a law requiring the payment of specie at the post offices, considered a resolution urging that the law be resisted, " 'peaceably' if it were possible, 'forcibly' if it were necessary—at any rate it should be AT ALL HAZARDS RESISTED." Abbott Lawrence, the cotton magnate, who had himself voted for the law when Congress enacted it a year before, now assured the meeting that "men with the feelings of men" could not repress their indignation: "THERE IS NO PEOPLE ON THE FACE OF GOD'S EARTH THAT IS SO ABUSED, CHEATED, PLUNDERED AND TRAMPLED BY THEIR RULERS, AS ARE THE PEOPLE OF THE UNITED STATES." From a fairly responsible source this was quite an indictment.

The Faneuil Hall outburst was no isolated episode. Such menaces and denunciations became the staple of the Whig press. "It is our right and our *duty* to resist oppression," declared a New York paper. ". . . never was our country in a position when it was absolutely necessary that this right should be exercised as at this moment." The word *revolution* had "no peculiar horror" for those who felt that it now meant "the preservation of our constitution and the protection of our lives and property. . . . Our fathers exercised it, and their descendants may and will resort to it, when necessary." (The Locofoco leaders might well blush at their diffidence in the Park in February.) "We unhesitatingly say," a Whig editor observed of the Specie Circular, "that it is a more high-handed measure of *tyranny* than that which cost *Charles* the 1st his crown and his head . . . one which calls more loudly for resistance than any act of Great Britain which led to the Declaration of Independence."

Philip Hone, with the conservative weakness for classical analogy, noted that Jackson, Van Buren and Benton formed a triumvirate more fatal to the prosperity of America than Caesar, Pompey and Crassus were to the liberties of Rome. "Where will it end?" he asked. "—In ruin, revolution, perhaps civil war." Robert Mayo published his *Chapter of Sketches on Finance,* the outpourings of a disappointed brain truster, and confirmed the worst suspicions of the merchants. "The conclusion is inevitable," wrote Mayo, "that *revolution is already more than half accomplished!"* The convictions were strong enough in his own mind, he added, to place Amos Kendall's head on the scaffold. . . . Everywhere government was charged with conspiring to destroy business, and always in the background were the ominous threats of direct action.

On May 10, in this atmosphere of gathering crisis, the banks of New York City suspended specie payments, refusing any

longer to redeem their paper bank notes in hard money. Within
a few days all the banks in the country had followed New
York's example.

The nationwide suspension brought events to a head. The
business community rushed to defend it as a natural and necessary step, some of its hangers-on even extolling it as an act
of virtue. "From a sense of duty to the public," cried the Reverend Andrew Preston Peabody in a sermon of May 14 on the
banks, "they spare their creditors, and themselves ask to be
spared. . . . Let institutions, that have never yet betrayed the
public confidence, still be a rallying point for those hopes, that
pierce the cloud and dissipate the gloom."

But not even all the conservatives could agree that the action of the banks exhibited a high sense of public duty. *
Nathan Appleton in 1841 was to define suspension as "the
gentle name applied to the failure or refusal to perform the
promise contained on the face of a bank note." When one bank
suspends, he said, it is stigmatized as bankrupt, but let a number suspend, "all the others follow, and the public submit, not
only without a murmur, but give it their commendation." Albert Gallatin was equally caustic, and other businessmen
shared their misgivings, especially as the political exploitation
of the crisis became more and more blatant.

Yet, for all the qualms of responsible Whigs and opposition
of radical Democrats, state legislatures enacted laws exempting
banks from the penalties of suspension just about as the business community specified. The time seemed ripe for an all-out
attack on the hard-money system. The Whig press grew increasingly violent and peremptory. Daniel Webster was ordered on a great speaking tour through the nation. Van Buren
and Benton were sent hundreds of parody bank-notes, in-
scribed *This is what you have brought the country to"* or *"The
gold humbug exploited"* or *"Behold the effects of tampering
with the currency"* or sentiments less printable.

Intimidation would have been wasted on General Jackson.
But a wily politician, a magician, a red fox, like Martin Van
Buren—could he hold out against an aroused people?

Or, did the business leaders, as so often, miscalculate? "They
will, with their accustomed wisdom, mistake the opinion of
stockholders and speculators for public sentiment," predicted
C. C. Cambreleng, "and think that they are going to carry

---

* Some felt perhaps the justice of Frank Blair's dry reminders that the
classes which had been loudest in condemning the relief laws of Kentucky were
now loudest in demanding that such laws be invoked in their own interest, and
that the very people who denounced workingmen for combining in trade-unions
were now combining themselves "for the purpose of sustaining each other in
setting the laws at defiance, and refusing to pay their debts." *Washington
Globe,* May 22, 27, 1837.

every thing before them. They forgot that [while] Wall St. may be converted into a Bedlam nations seldom run mad except in war or revolution."

XIX *Divorce of Bank and State*

VAN BUREN NOW FACED THREE POSSIBILITIES. HE could struggle on with the state-bank system. He could retreat gracefully, strike the Jacksonian flag and restore the big Bank. Or, he could head into the gale, fight the hard-money policy one step further and urge the separation of the fiscal affairs of the government from all banks. Each form of government cohabitation with banks had been tried twice, and twice was considered to have failed; but the business community as a whole was grimly convinced that one or the other relation was necessary. The third system—divorce of bank and state—was untried. It found its only backing among intellectuals and radicals.

A FEW DAYS AFTER THE PHILADELPHIA BANKS SUS-pended specie payments, Independence Square was filled with the largest crowd ever to assemble in the city, eventually total-ing twenty thousand persons, called together by John Ferral, Thomas Hogan and other union leaders. Henry D. Gilpin moved among the throng. "It was temperate and orderly . . . but the feeling was very strong. . . . I have never seen the working classes more deeply agitated and roused." Speakers denounced the paper system, and a committee was appointed to discuss resumption with the local banks. It was, as Gilpin wrote privately to the President, a spontaneous outburst of labor discontent, "projected and carried on *entirely* by the working classes."

Nicholas Biddle, still calm as a summer's morning, tried to induce the committee to recommend that the United States Bank be made a deposit bank, so that he and the government could once again be friends. "If *I* can forgive them," he said magnanimously, "they may forgive me." But the committee was unimpressed, and its report provoked the reconvened meeting to speak its mind. One resolution, noting the threats of violence from the business community, proposed the formation of a "volunteer legion of *ten thousand men*, to be as shortly as possible fully armed and equipped" and to hold itself ready, day and night, to "fly to the rescue of the public peace." Another simply demanded that the government sever its financial connections with the banks.

The pattern was repeating itself up and down the coast. Suspension set Theophilus Fisk's pen scratching in burning excitement in Charleston, till, early in June, he finished a pamphlet violently entitled *The Banking Bubble Burst; or the Mammoth Corruptions of the Paper Money System Relieved by Bleeding.*

On July 4 he struck again, in an oration, *Labor the Only True Source of Wealth,* another brisk summary of the radical position. Our constitution, he said, may have forbidden a dynasty of hereditary rank, but "it has not proved a safeguard against a dynasty of associated wealth." Since labor alone could produce wealth, this dynasty must exist on proceeds stolen from labor; and the chief instruments of this plunder were *"Incorporated companies;* and the worst of all incorporated companies are *banks."*

The solid citizens of Charleston had apparently heard enough. They packed the hall when Fisk was billed to address a meeting on the financial situation on July 8, howled him down, and, when he would not leave the platform, some of the more valiant spirits slugged him. The Mayor sat silently by, evidently in quiet approval. . . . The businessmen of Charleston could show the Locofocos a think or two about breaking up meetings.

In Massachusetts and New York the banking crisis precipitated the final struggles between the conservative and radical wings of the Democratic party.

IT WAS A SPRING AND SUMMER OF DECISION IN WASHington. From the first, Van Buren had apparently recognized that divorce was the only measure which would not mean surrender. Gouge's arguments impressed him, and he was also struck by the plan of a Virginia banker named Dr. John Brockenbrough, a friend of Randolph and Gordon, which provided for a system of federal depositories but did not insist on the "specie clause"—a right-wing version of the independent treasury. The President quietly meditated the possibilities, roughed out a preliminary scheme in May and submitted it to his advisers.

Cambreleng and Butler had already announced for separation. Silas Wright had doubts about the political risks, but made up his mind by June. Thomas Hart Benton, James K. Paulding and James Buchanan, A. C. Flagg and Robert Rantoul, Jr., gave additional support. Above all, resolutions poured in from meetings across the country, Bunker Hill and Tammany Hall and Independence Square, large towns and small, demanding the divorce of bank and state.

In retirement at the stately Hermitage, Andrew Jackson watched the progress of politics with a hawklike eye and regularly scrawled in his large indignant hand long letters of advice and encouragement to Blair, to Kendall, to the President. His instinct about his people was still unerring, and, as storms raged around the White House, the Hermitage counseled Van Buren to hold firm. "The people are everywhere becoming more aroused against the proceedings of the Banks and will sustain the Executive Government in any course that will coerce them to specie payments; and in any plan that will hereafter secure them from . . . the corrupt paper credit system." When Amos Kendall visited the Hermitage in 1838, driving up on a bitter-cold day, he found the venerable chief at his gate, a quarter of a mile from the house, without an overcoat, waiting for the mail carrier and the newspapers. "He looks as well as he usually did at Washington," Kendall reported, "but does not move with the same elasticity." Bones must stiffen, but the eyes still flashed with fire.

On July 7 the *Washington Globe* came out for divorce and printed the first installment of Gouge's pamphlet. The conservative Democrats retorted by setting up a paper in Washington, the *Madisonian,* devoted to Democratic principles "as delineated by Mr. Madison" (rather than by Mr Jefferson or General Jackson?). From the start the *Madisonian* assailed "visionary theories, and an unwise adherence to the plan for an *exclusive metallic* currency," attacked Gouge and his "spirit of Jacobinism and anarchy," and expounded with feeling the beauties of the state bank system.

In the early days of a still hot September Congressmen streamed back to Washington for the special session, and on September 4 came the long-awaited presidential message. After a trenchant analysis of the panic, Van Buren decisively rejected the system of deposit in banks, whether one large or many small, and declared for an independent treasury. Locofocoism now bore the *imprimatur* of the White House.

"TELL ME FRANKLY," VAN BUREN WROTE IN HIS sprawling script on a copy of the message intended for Theodore Sedgwick, "how near this comes to what you think it ought to be." The President need have had no doubts. A thrill of exultation burst through the ranks of the hard-money men. Frank Blair called it "the boldest and highest stand ever taken by a Chief Magistrate in defence of the rights of the people. . . . a second declaration of independence." Bryant and Leggett rejoiced, and the Locofocos promptly gathered for a special meeting to commend Van Buren. A. H. Wood of Boston expressed the general sentiment: "Like his predecessor he now stands at the head of radical democracy." Letters of congratulation poured into the White House: from Gideon Welles, from J. K. Paulding, from N. P. Trist, from Moses Dawson of Ohio, from Theodore Sedgwick, from a hundred others. And through the country humble men, drawing a precarious existence from some hillside farm, or supporting a family on the meager returns of bootmaking, or working long gray hours in a factory, felt a surge of renewing confidence in their government. It was still their country and not Nicholas Biddle's.

The horror of the business community was about as single-minded as the enthusiasm of the working people.

The message is a heartless, cold-blooded attack upon our most valuable and most cherished classes of citizens. (*New York Gazette*)

The people, the country, the business men have nothing to hope from the message, Mr. Van Buren, or any of his clan. (*New York Express*)

It is the incarnation of the Bentonian-Jacksonism—a sophistical sermon of the favorite text of "Perish commerce —perish credit," and an ungenerous appeal to the irrational passions of the worst party in the country. (*Philadelphia Natural Gazette*)

He has identified himself wholly with the loco-focos— come forth a champion of the most destructive species of ultraism—and aimed at the vital interests of the country a blow, which if it do not recoil upon the aggressor, must be productive to the country of lasting mischief, perhaps of irretrievable anarchy. (*Boston Atlas*)

He has gone full length with the Plaindealer, the Evening Post, the Washington Globe, Blair, Kendall, and General Jackson. (*New York Courier and Enquirer*)

ANOTHER CENTURY FINDS A STRANGE DISPROPORTION between the uproar over the independent treasury and the plan itself, which after all, simply proposed that the government take care of its own funds and require payment in legal tender. Why should the radical Democrats look on this innocent scheme as a second Declaration of Independance, and conservatives denounce it as wild, subversive and dangerous, deserving resistance almost on the barricades?

The plan was certainly vulnerable on economic grounds. It enforced a decentralization of the banking system which in the end would prove so cumbersome that the policy was reversed with the establishment of the Federal Reserve System. But this was not the cause of the outcry against it. Indeed, the economic objections were barely mentioned, and they would not become urgent till after the Civil War. Instead, the independent treasury was denounced for political and social reasons—as a movement toward despotism, and a conspiracy against private property.

The divorce of bank and state represented primarily—both for friends and foes—a further extension of the hard-money policy. That policy, it will be remembered, had three ends: the diminution of periodic economic crises; the destruction of irresponsible sovereignties within the political state; and the prevention of a moneyed aristocracy. The independent treasury served the policy in each respect. By removing the public funds from the banks, it reduced the amount of specie on which paper could be issued and thus had a sobering tendency on the economy. By rejecting bank notes in payment of the revenue, it considerably restricted the power of banks over the currency. By confining banks to the needs of the commercial community, it held them to "legitimate" economic operations and limited their capacity for redistributing wealth in favor of a single class.

Thus, the business community fought the project as the culmination of the whole hard-money campaign. The scheme "could only be founded," wrote one Whig pamphleteer, "upon the supposition, that the banks, and the currency which they supply, are of too unsafe a character to be employed by the government. If unsafe for the government, they must also be unsafe for the people." "What then, sir, is the policy of the administration?" asked a Whig orator. ". . . For myself, I believe it to be . . . a war of extermination on commerce and the currency." "Disguise it as you may," cried N. P. Tallmadge in the Senate, "it is no more nor less than a war upon the whole banking system."

But more yet was involved than simply hard money and the banking system. "Those who regard it in no higher aspect than a mere financial arrangement," as John M. Niles declared, ". . . cannot appreciate the motive of those who consider it as the first important step in the reform of our wretched paper money system, on the one hand, and of our political institutions on the other." Its object, he said, was "the entire separation and exclusion of the organized moneyed power from our political institutions."

For those who believed, with Hamilton, that the business class had a proprietary right to government favor, the bill thus seemed an assault on the very fabric of society. "Its leading feature," exclaimed Philip Hone in horror, "seems to be the total preclusion of the merchants, whose enterprise supports the government, from any participation in the use of money collected through their means." William M. Gouge made the repudiation of Hamilton inescapable. "If there ever should be a surplus of public funds," he wrote, "we know not what particular merit there is in the banking and speculating interests, that they should lay claim to its exclusive use. . . . If any classes of the community deserve the favor of the government, in any country, they are the farmers, mechanics, and other hard-working men."

The philosophy of Federalism was thus at stake. Said the *Madisonian,* "The contest now waging, we regard as a battle between civilization and barbarism." "We have reached that point of national existence," declared a respectable magazine, "when a much longer toleration of misrule . . . is impossible. Either revolution—a revolution of violence, and perhaps of blood—or renovation, must soon change the aspect of affairs."

Democrats answered in kind. Frank Blair declared the scheme put the axe "to the root of that complicated system of measures by which HAMILTON and his party sought to destroy the spirit, while maintaining the forms of the Constitution." Fanny Wright grew ecstatic. "It is the national independence realized. It is the effective, definitive annulment of this country's vassalage. It is the first practical, efficient, decisive realization of the Declaration of '76."

Depression drew the lines tight. In 1837 and 1838, American business men were as much united against their government as they ever have been. The ultimate question was whether, in the last resort, the government dared overrule this unanimity—and this was the obverse of the other question: who was to make the decisions for the nation, the business community or the government?

For a Jeffersonian there could be but one answer. The vital decisions must in the last resort be made by men responsible to the people, and not by irresponsible private groups. In last analysis, said Martin Van Buren by his refusal to yield on the subtreasury, the democratically elected government *must* have control over the business community, for this may be the only way to safeguard the life, liberty and property of the humble members of society.

XX *The Southern Dilemma*

JOHN C. CALHOUN WAS FACING A MAJOR DECISION, AS he rode north from Pendleton in the Indian summer of 1837, his lips compressed, his face drawn with concentration, his manner absent and taciturn, he weighed his future course with infinite exactness. Before him lay the special session of Congress and the battle over the independent treasury. On his decision—on every decision till the insoluble question was solved—might tremble the future of the South.

CALHOUN WAS NO LONGER MERELY THE ASPIRING politician who had feuded with Jackson in 1830. Personal ambition was now increasingly submerged in a cold monomania for South Carolina and slavery. Many, like Harriet Martineau, found they could no longer communicate with him. He felt so deeply that he rarely heard argument, so passionately that he never forgot his responsibility. "There is no *relaxation* with him," cried his devoted friend Dixon H. Lewis of Alabama (who weighed three hundred and fifty pounds, and spoke with feeling). "On the contrary, when I seek relaxation in him, he screws me only the higher in some sort of excitement." He appeared to subsist in an unimaginable intellectual solitude, his mind committed to his interminable obligation, focusing forever on a single shining point, which for him was the center of the universe. He was becoming "the cast-iron man," as Miss Martineau saw him, "who looks as if he had never been born, and never could be extinguished."

But he became a startling figure when he rose to speak in the Senate, eyes burning like live coals in his pale face, hair bristling and erect, skin loose over his prominent bones, words pouring out in an abrupt, condensed, closely reasoned flow. His voice was metallic and harsh, his gestures monotonous, and his ventriloquist's tones came from nowhere and sounded equally in all corners of the chamber. Yet the commanding eye, the grim earnestness of manner, the utter integrity of sentiment held the galleries in anxious attention. Standing in the narrow aisle of the Senate, bracing himself on the desks beside him, he averaged perhaps one hundred and eighty words a minute of terse and unconquerable argument.

His was the supreme intelligence among the statesmen of the day. Where Clay relied on a richness and audacity of feeling, Webster on a certain massiveness of rhetoric, Benton on the sheer weight of facts, and all indulged in orgies of shameless verbiage, Calhoun's speeches were stripped bare, arguing the facts with an iron logic drawn to the highest pitch of tension. Nourished on Aristotle, Machiavelli and Burke, he possessed an uncanny ability to cut through to the substance of problems. His processes of thought were intricate, merciless and unsentimental in a day when none of these qualities was in demand.

More than any of the others, he understood that he was living in one of the critical periods of history. It was, for him, a revolutionary age—"a period of transition, which must always necessarily be one of uncertainty, confusion, error, and wild and fierce fanaticism"—and he looked with anxiety on what was plainly a "great approaching change in the political and social condition of the country." "Modern society," he exclaimed, almost with horror, "seems to be rushing to some new and untried condition." The "great question" of the future would be that of "the distribution of wealth—a question least explored, and the most important of any in the whole range of political economy."

The emerging outlines of industrial society filled him with foreboding. The new economy, he felt, was enriching a small group of capitalists at the expense of the great mass of the people. The "tendency of Capital to destroy and absorb the property of society and produce a collision between itself and operatives" was a source of deep alarm. "In the North you are running into anarchy," he told Albert Brisbane. ". . . The capitalist owns the instruments of labor, and he seeks to draw out of labor all of the profits, leaving the laborer to shift for himself in age and disease. This can only engender antagonism; the result will be hostility and conflict, ending in civil war, and the North may fall into a state of social dissolution." Both the growing power of the capitalists and the growing frustration of the masses seemed to threaten the fabric of society.

And the consequences for the South? The business party placed a premium on conservatism and stability, yet no group was more concerned to expand the power of the central government and whittle away the rights of the states. If, as Calhoun believed, the union of bank and state would "inevitably draw all the powers of the system into the vortex of the general government," what safeguards would remain for the South? And a second danger lay in the inescapable economic clash between Northern finance and Southern cotton. As Francis W. Pickens candidly stated the hard facts which underwrote Calhoun's logic, the South must decide "whether cotton shall control exchanges and importations, or whether the banks and the stock interests shall do it. . . . Break down the swindling of bankers. . . . and cotton will do the exchanges of the commercial world."

On the other hand, the party which opposed the business class contained in itself ominous threats to Southern security. Equalitarian and radical, thriving on agitation and forever fomenting new projects of reform, it must prove an ever-flowing fount of libertarian dogma. Yet, for all its excesses, it was primarily interested in limiting the power of the business community, and in so doing it was employing the State-rights doctrine so vital to the South.

The Southern dilemma was this: which was the greater menace to the plantation system—radical democracy or finance capital? Should the ruling class of the South ally itself to the upper class of the North, and thus to broad construction, capitalism and conservatism, or to the lower classes of the North, and thus to State rights, agrarianism and reform? Should the South join the Whigs in their fight against radicalism, or should it join the Democrats in their fight against business rule?

MANY SOUTHERNERS HAD ALREADY MADE THEIR choice. Thomas Cooper voiced a profound planting conviction when he observed, in 1830, that universal suffrage was the root of political evil. Political power must fall thereby "into the hands of the operatives, mechanics and labouring classes, the men of no property." The consequence? "We say, without hesitation, the wealth of the wealthy is in danger." This was clearly no sectional problem, and Cooper himself by 1837 was turning to Nicholas Biddle, the very embodiment of finance capital, as the best hope for the South.

Yet Calhoun knew that the business community would in the end exact a price for its protection, and the price would be Southern acquiescence in the American System and broad construction. Could the South afford to pay it? Calhoun was skeptical. If the South surrendered its economic and constitutional bastions, it would exist only on the sufferance of the North.

And the alternative? In 1836 Calhoun could not bring himself to support the Democrats any more than the Whigs. But the panic of 1837 transformed the situation. If Van Buren remained faithful to the hard-money policy, he must come out for the divorce of bank and state. Should not the South seize this opportunity to strengthen its economic position, fortify its constitutional bulwarks and check Northern capitalism, even at the cost of giving more power to Northern radicals?

Van Buren's message sealed his intention. "We have now a fair opportunity to break the last of our commercial Shackles," Calhoun declared with delight. With a sense of vast relief, now restored to a position "much more congenial to my feelings," he broke his partnership with the Whigs, throwing his influence to what he had called not many months before the "more filthy" portion of the Democratic party, "under Benton, Kendall, Blair and Johnson," and backing the personal measure of his ancient enemy, Martin Van Buren. But he was a man of principle, and he would follow where principle led.

XXI *Radicalism at High Water*

THE REVEREND THEOPHILUS FISK PREACHED THE FIRST sermon in the Capitol after the independent-treasury message, but was defeated in the contest for the chaplaincy of the House—an omen for the special session. Silas Wright then introduced the subtreasury bill, Calhoun added the "specie clause," and angry debate began. The opposition was suitably horrified, but the country demanded action and the measure soon passed the Senate, complete with Calhoun's amendment. In the House, Henry A. Wise of Virginia, who, as the *New York Evening Post* observed, was seldom silent "except when forced to be so by organic disease," led a furious counterattack with a flow of invective unequaled since the days of Randolph. Flinging epithets about with riotous abandon— "Honest Iago" Kendall and "Big Bully Bottom" Benton were typical—Wise rallied the Whig and right-wing Democratic forces against what he called "the proposition . . . to destroy all banking institutions." The House responded, and the independent treasury was tabled.

THROUGH THE EAST THE BATTLE OVER THE INDEPEN-dent treasury precipitated the latent radicalism in the Jacksonian party. Orations, party addresses, convention resolutions voiced increasingly an open appeal to the humble members of society to arrest the might of the rich and powerful. The very name—Locofoco—hitherto confined to the little band in New York City, was soon applied by universal consent to the whole party. The frontier had watched the unfolding of the hard-money policy with increasing coolness.

So pronounced, indeed, was Western opposition that William Foster advanced the theory, which won the support of the *New York Evening Post*, that the independent treasury was really a sectional issue, with the East playing the liberal role and the West the conservative. Though a case can be made for Foster's thesis by an analysis of votes in Congress, Henry D. Gilpin answered it in language as conclusive for Foster's theory of Jacksonian democracy as for the frontier theory. It was not a "question between Atlantic and Western States," Gilpin declared, "—but between trade and productive labour . . . not a question of locality." It seems clear now that more can be understood about Jacksonian democracy if it is regarded as a problem not of sections but of classes. In 1837 Van Buren received what support he got from the West, apart from that of a few men like Benton and Polk, chiefly because of his control over the party organization.

AS PRESIDENT, VAN BUREN WAS WEAK IN THE VERY respect in which he might have been expected to excel—as a politician. For a man who in the past had been so skillful in party management, he showed himself negligent and maladroit during his own administration. His appointments failed to strengthen him. It was sheer indulgence, for example, to make James K. Paulding Secretary of the Navy, and it was worse to consider Washington Irving for the post (as Van Buren did) after Irving had come out against the independent treasury.

Nor did Van Buren show particular skill in dealing with disunity in the party. He allowed the Tallmadge split to grow almost into a rebellion, while similar splits under Jackson never became more than individual desertions. He coped badly with the slavery question, gaining an undeserved pro-Southern reputation in the North while failing to win the confidence of the South. This unexpected political ineptness weakened his administration and delayed until 1840 the passage of the independent treasury.

He had to face the final struggle with Nicholas Biddle before his policy achieved victory. The national resumption of specie payments in 1838 found Biddle's bank in an increasingly unstable position. "There is scarcely anything vicious and unsound in banking," wrote William Graham Sumner of Biddle's policy in these last years, "which the great bank did not illustrate." Biddle himself left the sinking ship in March, 1839, but his policy lingered on. For a time the Bank hoped to conceal its own condition by tricky financial operations which would cause the New York banks to suspend first. When this scheme failed, it closed its doors on October 9, carrying down with it most of the banks of the country except those of New York and New England.

The second suspension produced Gallatin's mature judgment of the Bank. It was the judgment of a man who in 1832 had supported recharter, and few businessmen of the day would have contradicted it.

That bank, subsequent to the first general suspension of May, 1837, has been the principal, if not the sole cause of the delay in resuming and of the subsequent suspensions. In every respect it has been a public nuisance. The original error consisted in the ambitious attempt to control and direct the commerce of the country; in the arrogant assumption of a pretended right to decide on the expediency of performing that which was an absolute duty; and in the manifest and deliberate deviation from the acknowledged principles of sound and legitimate banking. . . . The mismanagement and gross neglect, which could in a few years devour two-thirds of a capital of thirty-five millions, are incomprehensible, and have no parallel in the history of banks. . . . It is due to the moral feeling of this country, not less than to the security of its financial concerns, that this disgraced and dangerous corporation should not be permitted any longer to exist.*

The elder statesman of American finance had delivered his verdict. In the end it agreed strangely with that of General Jackson.

The second suspension heightened the public sentiment in

* Gallatin, "Suggestions on the Banks and Currency" (1841), *Writings*, III, 406. But many businessmen (and some historians) clung to the myth. Henry C. Carey, for example, a respected conservative economist as well as a man with "practical" business experience, wrote letter after letter to Nathan Appleton in 1840 begging him to desist from attacks on the Bank. See Appleton Papers.

favor of divorce. A new Congress was elected with the sub-treasury as an issue. The plan, tirelessly reintroduced by Silas Wright, went steadily through Senate and House, complete with a specie clause scheduled to go into full effect in 1843. On July 4, 1840, Van Buren finally signed what Blair had called the second Declaration of Independence.

In the meantime Van Buren performed by executive order the second great service of his administration. On March 31 he declared that no person should labor more than ten hours a day on federal public works, and that this should go into effect without a reduction of wages.* This measure was an unmis-takable declaration that the people's government would act on behalf of the people as freely as in the past the capitalists' gov-ernment had acted on behalf of the capitalists. The Whigs promptly cried that Van Buren was infringing on the right to work and demanded that pay be reduced correspondingly. Said Horace Greeley, the great alleged friend of labor: "We do not regard this measure as promising any great benefit." The length of a day's labour should be left to "mutual agreement. . . . What have Governments and Presidents to do with it?"

But Van Buren might have felt repaid for all the uproar if he could have read the words which Michael Shiner, the free Negro who worked in the Washington Navy Yard, wrote pain-fully years later: "the Working Class of people of the United States Mechanic and laboures ought to never forget the Hon ex president Van Buren for the ten hour sistom. . . . May the lord Bless Mr Van Buren it seemes like they have forgot Mr Van Buren his name ought to be Recorded in evry Working Man heart."†

The calm, smiling little President might have had a worse epitaph. He governed during years of strain and anxiety, bur-dened with stern decisions, cluttered by the wreck of friend-ships and the clash of loyalties. For those on the firing lines the years cast themselves inevitably in the image of a battlefield. In a poem in the *Democratic Review*, William Cullen Bryant ex-

---

* Richardson, *Messages and Papers*, III, 602. A ten-hour day already existed in the navy yards at New York and Philadelphia, but the hours were sunrise to sunset at Portsmouth, Boston, Norfolk, Washington and Pensacola. "Statement of the Working Hours at the Different Navy Yards," March 27, 1840, Van Buren Papers.

† Michael Shiner, manuscript diary, Library of Congress, p. 77. The omitted sentences read: "for when they youster have to work in the Hot Broiling sun from sun to sun when they wher Building the treasure office Befor he gave the time from six to 6 the laboures youster have to go ther and get the Bricks and Mortar up on the scaffold Befor the Masons came until the president ishued a proclamation that all the Mechanics and labourours that wher employed By the day By the federal government Should Work the ten hour Sistom."

pressed for all the fighters the sorrows, the misgivings, the terrible loneliness, and the ultimate hope:—

> A friendless warfare! lingering long
>   Through weary day and weary year;
> A wild and many-weaponed throng
>   Hang on thy front and flank and rear.
>
> Yet nerve thy spirit to the proof,
>   And blench not at thy chosen lot;
> The timid good may stand aloof,
>   The sage may frown—yet faint thou not!
>
>   *   *   *
>
> Truth, crushed to earth, shall rise again!
>   The eternal years of God are her's;
> But Error, wounded, writhes with pain
>   And dies among his worshippers.

XXII *The Whig Counter-reformation*

THE PRESIDENCY OF JACKSON ACCOMPLISHED A REVO-
lution of political values. It destroyed neo-Federalism as a public social philosophy and restated fundamentally the presup-
positions of American political life. No one ever again could
talk with hope of success in the language of Fisher Ames, of
Chancellor Kent, of Jeremiah Mason.

TO THOSE ACCUSTOMED TO REGARD THE VOCABULARY
of Federalism as absolutely descriptive of society, its disappearance meant the end of a world. Old-school conservatives
exchanged lamentations, looked darkly into the future and
sank into ever blacker gloom. "I think that our experiment
of self government approaches to a total failure," observed
William Sullivan of Massachusetts. "My opinion is," said
Chancellor Kent, "that the admission of universal suffrage
and a licentious press are incompatible with government and
security to property, and that the government and character

of this country are going to ruin." In 1837 Kent, drinking the waters of Saratoga in company with gentlemen of like mind, reported that all the talk was on the "sad hopes of self-governing democracies." "We are going to destruction," he summed it up with a kind of mournful relish, "—all checks and balances and institutions in this country are threatened with destruction from the ascendancy of the democracy of numbers and radicalism and the horrible doctrine and influence of Jacksonism."

The same year the aged conservative publicist Noah Webster set forth a plan to halt the disintegration and reconstruct society according to Federalist principles. While the American people, he said, were not divided into orders, like the nobility and commoners of Britain, "the distinction of rich and poor does exist, and must always exist; no human power or device can prevent it." Would it not be sensible, then, to recognize this distinction in the structure of government? After all, "the man who has half a million of dollars in property . . . has a much higher interest in government, than the man who has little or no property." Let us therefore end the popular election of Presidents, for the "great mass of people are and always must be very incompetent judges." Let us destroy the theory that the rich exploit the poor, and that corporations are "aristocratic in their tendency"; these are among the "most pernicious doctrines that ever cursed a nation." Let us divide the electorate into two classes, "the qualifications of one of which shall be superior age, and the possession of a certain amount of property," and let each class choose one house of Congress. Thus the supremacy of property may be assured, and America yet saved from democracy.

This proposal was the last gasp of Federalism. The mere act of stating such a program, after eight years of General Jackson, showed how unreal Federalism had become. No politician could espouse such ideas. No populace would submit to them. Not only were they dead, but the corpses were fatal to the touch.

Their death was not, however, as cataclysmic for everyone at it was for the Websters and Kents. Conservatism was a political party as well as a social faith; and, while the guardians of the faith were cherishing it in all its purity, the leaders of the party were quietly making a series of minor practical adjustments, entered into piecemeal and prescribed by the technical necessity of getting votes. Success rather than doctrinal soundness was their test: if the hallowed principles of Federalism did not work, they would have to go. Many conservatives, moreover, were themselves in part infected by the ideals of Jackson and hoped sincerely to reconcile these ideals with the continued rule of the business classes.

The result was the emergence of a new temper for conservatism—a temper whose characteristics paid tribute to both the political and moral strength of Jackson. It influenced first the neighborhood politicians, then the state organizations, and reached the heads of the party almost last, because the Websters and Clays were farthest from the people and most committed to the ancient dogmas. But it reached them too, and they modified, remolded and extemporized in conformity to the new moods they dimly felt. In this way, fresh elements made their way into conservative thought and almost transformed it before anyone knew what was happening.

BEFORE CONSERVATISM WAS STREAMLINED FOR THE post-Jacksonian world, it had to rid itself of the social exclusiveness so characteristic of Federalism. The Federalists had dressed differently, talked differently, behaved differently, and were exceedingly proud of the difference. Gentlemen, in their view, should enjoy a monopoly of government, and the lower orders must accept their place. "A farmer never looks so well as when he has a hand upon the plough," observed a Boston paper as late as 1834; "with his huge paw upon the statutes what can he do? It is as proper for a blacksmith to attempt to repair watches, as a farmer, in general to legislate."

Such expressions of aristocratic superiority, once the badges of gentlemanhood, were becoming more and more invitations to the abuse of the rising and irreverent democracy. Distinctions in dress began to disappear. Politicians found they must assume increasingly the manner and language of the common man.

THE WIDENING CHASM BETWEEN PRIVATE BELIEF AND public profession took all seriousness out of Whiggery as a social philosophy, turning it into a miscellaneous collection of stock political appeals, consistent only in a steady but muted enmity to change. It may be argued, of course, that the intellectual collapse of conservatism was unimportant, since the first criterion of a political creed is its success and not its profundity. Yet it may be speculated whether the repeated failure of conservatism in this country to govern effectively may not be related to the increasing flabbiness of conservative thought. Individuals might continue thinking in Federalist terms, reserving the Whig phrases for public consumption; but such a thoroughly Machiavellian position is difficult to sustain. When a party starts out by deceiving the people, it is likely to finish by deceiving itself.

In the end, as Whiggism became the dominant language, all conservatives more or less had to talk in it, and ultimately most came to believe it. Politicians so systematically misled as to the character of society were not likely to provide effective government, unless, like Mark Hanna, they were Machiavellians, or, like William Howard Taft, they were possessed of an executive instinct which could triumph over all illusions.

XXIII *1840*

THE ASSIMILATION BY CONSERVATISM OF THE NEW democratic moods came first in the West, where orthodox Federalism had never discovered a social basis. This democratization was, however, mainly an unconscious process. Western leaders like Clay and Harrison, however much they maintained the Hamiltonian policies, could feel no compulsion to repudiate a Hamiltonian social philosophy they had never really possessed. In the East, where class distinctions had kept the Federalist philosophy alive, assimilation of the new values was hardly possible without deliberate rejection of the old, an intellectual exercise not required on the frontier. Among the Whigs of the eighteen-thirties, as among the Democrats, the conscious assertion of radicalism came in the main from the seaboard, not from the forest.

THE TASK OF CONSERVATISM, IF IT WERE TO SUCCEED in post-Jacksonian America, was to purge itself of the discredited past—manners, principles, issues—and to set the case of the business community on fresh and unspoiled grounds. The conservatives of New York, kept from power for a quarter of a century by the dead hand of Federalism, saw with special clarity the need for a new departure, and two politicians of remarkable ability arose during the thirties to show the way. William H. Seward and Thurlow Weed represented accurately the double impulse behind the new conservatism. Seward, a man of passion and principle, had a genuine if qualified belief in Jacksonian ideals. Weed, a personal reactionary, had a cynical recognition that Jacksonian professions were necessary for political success. Where, for example, Seward thought New York's constitution of 1821, if anything too conservative, Weed strongly but privately disapproved of it as dangerously radical. Where Seward was a great believer in popular rule and frequent elections, Weed feared, to the end of his life, that universal suffrage would "occasion universal political demoralization, and ultimately overthrow our government"—though this fear never deterred him from encouraging the demoralization when it paid him to do so.

EIGHTEEN-FORTY FORCED THE PARTY TO THE CONcrete choice, should the campaign be fought once more with the issues and leaders with which the Whigs had repeatedly gone down to defeat? Or should the past be forgotten, and the party enter the canvass unencumbered by its former issues and leaders?

For the liberals the decision was clear. Early in Van Buren's administration they set out to knife the "aristocratic" possibilities and clear the field for a "democratic" candidate. The first victim was Daniel Webster. Webster's great opportunity had come in 1837 when the business community in its crisis had instinctively turned to him as the most formidable intellect among the Whigs. When he could provide no solution more stirring than a return to the Bank, he lost his chance. In 1838 the *Atlas* led the wolf-pack against him, declaring in a series of editorials that his nomination would ruin the party. Webster went unhappily to England in 1839 knowing that revolt in his home state had destroyed his availability. As for Henry Clay, Thurlow Weed personally conducted the campaign of elimination, imperturbably passing the word to the convention delegates that the people would have no more of him. Their own candidate had been settled by the popular vote in 1836. A Westerner, a military hero, and a plain man of the people, innocent of the Jacksonian controversies, who could be a better nominee than William Henry Harrison?

THROUGH THE FALL THE PARADES MARCHED, AND THE torches flared, and the hard cider flowed, and Whig operators stumped the country. One by one the states went to the polls.

One by one the returns came in. The result was decisive: Harrison, 234 votes, Van Buren, 60. The President, sitting silently in the White House through November gloom, heard the inevitable refrain in the streets outside. "Van, Van, is a used-up man. . . ."

Yet the majority was not as great as the electoral result indicated. Van Buren's 1,129,102 votes were an increase of 366,424 over the vote which had elected him in 1836; it was indeed a much larger total than any victorious President had polled before 1840. Out of nearly two and a half million votes cast, Harrison's margin was 145,914. A shift of a little over eight thousand votes, properly distributed, would have given Van Buren the election.*

The achievement of Whig hullabaloo lay, not in changing Democratic votes, but in bringing out people who had never been to the polls before. Few of the million new voters had much idea what all the shouting was about. "So far as ideas entered into my support of the Whig candidate," recollected one veteran of the campaign, "I simply regarded him as a poor man, whose home was in a log cabin, and who would in some way help the people . . . while I was fully persuaded that Van Buren was not only a graceless aristocrat and a dandy, but a cunning conspirator, seeking the overthrow of this country's liberties." "As to what the 'Sub-Treasury' really was," confessed another, "I had not the remotest idea; but this I knew;— that it was the most wicked outrage ever committed by a remorseless tyrant upon a long-suffering people."

The defeat threw many Democrats into deep dejection. They could not understand how their people could have forsaken them. But, though a long view is perhaps inadequately comforting in the short run, the election of 1840, if a setback for the Democrats, was not necessarily a setback for democracy. In a sense, it was the most conclusive evidence of the triumph of Jackson. Conservatism had carried the election, but it had to assume the manner of the popular party in order to do it. The champions of inequality were forced to take over the slogans of the new dispensation.

Jackson's success was not to mean the end of all conflict. Democracy cannot exist without conflict, and it becomes meaningless when one party can suppress all opposition. But the Jacksonian triumph did mean that the struggle would be renewed on Jackson's terms, and not on those of Daniel Webster or Nicholas Biddle.

* Van Buren lost New York, Pennsylvania, Maine and New Jersey by narrow margins. With a properly allocated shift of 8184 votes, he could have carried these states and won in the electoral college, 150-144. H. R. Fraser, *Democracy in the Making,* has similar, though somewhat inaccurate, calculations.

XXIV *Jacksonian Democracy as an Intellectual Movement*

THE JACKSONIAN REVOLUTION RESTED ON PREMISES
which the struggles of the thirties hammered together into a
kind of practical social philosophy. The outline of this way of
thinking about society was clear. It was stated and restated, as
we have seen, on every level of political discourse from presidential messages to stump speeches, from newspaper editorials
to private letters. It provided the intellectual background without which the party battles of the day cannot be understood.

THE JACKSONIANS BELIEVED THAT THERE WAS A DEEP-
rooted conflict in society between the "producing" and "non-
producing" classes—the farmers and laborers, on the one
hand, and the business community on the other. The business
community was considered to hold high cards in this conflict
through its network of banks and corporations, its control of
education and the press, above all, its power over the state:
it was therefore able to strip the working classes of the fruits
of their labor. "Those who produce all wealth," said Amos
Kendall, "are themselves left poor. They see principalities
extending and palaces built around them, without being aware
that the entire expense is a tax upon themselves."

If they wished to preserve their liberty, the producing classes
would have to unite against the movement "to make the rich
richer and the potent more powerful." Constitutional prescriptions and political promises afforded no sure protection. "We
have heretofore been too disregardful of the fact," observed
William M. Gouge, "that social order is quite as dependent on
the laws which regulate the distribution of wealth, as on political organization." The program now was to resist every attempt to concentrate wealth and power further in a single
class. Since free elections do not annihilate the opposition, the
fight would be unceasing. "The struggle for power," said C. C.
Cambreleng, "is as eternal as the division of society. A defeat
cannot destroy the boundary which perpetually separates the
democracy from the aristocracy."

The specific problem was to control the power of the capitalistic groups, mainly Eastern, for the benefit of the non-

capitalist groups, farmers and laboring men, East, West and South. The basic Jacksonian ideas came naturally enough from the East, which best understood the nature of business power and reacted most sharply against it. The legend that Jacksonian democracy was the explosion of the frontier, lifting into the government some violent men filled with rustic prejudices against big business, does not explain the facts, which were somewhat more complex. Jacksonian democracy was rather a second American phase of that enduring struggle between the business community and the rest of society which is the guarantee of freedom in a liberal capitalist state.

Like any social philosophy, Jacksonian democracy drew on several intellectual traditions. Basically, it was a revival of Jeffersonianism, but the Jeffersonian inheritance was strengthened by the infusion of fresh influences; notably the anti-monopolistic tradition, formulated primarily by Adam Smith and expounded in America by Gouge, Leggett, Sedgwick, Cambreleng; and the pro-labor tradition, formulated primarily by William Cobbett and expounded by G. H. Evans, Ely Moore, John Ferral.*

THE NEW INDUSTRIALISM HAD TO BE ACCEPTED: banks, mills, factories, industrial capital, industrial labor. These were all distasteful realities for orthodox Jeffersonians, and, not least, the propertyless workers. "The mobs of great cities," Jefferson had said, "add just so much to the support of pure government, as sores do to the strength of the human body." The very ferocity of his images expressed the violence of his feelings. "When we get piled upon one another in large cities, as in Europe," he told Madison, "we shall become corrupt as in Europe, and go to eating one another as they do there." It was a universal sentiment among his followers. "No man should live," Nathaniel Macon used to say, "where he can hear his neighbour's dog bark."

Yet the plain political necessity of winning the labor vote obliged a change of mood. Slowly, with some embarrassment, the Jeffersonian preferences for the common man were enlarged to take in the city workers. In 1833 the *New York Evening Post,* declaring that, if anywhere, a large city of mixed population would display the evils of universal suffrage, asked if this had been the case in New York and answered: No. Amasa Walker set out the same year to prove that "great cities

* The experience of Samuel Clesson Allen, reaching Jacksonian conclusions along paths altogether independent of the main Jacksonian influences, is an important reminder that the vital origins of an effective social philosophy are the concrete needs of the day.

are not *necessarily*, as the proverb says, 'great sores,' " and
looked forward cheerily to the day when they would be "great
fountains of healthful moral influence, sending forth streams
that shall fertilize and bless the land." The elder Theodore
Sedgwick added that the cause of the bad reputation of cities
was economic: "it is the sleeping in garrets and cellars; the living in holes and dens; in dirty, unpaved, unlighted streets,
without the accommodations of wells, cisterns, baths, and
other means of cleanliness and health"—clear up this situation, and cities will be all right.

Jackson himself never betrayed any of Jefferson's revulsion
to industrialism. He was, for example, deeply interested by the
mills of Lowell in 1833, and his inquiries respecting hours,
wages and production showed, observers reported, "that the
subject of domestic manufactures had previously engaged his
attentive observation." His presidential allusions to the "producing classes" always included the workingmen of the cities.

THE ACCEPTANCE OF THE PROPERTYLESS LABORING
classes involved a retreat from one of the strongest Jeffersonian positions. John Taylor's distinction between "natural" and
"artificial" property had enabled the Jeffersonians to enlist
the moral and emotional resources contained in the notion of
property. They could claim to be the protectors of property
rights, while the business community, by despoiling the producers of the fruits of their labor, were the enemies of property. Yet, this distinction, if it were to have other than a meta-
phorical existence, had to rest on the dominance of agriculture and small handicraft. The proceeds of the labor of a
farmer, or a blacksmith, could be measured with some exactness; but who could say what the "just" fruits of labor were
for a girl whose labor consisted in one small operation in the
total process of manufacturing cotton cloth? In what sense
could propertyless people be deprived of their property?

The Whigs diligently set forth to make every attack on
"fictitious" capital an attack on all property rights.

The Whigs slowly won the battle. The discovery of the
courts that a corporation was really a person completed their
victory. By 1843 William S. Wait could strike the Jeffersonian
flag: " 'Security to property' no longer means security to the
citizen in the possession of his moderate competency, but security to him who monopolizes thousands—security to a few,
who may live in luxury and ease upon the blood and sweat of
many."

Jacksonians now tended to exalt human rights as a counterweight to property rights. The Whigs, charged Frank Blair, were seeking such an extension of "the rights of property as to swallow up and annihilate those of persons"; the Democratic party would "do all in its power to preserve and defend them." "We believe property should be held subordinate to man, and not man to property," said Orestes A. Brownson; "and therefore that it is always lawful to make such modifications of its constitution as the good of Humanity requires." The early decisions of Roger B. Taney's court helped establish the priority of the public welfare. But the Democrats had surrendered an important ideological bastion. The right to property provided a sturdy foundation for liberalism, while talk of human rights too often might end up in sentimentality or blood.

In several respects, then, the Jacksonians revised the Jeffersonian faith for America. They moderated that side of Jeffersonianism which talked of agricultural virtue, independent proprietors, "natural" property, abolition of industrialism, and expanded immensely that side which talked of economic equality, the laboring classes, human rights and the control of industrialism. This readjustment enabled the Jacksonians to attack economic problems which had baffled and defeated the Jeffersonians. It made for a greater realism, and was accompanied by a general toughening of the basic Jeffersonian conceptions. While the loss of "property" was serious, both symbolically and intellectually, this notion had been for most Jeffersonians somewhat submerged next to the romantic image of the free and virtuous cultivator; and the Jacksonians grew much more insistent about theories of capitalist alienation. Where, for the Jeffersonians, the tensions of class conflict tended to dissolve in vague generalizations about the democracy and the aristocracy, many Jacksonians would have agreed with A. H. Wood's remark, "It is in vain to talk of Aristocracy and Democracy—these terms are too variable and indeterminate to convey adequate ideas of the present opposing interests; the division is between the rich and the poor—the warfare is between them."

This greater realism was due, in the main, to the passage of time. The fears of Jefferson were now actualities. One handled fears by exorcism, but actualities by adjustment. For the Jeffersonians mistrust of banks and corporations was chiefly a matter of theory; for the Jacksonians it was a matter of experience. The contrast between the scintillating metaphors of John Taylor and the sober detail of William M. Gouge expressed the difference. Jefferson rejected the Industrial Revolution and sought to perpetuate the smiling society which preceded it (at least, to the philosopher; facts compelled the President toward a different policy), while Jackson, accepting industrialism as an ineradicable and even useful part of the economic land-scape, sought rather to control it. Jeffersonian democracy looked wistfully back toward a past slipping further every minute into the mists of memory, while Jacksonian democracy came straightforwardly to grips with a rough and unlovely present.

The interlude saw also the gradual unfolding of certain con-sequences of the democratic dogma which had not been so clear to the previous generation. Though theoretically aware of the relation between political and economic power, the Jeffersonians had been occupied, chiefly, with establishing political equality. This was their mission, and they had little time to grapple with the economic questions.

But the very assertion of political equality raised inevitably the whole range of problems involved in property and class conflict. How could political equality mean anything without relative economic equality among the classes of the country? This question engaged the Jacksonians. As Orestes A. Brown-son said, "A Loco-foco is a Jeffersonian Democrat, who having realized political equality, passed through one phase of the revolution, now passes on to another, and attempts the realiza-tion of social equality, so that the actual condition of men in society shall be in harmony with their acknowledged rights as citizens." This gap between Jeffersonian and Jacksonian de-mocracy enabled men like John Quincy Adams, Henry Clay, Joseph Story and many others, who had been honest Jeffer-sonians, to balk at the economic extremities to which Jackson proposed to lead them.

Jacksonians thus opened irrevocably the economic question, which the Jeffersonians had only touched halfheartedly. Yet, while they clarified these economic implications of democracy, the Jacksonians were no more successful than their predeces-sors in resolving certain political ambiguities. Of these, two were outstanding—the problem of the virtue of majorities, and the problem of the evil of government. Since the Jacksonians made useful explorations of these issues after 1840, they will be reserved for later discussion.

A SECOND SOURCE OF INSPIRATION FOR THE JACKSONI-ans was the libertarian economic thought stirred up by Adam Smith and *The Wealth of Nations*. Believers in the myth of Adam Smith, as expounded by present-day publicists both of the right and of the left, may find this singular; but the real

Adam Smith was rich in ammunition for the Jacksonians, as for any foe of business manipulation of the state.

The Wealth of Nations quietly, precisely and implacably attacked the alliance of government and business, showing how monopoly retarded the economic growth of nations and promoted the exploitation of the people. It was, in effect, a criticism of the kind of mercantilist policy which, in modified form, Hamilton has instituted in the Federalist program of the seventeen-nineties. Smith's classic argument against monopoly appealed strongly to the Jacksonians, and his distinction between productive and unproductive labor converged with the Jacksonian distinction between the producers and the nonproducers.

In the end, business altogether captured the phrases of *laissez faire* and used them more or less ruthlessly in defense of monopoly, even coupling them with arguments for the protective tariff, a juxtaposition which would at least have given earlier conservatives a decent sense of embarrassment. Adam Smith himself doubted whether large businessmen really believed in free competition. The sequel confirmed his doubts. The irony was that the slogans of free trade, which he developed in order to destroy monopoly, should end up as its bulwark.

A THIRD IMPORTANT STIMULUS TO THE JACKSONIANS was the foaming tide of social revolt in Britain, reaching them primarily through the writings of William Cobbett.

A vehement advocate of the rights of workers to the full fruits of their industry, and a savage enemy of the new financial aristocracy, he found a rapt audience in America, especially in the labor movement. *Paper against Gold,* reprinted in New York in 1834, helped the hard-money campaign. William H. Hale of New York, the author of *Useful Knowledge for the Producers of Wealth,* and Thomas Brothers, the editor of the *Radical Reformer* of Philadelphia, were perhaps his leading disciples, but his unquenchable vitality inspired the whole radical wing.

THE RADICAL DEMOCRATS HAD A DEFINITE CONCEPTION of their relation to history. From the Jeffersonian analysis, fortified by the insights of Adam Smith and Cobbett, they sketched out an interpretation of modern times which gave meaning and status to the Jacksonian struggles.

Power, said the Jacksonians, goes with property. In the Mid-

dle Ages the feudal nobility held power in society through its
monopoly of land under feudal tenure. The overthrow of
feudalism, with the rise of new forms of property, marked the
first step in the long march toward freedom. The struggle was
carried on by the rising business community—"commercial,
or business capital, against landed capital; merchants, traders,
manufacturers, artizans, against the owners of the soil, the
great landed nobility." It lasted from the close of the twelfth
century to the Whig Revolution of 1688 in Britain.

What of the future? The Jacksonians were sublimely confident: history was on their side. "It is now for the yeomanry
and the mechanics to march at the head of civilization," said
Bancroft. "The merchants and the lawyers, that is, the
moneyed interest broke up feudalism. The day for the multitude has now dawned." "All classes, each in turn, have possessed the government," exclaimed Brownson; "and the time
has come for all predominance of class to end; for Man, the
People to rule."

XXV *Jacksonian Democracy and the Law*

DEFEATED IN THE OPEN FIELD BY JEFFERSON, FED-
eralism had retreated to prepared defenses. Under the resourceful leadership of John Marshall it entrenched itself in the courts
of law and sought to make them unshakable bulwarks against
change. Like every great democratic movement in American
history, Jacksonian democracy eventually collided with the
courts, running up sharply against their inclination to devise
new guarantees for property and throw up new obstacles to
popular control. The ensuing conflict had two main aspects:
the struggle to change the personnel of the courts, and the
struggle to simplify and reform the law itself.

THE BATTLE OF THE SUPREME COURT PRESENTED THIS
conflict in its most compact and dramatic form. The long and
superb series of decisions written by Marshall, or under his influence, had pretty well established the Constitution as a document which forbade government interference with private
property, even on the ground of the public welfare. The jur-
ists of many of the states were cast more or less crudely in

Marshall's image. All agreed in repeating his prejudices, though rarely with his profundity, and all, operating as a kind of high priesthood of the law, agreed in detesting Jacksonian democracy.

The death of Marshall in the summer of 1835 perfected the conservative despair. The last bulwark of their cause, or, as they preferred to describe it, their country's liberties, had fallen. With his next appointment Jackson would have not only the Chief Justice but a majority of the Court. William Leggett candidly observed for the Democrats that Marshall's power on the Court had always been "an occasion of lively regret. That he is at length removed from that station is a source of satisfaction."

Some Whigs began to torment themselves with the thought of Benton as Marshall's successor, but the Missouri colossus himself exploded at the idea. "These fellows are no more able to comprehend me," he wrote, ". . . than a rabbit, which breeds twelve times a year, could comprehend the gestation of an elephant, which carries two years. So of these fellows and me. Dying for small offices themselves, they cannot understand that I can refuse all. . . . Taney is my favorite for that place." Taney was also Jackson's favorite, and in every respect the logical choice. Marshall himself had favored him for an earlier appointment as Associate Justice, for which he had been rejected by the Senate, and the conservatives could hardly have expected a better selection. But they remained angry and unforgiving. "The pure ermine of the Supreme Court," observed the *New York American* after Taney's confirmation, "is sullied by the appointment of that political hack."

THE NEW CHIEF JUSTICE WORE TROUSERS INSTEAD OF the traditional knee breeches, and he showed in other ways that he was prepared to ignore the past. Two important issues in his first term gave him the chance to start breaking new trails. One involved the question whether corporate charters should be construed in favor of the corporation or in favor of the community. The second involved questions of the power of states to enforce laws affecting interstate commerce. Taney's answers, formulated with the same realism and lucidity, the same powerful appeal to principles rather than to precedents, the same classic finality as Marshall's, revealed the drift of the Court in the direction of narrowing the immunities of corporations and enlarging the scope of social legislation.

The crucial case in the retreat from Federalism was the fight, so long a staple of Massachusetts politics, between the

Charles River Bridge and the Warren Bridge. The question was whether the legislature of Massachusetts, by authorizing the construction of a free bridge over the Charles River at a point where it would interfere with the profits of a privately owned toll bridge, had impaired the contract of the toll-bridge corporation. The case had been argued before the Supreme Court in 1831, but no decision was handed down. It was re-argued in 1837, with Daniel Webster as one of the counsels for the bridge company. The fact that Harvard College, as well as many leading citizens of Boston, held stock in the Charles River Bridge increased the general tension.

The issue brought the Federalist and Jeffersonian views of the place of corporations in society into sharp collision. "I consider the interference of the legislature in the management of our private affairs, whether those affairs are committed to a company or remain under individual direction," John Marshall had written, "as equally dangerous and unwise." His decision in the Dartmouth College case that a charter was a contract which a state could not impair was designed to put corporations safely out of reach of state intervention.

Taney, on the other hand, had made clear as Attorney General that in his mind an act of incorporation—particularly in the case of corporations which perform essential public services, such as constructing roads and bridges—could "never be considered as having been granted for the exclusive benefit of the corporators. Certain privileges are given to them, in order to obtain a public convenience; and the interest of the public must, I presume, always be regarded as the main object of every charter for a toll-bridge or a turnpike road."

He had furthermore informed Jackson privately that, with regard to other than strictly public-utility corporations:—

It would be against the spirit of our free institutions, by which equal rights are intended to be secured to all, to grant peculiar franchises and privileges to a body of individuals merely for the purpose of enabling them more conveniently and effectively to advance their own private interests. . . . The consideration upon which alone, such peculiar privileges can be granted is the expectation and prospect of promoting thereby some public interest.

An advanced radical Democrat, Taney, like Marshall for the quarter century preceding, set out to read his "economic predilections" into the Constitution.

The Supreme Court handed down the bridge decision on February 14, 1837, with Taney holding in the majority opinion that no rights were granted in a corporate charter except those explicitly conferred by the words of the charter. Charters of incorporation, in other words, could not be construed inferentially against the community. "The object and end of all government," Taney declared in words central to an understanding of Jacksonian democracy, "is to promote the happiness and prosperity of the community by which it is established; and it can never be assumed, that the government intended to diminish its power of accomplishing the end for which it was created. . . . The continued existence of a government would be of no great value, if by implications and presumptions, it was disarmed of the powers necessary to accomplish the ends of its creation; and the functions it was designed to perform, transferred to the hands of privileged corporations." But what of the rights of property? "While the rights of private property are sacredly guarded," rejoined Taney, "we must not forget that the community also have rights, and that the happiness and well being of every citizen depends on their faithful preservation."

WHEN CHANCELLOR KENT FIRST LOOKED INTO TANEY'S opinion, he "dropped the pamphlet in disgust and read no more." Two months later he steeled himself to try again "and with increased disgust. . . . I have lost my confidence and hopes in the constitutional guardianship and protection of the Supreme Court." What, then, was left? A few months later Kent poured out his melancholy at length. The Charles River Bridge decision, he said, "undermines the foundations of morality, confidence, and truth." The doctrine of strict construction of corporate charters was appalling: "what destruction of rights under a contract can be more complete?" The old man was beyond consolation. "When we consider the revolution in opinion, in policy, and in numbers that has recently changed the character of the Supreme Court, we can scarcely avoid being reduced nearly to a state of despair of the commonwealth."

THE SPREADING DISSATISFACTION BRED A MOVEMENT toward codification, both of the common law and of the statutes, led by Edward Livingston of Louisiana. A friend of Bentham's, a careful student of jurisprudence and an able lawyer, Livingston made proposals of codification in Louisiana which attracted national attention. His close friendship with

Jackson and his place in the cabinet helped the doctrines of legal reform to penetrate the Democratic party.

The fight for codification took place against strong conservative opposition. As Chancellor Kent observed to Livingston, "I have spent the best years of my life in administering the old common law . . . *with all its imperfections on its head.*" Why change it? But the pressure for change was too strong. In 1827 Benjamin F. Butler took a leading part in the preparation of the *Revised Statutes of the State of New York,* the first successful attempt to put together in a systematic code the common law and the existing colonial and state laws. Pennsylvania followed suit in the early eighteen-thirties; in 1833-1834 Salmon P. Chase produced the *Revision of the Statutes of Ohio;* and, in 1836, Robert Rantoul's tireless agitation in Massachusetts resulted in the appointment of a committee on the expediency of codifying the common law, though Justice Story, as chairman, was able to keep it from doing very much. "We have not yet become votaries to the notions of Jeremy Bentham," Story said privately. "But the present state of popular opinion here makes it necessary to do something on the subject." Where the Jacksonian attack did not achieve immediate consolidation of the statutes, it often succeeded in simplifying procedure and particularly in reforming the baffling systems of special pleading and practice. The constitutions of the new Western states also showed the mark of the Jacksonian reforms.

XXVI *Jacksonian Democracy and Industrialism*

FROM THE START OF THE CENTURY, FIRST IN BANKING and insurance, then in transportation, canals, bridges, turnpikes, then in manufacturing, the corporation was gradually becoming the dominant form of economic organization. The generation of Jackson was the first to face large-scale adjustment to this new economic mechanism. For owners and large investors, the adjustment presented no particular problem. But those on the outside had a feeling of deep misgiving which was less an economic or political than a moral protest: it was basically a sense of shock.

ECONOMIC LIFE BEFORE THE CORPORATION, AT LEAST according to the prevalent conceptions, was more or less controlled by a feeling of mutual responsibility among the persons concerned. Economic relationships were generally personal—between master and workman laboring together in the same shop, between buyer and seller living together in the same village. The very character of this relation produced some restraints upon the tendency of the master to exploit the workman, or of the seller to cheat the buyer. Reciprocal confidence was necessarily the keynote of a system so much dominated by personal relations. Business and private affairs were governed by much the same ethical code.

But industrialism brought the growing depersonalization of economic life. With the increase in size of the labor force, the master was further and further removed from his workmen, till the head of a factory could have only the most tenuous community of feeling with his men. With the development of manufacturing and improved means of distribution, the seller lost all contact with the buyer, and feelings of responsibility to the consumer inevitably diminished. The expansion of investment tended to bring on absentee ownership, with the divorce of ownership and management; and the rise of cities enfeebled the paternal sentiments with which many capitalists had regarded their own workers in towns and villages. Slowly the vital economic relationships were becoming impersonal, passing out of the control of a personal moral code. Slowly private morality and business morality grew apart. Slowly the commercial community developed a collection of devices and ceremonials which enabled businessmen to set aside the ethic which ruled their private life and personal relations.

Of these devices the most dramatic and generally intelligible was the corporation. For a people still yearning for an economy dominated by individual responsibility, still under the spell of the Jeffersonian dream, the corporation had one outstanding characteristic: its moral irresponsibility. "Corporations have neither bodies to be kicked, nor souls to be damned," went a favorite aphorism. Beyond good and evil, insensible to argument or appeal, they symbolized the mounting independence of the new economy from the restraints and scruples of personal life.

In 1840 Amos Kendall urged the inculcation of the belief that "there is but one code of morals for private and public affairs." His very concern was a confession that two codes existed.

As long as individual responsibility existed in the economic system, as long as a single code more or less governed business and personal life, the Jeffersonians were right, and that government was best which governed least. But these were the moral characteristics of a society of small freeholds, as Jefferson well understood. When the economy became too complex to admit of much personal responsibility, when ownership became attenuated and liability limited and diffused, when impersonality began to dominate the system and produce irresponsibility, when, in short, economic life began to throw off the control of personal scruple, then government had to extend its function in order to preserve the ties which hold society together. The history of government intervention is thus a history of the growing ineffectiveness of private conscience as a means of social control. With private conscience powerless, the only alternative to tyranny or anarchy was the growth of the public conscience, and the natural expression of the public conscience was the democratic government.

IN SPITE OF JEFFERSONIAN INHIBITIONS, THEN, THE Jacksonians were forced to intervene in the affairs of business. Their ultimate aim was to safeguard the equitable distribution of property which they felt alone could sustain democracy, but this effort inevitably required a battle against the concentration of wealth and power in a single class.

THE FATE OF THE JACKSONIAN ECONOMIC LEGISLA-tion was that common historical irony: it on the whole promoted the very ends it was intended to defeat. The general laws sprinkled holy water on corporations, cleansing them of the legal status of monopoly and sending them forth as the benevolent agencies of free competition.

Yet the fact that the Jacksonian program was eventually beneficial to economic enterprise does not mean that the business world was astute enough to recognize this in advance. In fact, businessmen fought the Jacksonian program bitterly, step by step, and indulged in interminable wails of calamity and disaster.

THE FRONTAL ATTACK ON CAPITALIST DOMINATION had to be supported by the full mobilization of the noncapitalist groups. The Jeffersonian tradition had already rallied the farmers and the artisans. But the Jeffersonians, no less than the Federalists, looked on industrial labor as an element, fortunately small, to be regarded with mistrust and abhorrence.

THE DEBATE OVER UNIONISM EXHIBITED ANOTHER ASpect of the struggle for *laissez faire*. From the first, conservatism had rested part of its case on the ground that unions interrupted the freedom of trade.

Yet these doctrines immediately caused contradictions if they were applied only to unions and not to corporations. What, for example, of the policy of Hamilton? What of the United States Bank? For men like Thacher and Savage, who rejected the broad application, free competition was obviously an exorcism, not a faith.

THE DEMOCRATS ALSO SUPPORTED THE WORKINGmen's struggle for a shorter day. The average length of the working day in Lowell in 1845 varied from eleven hours and twenty-four minutes in December and January to thirteen hours and thirty-one minutes in April—ordinarily from sunrise to sunset. In the eighteen-thirties labor organizations raised the cry for reduction, and radical Democrats took it up with enthusiasm.

Van Buren's executive order of 1840 gave the movement official blessing. In Massachusetts in the next fifteen years Democrats several times presented ten-hour laws to the legislature. But the proposals were killed by Whig committees, like the one which visited Lowell in 1845 and returned "fully satisfied, that the order, decorum, and general appearance of things in and about the mills, could not be improved by any suggestion of theirs, or by any act of the Legislature." *

Another part of the Jacksonian effort sought to guarantee the political rights of labor. Having gained the ballot, the workingman now faced the problem of making sure he voted as he pleased. Employers not seldom threatened to discharge those who dared vote the radical ticket, and Fenimore Cooper reported that he had heard this practice openly defended.

* Massachusetts *House Document*, no. 50 (1845), 8. The chairman of the committee was William Schouler, father of the historian and editor of the principal paper in Lowell. The report exploited the tricks of pastorialism to a high degree. "Labor is on an equality with capital," it said, "and indeed controls it, and so it ever will be while free education and free constitutions exist. . . . Labor is intelligent enough to make its own bargains, and look out for its own interests without any interference from us." The evidence for the abuses was impressive, and the committee concluded: "We acknowledge all this, but we say, the remedy is not with us. We look for it in the progressive improvement in art and science, in a higher appreciation of man's destiny, in a less love for money, and a more ardent love for social happiness and intellectual superiority." *Ibid.*, 16. This last passage might almost have come from the writings of Dr. William Ellery Channing.

THE PROBLEM OF LABOR FOR THE JACKSONIANS, then, consisted in mobilizing the votes of the workingmen to support a policy which would increase their share in the national income. In their attempt to preserve the economic base of labor action they had a potent ally—the public domain in the West. The broad expanse across green forests and illimitable prairies and fertile plains offered inviting refuge to the discontented and underprivileged of the East; and the greater the number drawn to the frontier from the settled states, the higher the wages and the easier the life for those who stayed behind.

Whatever broad effects the frontier had on the price level, the labor supply, the incentives toward capital investment or the general economic atmosphere, it had ceased even by the time of Jackson to serve as a real alternative for the workers of the Eastern states.

THE JACKSONIANS THUS REGARDED THE KEEPING OPEN of the public domain as a democratic imperative.

Though the national domain may have been in the narrow sense a Western problem, the needs and energies which shaped the national policy toward it were by no means exclusively Western. The opening up of the public lands was nearly as vital for Eastern workingmen and farmers as for the people of the West. The importance of the land question is evidence less of the Western character of Jacksonianism than of its overmastering desire to preserve everywhere the economic democracy which alone could give political democracy meaning.

XXVII Jacksonian Democracy and Religion

FEDERALISM HAD VALUED THE CLERGY, AS WELL AS the judiciary, as a great stabilizing influence in society, hoping thus to identify the malcontent as the foe both of God and the law. Hamilton's curious project, in 1802, of a "Christian Constitutional Society" disclosed the fervor with which conservatism, when defeated at the polls, was turning to religion and law for salvation. In the next quarter-century conservatism, in collaboration with the pulpit, worked out a systematic view of America as essentially and legally a religious nation in which the church should assist the state in preserving the existing social order. Jacksonian democracy ran sharply up against these conceptions both of religion and of government.

THE SABBATARIAN CONTROVERSY OF THE LATE eighteen-twenties revived the religious community as a national political-pressure group; and the very defeat of the campaign against the Sunday mails only strengthened the conviction that religious-minded persons must unite to save the country from infidelity and radicalism.

AGAINST THE WHIG THEORY OF THE "NATIONAL RELIGION" the Democrats set up a theory of religious nonintervention.

Total separation of church and state was considered the best safeguard for the health of each.

This principle did not enjoin an exclusively defensive policy. Church and state were not, in fact, completely separated; and a part of the Jacksonian program became not only to guard against new clerical interference, as in the case of the Sunday mails, but to eradicate the lingering traces of theocracy.

The Democratic theory of the relations of church and state did not necessarily imply a weaker personal faith.

Yet the Whig charges that the Democratic party was the party of irreligion were not without basis. The unrelenting conservatism of so many of the clergy had poisoned not a few liberals. "The clergy, as a class," Samuel Clesson Allen put it, "have always been ready to come in for a share in the advantages of the privileged classes, and in return for the ease and convenience accorded to them by these classes, to spread their broad mantle over them."

Tom Paine, whom the Whigs were already busy turning into a filthy little atheist, was still a Democratic hero, admired by Jackson, toasted at party celebrations and defended from conservative smears.

FOR SOME DEMOCRATS, HOWEVER, CHRISTIANITY, FAR from being the partner of privilege, was potentially, the most radical of all faiths. Realization of the typically conservative role of the clergy made them advocate the separation of church and state; but true Christianity, in their minds, could alone release the energies of reform in all their strength.

Jacksonianism thus assisted the growing secularization of society. Its substantial effect was to divert the church toward

what many in this country believe its true function: to lead the
individual soul to salvation, not to interfere in politics. Religion, the Jacksonians felt, could best serve itself by ending its
entangling alliances with political reaction.

XXVIII *Jacksonian Democracy and Utopia*

THE DECADE OF THE EIGHTEEN-FORTIES WAS MARKED
by outbursts of Utopian enthusiasm. Literary men, appalled by
the drabness of life around them, sought refuge in social orders
of their own fabrication. Some fled physically, as well as intellectually, retiring to model communities where the contempla-
tion of their own principles would protect them from the
challenges of the new industrialism. Literary men of later generations, perhaps equipped by their own timidities to sympa-
thize with this earlier retreat from responsibility, have since
glorified the movement until the impression has passed into
the tradition that these fugitives had almost a monopoly of the
reform impulse. It is pertinent to inquire into the relations of
Jacksonian democracy and the passion for Utopia.

THE MOST POPULAR OF THE UTOPIAN FAITHS IN AMER-
ica was the gospel of Fourier, of which the prophet was Albert
Brisbane. A tall, slim, round-shouldered man, with jutting chin
and deep-set eyes, he had gone to Europe in the late eighteen-
twenties, spurred on by "an irresistible desire to solve the mystery of man's destiny." When he returned a few years later,
man's destiny had become an open book. The book was written by Fourier.

As a diagnosis of industrial society, Fourierism was filled
with many keen insights. It insisted at bottom that man must
be accepted as a whole, with all his needs, passions and in-
stincts. No society, it emphasized, which regularly ignored,
stifled or thwarted the basic drives of man could be stable or
happy.

LITERARY FASHION HAS BEEN A DISTORTER OF HIS-
tory. Much more important for the national democratic tradition than this intellectual dalliance with pseudo-reform was

the tainted, corrupt, unsatisfactory work performed by the Locofoco politicians. The emotions of Utopia have been admired long enough. It is time to pass along from the sideshows into the main arena and watch the men who were actually fighting the battles of reform in the place where they had to be fought. All the prose about brotherhood and the pretty experiments in group living made no conservative sleep less easily at night. The politicians might have sold their souls to Party, but at least they had something to show for it.

Yet, let no one forget the generous and humane aspirations which animated the Utopian faith. Some people must dream broadly and guilelessly, if only to balance those who never dream at all.

XXIX   *Jacksonian Democracy and Literature*

HISTORIANS OF REVOLUTION DESCRIBE A PHENOME-non they have named the "desertion of the intellectuals." This is the stage in society when the artists, the writers, the intellectuals in general, no longer find enough sustenance in the established order to feel much loyalty to it. They are filled with a pervading sense at once of alienation and of longing, which, one way or another, controls their work, directly if they are political writers, obliquely and at many removes if they are poets. The age of Jackson was such a period. One world was passing away, while another struggled to be born, and the political battles of the Jacksonians helped set in motion a whole train of changes in other spheres. "The strife has been of a character to call forth all the resources of the popular intelligence," Theodore Sedgwick, Jr., wrote in 1835. ". . . It has urged forward the whole American mind."

NOT ALL WRITERS WERE POLITICALLY ACTIVE, NOT even all those possessed by visions of a new world. Some, like Emerson and Thoreau, preoccupied most profoundly with the questions raised up by the change, spent years quietly ignoring politics. But, even with such important exceptions, it is yet remarkable how many of the leading authors and artists publicly aligned themselves with the Jacksonian party. Nathaniel Hawthorne, William Cullen Bryant, Walt Whitman, James Fenimore Cooper, George Bancroft, Washington Irving (until the pressure became too great), James K. Paulding, Orestes A. Brownson, William Leggett, John L. O'Sullivan, John L. Stephens, Horatio Greenough, Hiram Powers, Edwin Forrest, Frances Wright, Robert Dale Owen, for example, were all Jacksonians. As Harriet Martineau observed, the Democratic party included the underprivileged classes, the careerists, the humanitarians and "an accession small in number, but inestimable in power,—the men of genius."

The Democrats were exceedingly proud of their intellectuals. Van Buren himself offered government jobs to Bancroft, Hawthorne, Irving, Paulding, Brownson and Leggett.

Many of the authors regarded a position of political liberalism as an artistic imperative. They felt that the Whigs cared only to preserve the tame, reliable and derivative culture of which men like Everett and Longfellow were faithful representatives. The only future for a powerful native literature, dealing fearlessly in truth and reality, seemed to lie in a bold exploration of the possibilities of democracy.

A FIRST REQUISITE FOR A LITERATURE IS A MEDIUM for publication. The respectable magazines—the *North American*, the *American Quarterly*, the *New-England Magazine*, and so on—were in Whig hands, and during the eighteen-thirties the need for a monthly journal of liberal sympathies became increasingly pronounced. At this juncture a bright young man named John L. O'Sullivan, who had been running a small newspaper in Washington, appeared with the project of a Democratic review.

O'Sullivan was descended from a long line of picaresque Irishmen whose actual careers remain buried under family legend. O'Sullivan's sister (handsome enough to provoke even Emerson to enthusiastic comment) had married another young writer named S. D. Langtree, and together in 1837 the two approached Benjamin F. Butler with the proposal of a Democratic literary magazine.

Butler, who was given to cultural dabbling and even wrote verse for publication, took fire at the idea, subscribed five hundred dollars himself and urged other Democratic politicians to aid in financing the *Democratic Review*. Henry D. Gilpin also took an active part in the search for backing. Jackson, who had long hoped for such a journal, encouraged the project and became the first subscriber. During the summer the editors approached writers the country over, and in October a preliminary number appeared, with contributions by Bryant, Hawthorne, Whittier and others.

Whatever O'Sullivan's failings, he was an excellent editor. He was assiduous in seeking out new talent, and he quickly made the *Democratic Review* by far the liveliest journal of the day. His authors included Bryant, Hawthorne, Thoreau, Whittier, Walt Whitman, Poe, Longfellow, Lowell, Paulding, William Gilmore Simms, Bancroft, Brownson, A. H. Everett and many more. Politically the magazine aligned itself vigorously with the radical wing of the party.

In the meantime Orestes Brownson had provided the liberals with another organ in his *Boston Quarterly Review*. The concurrence of motives behind this journal showed the wide front of the cultural revolt. His object, Brownson said, was to support the new movement in all its manifestations, "whether it be effecting a reform in the Church, giving us a purer and more rational theology; in philosophy seeking something profounder and more inspiring than the heartless Sensualism of the last century; or whether in society demanding the elevation of labor with the Loco foco, or the freedom of the slave with the Abolitionist."

The *Boston Quarterly* thus became a compendium of the desertion of the intellectuals, defending in detail the repudiation of the old order in religion, philosophy and politics.

In 1842 the *Democratic Review* and the *Boston Quarterly* merged, but not before each had left a distinct mark on the development of American letters. Each journal, on its own level, was the best of its day, and both gained much of their energy, courage and free vigor from their immersion in the political ideals of Jacksonian democracy.

THE TRANSCENDENTALISTS OF MASSACHUSETTS CONconstituted the one important literary group never much impressed by Jacksonian democracy. This immunity was all the more singular because for two occasional members, George Bancroft and Orestes A. Brownson, the relations between transcendentalism and democracy seemed close and vital. The Jacksonians, in the minds of Bancroft and Brownson, were carrying on the same revolt against the dead hand of John Locke in politics which the transcendentalists were carrying on in religion. Both Democrat and transcendentalist agreed in asserting the rights of the free mind against the pretensions of precedents or institutions. Both shared a living faith in the integrity and perfectibility of man. Both proclaimed self-reliance. Both detested special groups claiming authority to mediate between the common man and the truth.

Yet, for all the inspiration some Democrats found in transcendentalism, the transcendentalists remained singularly unmoved by the exertions of the Democrats. From their book-lined studies or their shady walks in cool Concord woods, they found the hullabaloo of party politics unedifying and vulgar.

BEYOND THE TRANSCENDENTALISTS, ACCEPTING THEIR inspiration but safe from their illusions, was Emerson, the wisest man of the day. He was too concretely aware of the complexities of experience to be altogether consoled by vagueness and reverie. The doctrine of compensation had its limits, and he was not deceived by Ripley's community. "At Education Farm, the noblest theory of life sat on the noblest figures of young men and maidens, quite powerless and melancholy. It would not rake or pitch a ton of hay; it would not rub down a horse; and the men and maidens it left pale and hungry." Yet politics represent his greatest failure. He would not succumb to verbal panaceas, neither would he make the ultimate moral effort of Thoreau and cast off all obligation to society. Instead he lingered indecisively, accepting without enthusiasm certain relations of government but never confronting directly the implications of acceptance.

He acknowledged the claims of the Democratic party expounded so ardently by Bancroft and Brownson. "The philosopher, the poet, or the religious man, will, of course, wish to cast his vote with the democrat, for free-trade, for wide suffrage, for the abolition of legal cruelties in the penal code, and for facilitating in every manner the access of the young and the poor to the sources of wealth and power." He recognized, too, the inevitable drift of transcendentalism toward the democratic position. The first lecture of his series in 1839 on the "Present Age" was reported by Theodore Parker as *"Democratic-locofoco* throughout, and very much in the spirit of Brownson's article on Democracy and Reform in the last *Quarterly."* Bancroft left "in ecstasies . . . rapt beyond vision at the *locofocoism,"* and one Boston conservative could only growl that Emerson must be angling for a place in the Custom House.

Yet Emerson would go no further. "Of the two great parties, which, at this hour, almost share the nation between them," he would lamely conclude, "I should say, that one has the best cause, and the other contains the best men." This would have provided no excuse for inaction, even if it were true, for a man of Emersonian principle should follow his principle; but it was not even true.

Fundamentally he did not care, and thus he was betrayed, almost without struggle, into the clichés of conservatism which had surrounded him from birth. In a flash of insight he could see that "banks and tariffs, the newspaper and caucus" were "flat and dull to dull people, but rest on the same foundations of wonder as the town of Troy, and the temple of Delphos." Yet, in life at Concord, day in, day out, banks and tariffs were flat and dull to him. As he glanced at party contests, he was most impressed by "the meanness of our politics."

OF ALL THE NEW ENGLAND GROUP WHO SHUNNED political choice, Thoreau alone lived at a degree of moral tension which imposed responsibilities equivalent to those borne by men who sought to govern. He could not delude himself with fantasies of easy salvation, like Alcott or Ripley, nor could he accept the status of citizenship, like Emerson, and dally with its obligations. For him the moral life admitted but one possibility: the complete assumption of all responsibility by the individual. The highest good, said Thoreau, was the living unity of the ethical consciousness and its direct, solid expression in art and life.

In practice he achieved the goal best by a deliberate reduction of life to its essentials—a cabin by blue Walden, blackberries in the summer, the indomitable woodchuck, the wild sweet song of the evening robin, the geese flying low over the woods, the last blaze of sun in the west. But he could not dwell forever at Walden; he had other lives to live; and he returned to society, now fulfilling his singleness of feeling by fusing his superb style till the words, as he said, fell like boulders across the page. Back in the world again, he was face to face with the enemies of the moral life: the new industrialism, which would deform the moral self, and the state, which would corrupt it. In society people lived in quiet desperation, sick at heart, their integrity menaced, clouded and compromised. The only man worth having, thought Thoreau, was the man of principle, and he was worth any expense to the state.

THOREAU SAID NAY TO THE CLAIMS OF DEMOCRACY, but Walt Whitman sent back the thunderous affirmation, echoing off the roof-tops of the world. Twenty-one in the year of

Tippecanoe, Whitman was already up to his neck in radical Democratic politics. In a year, he would be speaking at a huge party mass meeting and contributing to the *Democratic Review*. In 1844 he would join the movement to draft Silas Wright for Governor and elect James K. Polk. In 1846 he would become editor of the *Brooklyn Daily Eagle,* and while in Brooklyn serve on the Democratic General Committee and the Fourth of July Celebration Committee.

Brooklyn knew him as Walter Whitman, an amiable and relaxed young man, with a ruddy pleasant face and a short beard, wandering indolently through the bustling streets with an easy word for everyone, from merchant to cartman. After his stint for the *Eagle* he would go down to Gray's Swimming Bath at the foot of Fulton Street and lounge for twenty minutes in the water. Then the office boy would give him a shower, and he would take the evening ferry back to New York through the dying sunset. ("Flood-tide below me! I see you face to face! Clouds of the west—sun there half an hour high —I see you also face to face.")

These were days of quiet immersion in the flood of experience which would later sweep aside the conventions of verse to achieve their own expression, poignant, tender, gusty, barbaric, incoherent and magnificent. He drank in not just the sea gulls, floating high in the air on motionless wings, their bodies lit up glistening yellow by the setting sun, not just the men and women on the street, "the blab of the pave, tires of carts, sluff of boot-soles, talk of the promenaders." He drank in the feelings of the people themselves, their anxieties, hopes, aspirations.

For Whitman none of the doubts of Thoreau. For him only a vigorous acceptance and mastery of the democratic opportunity. "To attack the turbulence and destructiveness of the Democratic spirit," he said, "is an old story. . . . Why, all that is good and grand in any political organization in the world, is the result of this turbulence and destructiveness, and controlled by the intelligence and common sense of such a people as the Americans, it never has brought harm, and never can."

Politics a noisy show, unworthy of the attention of serious men? "It is the fashion of a certain set to assume to despise 'politics' . . . they look at the fierce struggle, and at the battle of principles and candidates, and their weak nerves retreat dismayed from the neighborhood of such scenes of convulsion. But to our view, the spectacle is always a grand one—full of the most august and sublime attributes."

The enthusiasm of democracy an evil? "All the noisy tempestuous scenes of politics witnessed in this country—all the excitement and strife, even—are *good* to behold. They evince that the *people act;* they are the disciple of the young giant, getting his maturer strength."

Is democracy then perfect? Let no one be distracted by detail. "We know, well enough, that the workings of Democracy are not always justifiable, in every trivial point. But the great winds that purify the air, without which nature would flag into ruin—are they to be condemned because a tree is prostrated here and there, in their course?"

Through the blast of Whitman's prose sounded the answer to Thoreau. Man, he affirmed, could have a relation of moral significance to the state, so long as the state was truly the expression of the popular will and the best in man. Perfection? No, for the state, like the people which created it, had failings and flaws. (Whitman, unlike Thoreau, had a certain sympathy for imperfections.) Belief in the people should not be discouraged by trivialities or weakened by petty disappointments. In the greatness of his faith in the people Whitman could not but declare his faith in the possibilities of democratic government.

XXX *Tyler Too*

AMERICAN HISTORY HAS BEEN MARKED BY RECURRENT swings of conservatism and of liberalism. During the periods of inaction, unsolved social problems pile up till the demand for reform becomes overwhelming. Then a liberal government comes to power, the dam breaks and a flood of change sweeps away a great deal in a short time. After fifteen or twenty years the liberal impulse is exhausted, the day of "consolidation" and inaction arrives, and conservatism, once again, expresses the mood of the country, but generally on the terms of the liberalism it displaces. So with Jacksonian democracy. In time it satisfied the popular desire for change. As it developed vested party interests of its own, and its internal paths to power became choked up, able younger men—the Sewards, Lincolns, Thaddeus Stevenses—began to go into the opposition. Partly because of this infusion of fresh blood, and partly because of the lessons of defeat, the Whigs soft-pedaled their diehard aims and began to borrow the Jacksonian phrases. They prepared for the popular reaction. Their reward was victory in 1840.

DEFEAT WAS A TERRIFIC BLOW TO DEMOCRATIC MORALE. Not since 1796, nearly half a century before, had a conservative candidate gained the presidency.

The administration was plunged in dejection.

The President himself, quiet and urbane in the White House, took refuge in what became the official explanation: that he had lost because of fraud and corruption—the only theory which accounted for the defeat without impugning the party faith in the masses. "The sober, second thought of the people," he had said some years before, "is never wrong, and always efficient." Democrats now retired from office to await the fruits of this consoling maxim.

WILLIAM HENRY HARRISON HAD BEEN ELECTED AS A figurehead, whom Clay and Webster and doubtless others had severally calculated on controlling. His early death installed John Tyler of the Virginia State-rights school in the White House. While Tyler's training had allowed him to join the Whigs in attacking executive despotism, it did not incline him to support the more arrantly Federalist items in the Whig program. He submitted to the repeal of the independent treasury; but, when Henry Clay pushed through a new Bank charter, Tyler returned it with a resolute veto.

The fate of Biddle himself, standing wearily under criminal indictment in the dock in the city where once he had been toast and hero, was not encouraging to recharter. Lawyers obtained his release on a technicality, but he was a broken man. "The anti-Biddle feeling is very strong," reported Fenimore Cooper with delight, "and quite as ferocious as the pro-Biddle feeling was formerly."

While Clay and his followers still dallied with the Federalist dreams, Tyler went briskly ahead on the basis of his vetoes to make a palace guard out of such liberal Whigs as Caleb Cushing and Henry A. Wise, such conservative or complaisant Democrats as David Henshaw and Robert J. Walker, such men without parties as N. P. Tallmadge and William Cabell Rives. By directing his course about midway between the haughty conservatism of Clay and the Locofoco radicalism of Van Buren, Tyler hoped to create a strong middle-of-the-road party for himself. His power as President won him a small following, but his prestige as a political leader, none at all. Whigs, even liberal ones, tended to prefer Clay. Democrats, even conservative ones, tended to prefer Van Buren or Calhoun. Tyler lingered affably in the middle, a President with a policy but without a party.

XXXI *Minorities and Majorities*

LISTING "THE ESSENTIAL PRINCIPLES OF OUR GOVERNment" in his first inaugural, Thomas Jefferson made vigorous affirmation of what he called the "vital principle of republics" —"absolute acquiescence in the decisions of the majority." But what were the other "essential principles" of his enumeration but a bill of exceptions to this "vital principle"? They were, in fact, a catalogue of rights placed out of reach of the majority, for fear that the majority might destroy them. Elsewhere in the same address Jefferson even declared explicitly that though the will of the majority was "in all cases" to prevail, that will "to be rightful must be reasonable." "The minority possess their equal rights . . . and to violate [them] would be oppression."

If the will of the majority was entitled to "absolute acquiescence," if it was "in all cases" to prevail, what safeguard was there for the rights of minorities? Yet if minorities were indulged in their claims, how was the maintenance of their "equal rights" to be restrained from leading to minority rule? These questions from the start constituted a basic ambiguity in American democratic theory.

THE DEMOCRATIC PARTY, AS THE PARTY OF THE LAboring classes, was beginning to split into two wings. Some friends of labor, like Bancroft and Van Buren, felt that the "people", though misled in 1840, were fundamentally sound, and could be relied on most of the time to back a democratic policy. Their sober second thoughts, in other words, would atone for occasional transgressions. Others, however, like Brownson, commenced to regard the "people" as an inchoate mass which would probably follow the side with the loudest songs and biggest torchlight processions. The real proponents of democracy, they believed, were a small group who would often have to save the people in spite of themselves.

The majoritarian Democrats clustered around Van Buren as their candidate for 1844. The minoritarians, accepting the logic of the Southern alliance, turned to Calhoun.

SUDDENLY IN THE SPRING OF 1842, THE PROBLEM OF majorities and minorities ceased to be an academic question. Rhode Island had been the only state without fairly wide manhood suffrage. It was still operating in 1841 on the colonial charter of 1663, which disfranchised everyone who did not own $134 in land. Over half the adult male population could not vote, and the spread of manufacturing was rapidly decreasing the proportion of the elect. The apportionment of seats in the legislature, moreover, gravely penalized the growing industrial towns to the advantage of the older villages.

In the middle eighteen-thirties a young man of conservative antecedents named Thomas Wilson Dorr came onto the scene. A Whig, a graduate of Exeter and Harvard, but singularly high-principled and conscientious, he became interested in remedying the suffrage inequities. Finding no support in his own party, he joined the Democrats in 1837. When the reform movement had one of its periodic spurts in 1841, Dorr emerged as its natural leader.

The new agitation abandoned from the first all resort to the existing government, proposing instead to appeal to the original sovereign rights of the people which underlay all government. By July, 1841, this strategy produced two constitutional conventions: one called hastily by the legislature to appease the popular resentments, and the other called by extraconstitutional procedures finding their sanction in the basic "constituent power" of the people.

The result was two state administrations, one under the old charter, the other under the People's Constitution. During the early months of 1842 the state remained quiet but tense. Then, on May 3, Dorr, as the People's Governor, started to organize his government. The charter government, under a severe punitive measure known as the "Algerine" law, began to arrest Dorr leaders.

On the foggy night of May 17, Dorr at the head of 234 men stormed the Providence Arsenal. With him, as "organizational secretary," was Seth Luther, the veteran agitator. When the men in the arsenal refused to surrender, Dorr ordered his cannon to be fired. They flashed out twice through the black night, but without result. Soon the bells of Providence were ringing wildly, and the streets began to fill with bewildered people. As the gray dawn broke, Dorr's following started to go home. By sunrise he had only about fifty men, and at breakfast time he was told that his government had resigned. His friends advised him to leave. Before nine o'clock he was heading for the border.

In 1843 a new and somewhat more equitable constitution was adopted by the legal voters. Dorr now declared that he would return to the state after the fall elections. On October 31 he quietly stepped off the train at Providence and was shortly after arrested under indictment of high treason. Dorr's trial took place in Newport in March, 1844. Of the entire panel of 118 available jurors, only three were Democrats; and Dorr's own jury was exclusively Whig. He was speedily found guilty, sentenced to solitary confinement at hard labor for life and denied a new trial.

The summariness of the proceedings, the vindictiveness of the sentence and Dorr's own obvious high-mindedness soon caused a revulsion of feeling. "Liberation" became the dominant political issue, and in June, 1845, Dorr was released by the act of a Democratic legislature, elected for that purpose. In 1851 his civil and political rights were restored, and in 1854 the court judgment against him was annulled.

THE DORR WAR WAS ONE OF THOSE CASES WHERE technical right lay on one side, substantive right on the other. There can be small doubt that a stubborn and obtuse minority was determined to keep the control of the government to itself, and that the reformers had fairly well exhausted the possibilities of legal change. Nonetheless, in carrying out the reform, Dorr, perhaps too loyal to his state to admit that revolt against it was the only course left, invoked a theory of sovereignty which was, in fact, the "right" of revolution thinly disguised, and not a "right" of society.

The Rhode Island dilemma could not have been solved within the law in 1842, and without the Dorr War there would have been no constitution as useful as the one finally adopted in 1843. This somewhat immoral result must be blamed on the conservatives, who at no time showed any sense of responsibility about governing their state.

THE JEFFERSONIAN AMBIGUITY THUS MAY BE IN FACT a source of strength and stability. The circumstances of politics and the sentiments of the people will always set more effective limits on the tyranny of majorities or the obstinacy of minorities than any parchment formula. Like most important problems, the question of majorities and minorities is insoluble.

XXXII *Cloud on the Horizon*

THE POLITICAL STRUGGLES OF THE EIGHTEEN-THIRTIES had revolved around questions of banking and the currency. The Democrats had been, in the main, victorious. Jackson destroyed the Bank of the United States, Van Buren terminated the title of the banking system to the free use of government funds, and in many of the states Jacksonians tamed the political ambitions of the banks. While it was possible to repeal the independent treasury after 1840, it was not possible to charter a new Bank. The banking interest was temporarily checked, and banking questions receded as a new issue began to demand the center of the stage.

THE TARIFF, WHEN IT HAD BEEN EXTENSIVELY DEBATED in 1833, had aroused such violent emotions that Clay and Calhoun, leaders of the opposing parties, hastily collaborated on a negotiated peace.

The Jacksonian analysis of industrial society was perfectly clear in its estimate of protection.

The protective tariff, in Kendall's analysis, made "the whole population contribute to the wealth of the Factory owners," some by working in the factories, the rest by paying higher prices for manufactured goods. Was this just a Southern grievance?

Many Jacksonians in the past had temporized and straddled on the tariff out of deference to its supposed popularity. But the inner tendencies of their social thought were hard to resist. Jackson had, long since, abandoned his tolerance of 1824, and Van Buren, who as representative of an industrial state had been responsible for much of the skittishness, finally committed himself against protection in 1843.

Yet, even as lines were drawing taut on the tariff, a more imperative issue began to shoulder it aside. And the new issue, unlike the tariff, had no clear place in the Jacksonian social analysis.

AT FIRST, IT WAS LIKE A CLOUD ON THE HORIZON, AS they said in later years, no bigger than a man's hand. Then it rose, black and threatening. Soon it would fill the sky. Who could escape the shadow it promised to cast across the Union? . . . But the wise had long known that America must sometime face its conscience. The promises of democracy might be slow to exert their force; but, if America was to justify the dream, those promises had to be redeemed. Negro bondage was a living challenge to the American ethic—it was, said John Quincy Adams in 1820, "the great and foul stain upon the North American Union." Eventually the moral feeling of the land must wash it away, or the nation would lose its soul. "The seeds of the Declaration of Independence are yet maturing," wrote Adams as he watched the swirl of fear and hatred around the question of the admission of Missouri as a slave state. "The harvest will be what West, the painter, calls the terrible sublime."

Slavery was the most accusing, the most tragic and the most dangerous of all questions. It was implacable, it could not be winked away by compromise, and, as Adams knew in 1820, no man ought ever to agitate it without being prepared for the dissolution of the Union, "and reconciled to it, because it must end in that." The nation knew this, too, in its heart of hearts, and like a man banishing a dreaded image from consciousness, it turned and twisted desperately to suppress and deny and bury the terrible fact.

XXXIII *Gathering of the Storm*

JOHN TYLER'S LAST IMPORTANT LINK WITH THE WHIG party had broken when Webster resigned in May, 1843, His remaining hope for re-election was to build a personal party out of the disgruntled politicians of the Democracy and aim for the Democratic nomination of 1844. This strategy soon led him into close relations with Calhoun. While each, in the long run, intended to use the other, the two could work together for the moment in harmony, on patronage as well as on policy. The conservative wing of the party, starved during the years of Van Buren's ascendancy, thus began in 1843 to receive again the nutriment of office. In Massachusetts, for example, Robert Rantoul became Collector of the Port, and David Henshaw went to Washington as Secretary of the Navy. These men, with B. F. Hallett, Charles Gordon Greene and Isaac Hill of New Hampshire, headed the Tyler-Calhoun party in New England, and they proceeded to revive the old Henshaw machine under the noses of Bancroft, Marcus Morton and the Van Buren group. The appointment of Calhoun as Secretary of State in March, 1844, belatedly acknowledged the alliance.

THE JACKSONIAN UNITY WAS BREAKING DOWN. AND Old Hickory himself? The old man still refused to die. His body was racked by the pain of old wounds, his constitution undermined by the hardships of the Creek campaign thirty years before, but his will was adamant, and on he lived. Years of tobacco chewing had left him with throbbing temples and shattering headaches. Tuberculosis had wasted away one lung and diseased the other. Dropsy and diarrhea had reduced him to helplessness, and his remedies were primitive—bleeding to check hemorrhage, and calomel. Tall, ghostlike and fleshless, with his brush of snow-white hair, he could eat little more than rice and milk.

Yet he clung to life with unconquerable toughness. No stab of suffering could extract from him a word of irritation or self-pity. His intellect remained as keen and vigorous as ever, and his manner, as Paulding noted when visiting the Hermitage in 1842, "more kind, graceful, and benevolent, than that of any man who has ever fallen under my observation." He ruled his plantation like a patriarch. In the morning, when he could rise, he would ride around the land, pausing to talk with his favorite groom about the colts, then to the fields, where the Negroes picking cotton gave three cheers for him. In the evening he conducted family prayers. And always he followed politics with avidity, never ceasing to make fierce and decisive suggestions about the destiny of his nation. . . . But death was irresistible and even General Jackson could not stay its hand.

The shadows fell longer over the Hermitage, and in the late afternoons the old General, leaning on his tall ebony cane, would walk up and down the long porch; then, in the last flare of sunset, he would stride, erect and steady, across the green lawns to his wife's grave. Eighteen-forty-four gave way to 1845, and Mr. Polk was safely installed in the presidency. June came, with the still, heavy heat of Tennessee summer. On the morning of Sunday, June 8, after a week of unusual feebleness, the General fell into dead-pale unconsciousness. A long wail of anguish rose up from the slaves in the house and echoed through the fields and stables. "Oh, Lord! Oh, Lord!

Old Massa's dead! Old Massa's dead!" But soon the mists fell away, and the old man recovered consciousness. Major Lewis arrived at the bedside at noon to receive messages for Benton, for Blair, for Sam Houston.

On pressed the afternoon, and around the high bedstead with the tall mahogany posts his friends stood in tears. Outside the windows the slaves clustered in lamentation, and his body servants joined the group in the room. "Do not cry," said the dying man, rousing himself for a moment, "I shall meet you in heaven, yes I hope to meet you all in heaven white and black." A new burst of moaning greeted his words. He looked around. "Why should you weep? I am in the hands of the Lord! who is about to relieve me, you should rejoice, not weep!" "Oh, do not cry. Be good children, and we will all meet in heaven." He was given an anodyne and did not speak again. At six o'clock, with the evening sun flooding through the windows, he had a slight convulsion, his underjaw dropped, and his breathing faded so gently that they hardly knew when he died. Sarah Yorke Jackson, who was holding his hand, suddenly fainted, and they carried her away. Through the plantation spread the moan of death.

The funeral was a great mass meeting, white and black jostling together in an agony of grief, cramming the house and waiting patiently outside to follow the body to its resting place in the shade beside his beloved Rachel. Between the funeral sermon and the burial a wildly twittering parrot, a household pet, broke into raucous profanity and was taken away. When the body was lowered into the grave, the stone was left off for all to look a last time. The slave women in their anguish pressed in among the friends of their old master, leaving the laces and shawls of white women wet with tears. "Death did not make all equal," said one observer, "more completely than did this funeral."

Pondering a day later on Jackson's greatness, Justice Catron was tempted to ascribe it all to the magnificence of his leadership. "The way a thing should be done struck him plainly—& he adopted the plan." If it were not the best, it would still do, if well executed. "To the execution he brought a hardy industry, and a sleepless energy, few could equal." But most of all "his awful *will*, stood alone, & was made the will of all he commanded." "If he had fallen from the clouds into a city on fire, he would have been at the head of the extinguishing host in an hour, & would have blown up a palace to stop the fire with as little mis-giving as another would have torn down a board shed. In a moment he would have willed it proper—& in ten minutes the thing would have been done. Those who never worked before, who had hardly courage to cry, would have rushed to the execution, and applied the match."

"Hence it is," said Catron, "that timid men, and feeble women, have rushed to onslaught when he gave the command —fierce, fearless, and unwavering, for the first time." Hence it was that for fifty years he had been followed by the broad land; hence it was that he had swept over all opposition, "terrible and clean as a prairie fire, leaving hardly a smoke of the ruin behind."

The people felt an emptiness in their hearts. Michael Shiner, the poor free Negro of the Washington shipyards, set forth their aching sorrow. "the Hon Major General andrew Jackson is gone and his voice are heared no moore on earth. But his name still lives in the heart of the American people his spirit has takein its fligth it has gone to the one that first gave it and now i trust he is setting on the Right hand of god reaping his reward."

XXXIV *Free Soil*

TEXAS WAS ANNEXED EARLY IN 1845 BY JOINT CONgressional resolution, and in January, 1846, Polk ordered American troops under Zachary Taylor to advance through territory claimed by Mexico to the Rio Grande. Manifest Destiny was coming to a boil, and Van Buren, at ease in Lindenwald, deserved congratulation for clairvoyance. General Taylor waited at the head of the rabble army in the disputed land, while Polk tried vainly to buy the northern provinces of Mexico. Then, on April 24, Mexican and American soldiers clashed. The news arrived in Washington just in time to destroy all opposition to Polk's plan of gaining by war what he could not gain by negotiation. From South to North the common man lined up at recruiting offices and said farewell to his tearful family: in New England, far indeed from the Rio Grande, Seth Luther, the veteran agitator for the rights of labor, claimed to be the first Yankee volunteer. The American democracy prepared to broaden the area of freedom. "It is for the interest of mankind," wrote Walter Whitman, the Brooklyn editor, "that its power and territory should be extended—the farther the better."

EARLY IN THE EVENING OF A HUMID AUGUST DAY, with candles and lamps burning brightly in the dark chamber of the House, while members sat about drinking ice water and fanning themselves with folded newspapers, David Wilmot moved that the appropriations bill be amended so as to exclude slavery from all territory acquired in the war. "I would preserve for free white labor," he later declared, "a fair country, a rich inheritance, where the sons of toil, of my own race and color, can live without the disgrace which association with negro slavery brings upon free labor."

The Proviso failed of passage, but the free-soil issue was now formulated and laid before the country in terms which invoked deep Jacksonian sentiments. "The question," cried Walter Whitman, ". . . is a question between *the grand body of white workingmen, the millions of mechanics, farmers, and operatives of our country,* with their interests on the one side—and the interests of the few thousand rich, 'polished,' and aristocratic owners of slaves at the South, on the other side."

But another Jacksonian thought differently. "The agitation of the slavery question is mischievous & wicked," declared James K. Polk, "and proceeds from no patriotic motive by its authors." The Wilmot Proviso appeared, to him, "mischievous & foolish," and the whole movement seemed a gratuitous disturbance by which "demagogues & ambitious politicians hope to promote their own prospects."

This hostility did not arise from any particular solicitude for slavery. Polk refused to be, in any active sense, proslavery or antislavery; he was simply trying to carry on in terms of the Jacksonian unity—to extend into the eighteen-forties the neutrality of the eighteen-thirties.

BUT NORTHERN ANXIETY OVER THE QUESTION OF slavery was increasing. The agitations of two decades were beginning to tell. The religious antislavery men, who were mostly conservative on economic issues, caring more about the Negro than about the white man at home, were infecting large sectors of the Whig party, while the political antislavery men, who were primarily concerned for the future of white labor, were having increasing influence among the Democrats.

EIGHTEEN-FORTY-EIGHT WAS DRAWING NEAR, AND through the North, men were pondering how best to bring the free states to act as "an entire body" in defense of free territory.

The question of the relations of slavery and democracy had now arisen "in a practical form. It can no longer be evaded or postponed. It is upon us. We must decide it. Shall these vast communities [acquired from Mexico] be the creations of free or slave labor?" The two systems, Van Buren pointed out, could not coexist. Which to exclude, the planter or the free laboring man?

AT NO TIME COULD THE FREE SOILERS HAVE HAD much hope of electing Van Buren president, but they swept into the campaign with as much zeal as if victory lay around the corner. Conscience Whigs and abolitionists worked shoulder to shoulder with Van Buren Democrats. In Massachusetts the Van Buren organization had been crippled by the erratic behavior of George Bancroft, who, after joining Polk's cabinet, effected an alliance with Henshaw and Hallett. But Amasa Walker provided energetic leadership for the Free Soil Democrats, and Marcus Morton strong moral support. Though the Conscience Whigs, under Sumner and Charles Francis Adams, tended to dominate the Massachusetts Free Soil party, and the party included more Whigs than Democrats, the Whig representation was a much smaller proportion of the state Whig party.

November came, and the smoke cleared to show that Taylor and Fillmore had carried New York and consequently the election. The Free Soil ticket had polled nearly three hundred thousand votes, an almost fivefold increase in the antislavery vote from 1844. How much longer could the government ignore the question which its people were every year asking more insistently?

XXXV *The Storm Approaches*

AS THE SECTIONAL TENSION INCREASED, THE SENSE OF irrepressible differences, long buried in the national consciousness, began to burst into the clear. The growing pressure on the North had finally persuaded many Northerners that the slavery system embodied a fundamental threat to free society. The growing presure on the South had finally persuaded many Southerners that democracy constituted a fundamental threat to slavery. On both sides the pressure compelled a reconsideration of political premises; and, as the reconsideration progressed, the conviction of irreconcilability became more intense and more alarming. "Slavery," declared David Wilmot, "is the deadly enemy of free labor." *"Democracy,"* wrote a member of the Virginia constitutional convention, *"in its original philosophical sense, is, indeed, incompatible with slavery, and the whole system of Southern society."* Inevitably, radical democracy and slavery were coming to find in each other the fatal obstacle to security and power.

THE INCREASING SHARPNESS OF THE ISSUE MADE Northern opponents of democracy look more longingly than ever before toward an alliance with the slave power. The business community dreaded sectional conflict lest the delicate and shimmering web of commerce and credit, spread wide across the country, be rudely broken, with consequent convulsions on the stock market, destruction of assets and dissolution of contracts. Many merchants were, in addition, bound specifically to the South by profitable economic ties. In any case, the avidity with which the South moved to rebuke Northern radicalism after the Free Soil activity of the radical Democrats in 1848 markedly increased conservative solicitude for the future of the slave power.

Looking at the world through a haze of profit sheets and counting-houses, the Cotton Whigs could see only that property was in danger, a revelation which closed the discussion. But other Whigs had other values. Property, they felt, was not so much at stake as free society, and the maintenance of free society was as essential for business as for reform.

This leftward drift was exhibited all the more clearly on the level of political philosophy. Antislavery conservatives found themselves obliged by the intellectual necessity of sustaining themselves as champions of freedom and democracy to abandon, increasingly, the premises of Hamilton.

The Cotton Whigs, their hands forced by these heresies, had finally to disclose their own fundamental aversion to the maxims of democracy.

The conservatives of the North were thus compelled increasingly to decide whether, like Seward and Lincoln, they would move toward the politics and philosophy of Jefferson, or, like Webster and Choate, toward the politics and philosophy of the slave power. The pressures of the day permitted fewer and fewer alternatives between appeasement and resistance.

XXXVI *"Our Federal Union..."*

BUCHANAN CARRIED THE ELECTION OF 1856, AND THE last fateful days of uneasy peace set in. The Jacksonians who had voted for Buchanan now watched hopefully for signs of his delivery from Southern influence. Kansas—"Bleeding Kansas"—remained the critical issue, and the submission in 1857 of a proslavery constitution, drawn up at Lecompton by a small minority of the settlers, brought affairs to a test. When Buchanan recommended the admission of Kansas under the Lecompton constitution, no one could doubt his fidelity to Doughface principles. Even Stephen A. Douglas, the father of the Kansas-Nebraska bill, turned against the administration.

IN THE DAYS OF JACKSON—INDEED, TILL ABOUT 1850 —the bulk of the slaveholding aristocracy had been Whigs. Then why was the Democracy now the citadel of the slave power?

The answer to this question is complex. The Democratic party was paying the price of its own radicalism. It had been the first party to divide over slavery; and those remaining in control of the organization after the Free Soil exodus were, in the main, reliable on the slavery issue. The Whig party did not split in 1848. Consequently, from being the more dependable party in 1840, from the Southern viewpoint, it became the less dependable in 1850. As Seward and his followers gained in power, the Southern Whigs wondered increasingly what they were doing in that gallery—at the very moment that the Southern Democrats were for the first time breathing easily in the party of Jefferson.

Moreover, John C. Calhoun had prepared within the Democratic party a more elaborate and conclusive set of constitutional defenses for slavery than anything devised by the Whigs. Indeed, the Southern Whigs had sacrificed a good deal of the State-rights dogma as their price for an alliance with Northern conservatism. Thus the Democratic party was more quickly rid of its antislavery sections, and it had more formidable equipment for the protection of slavery: as a result, after 1848 it became increasingly attractive to the slave power.

The fact was that by the fifties both the old parties had disappeared. The election of 1844, as Gideon Welles observed many years later, was "the final struggle between the two opposing elements known as democrats and whigs" which had sprung into life over the great economic questions of the thirties. "The names of these two parties," Welles added, "were continued as rallying cries several years later, but little, save the prejudices growing out of former antagonisms, remained to stimulate action." From the introduction of the Wilmot Proviso politics turned on the slavery issue.

Whatever remained of the live Jacksonian tradition had in the main, by 1858, entered the Republican party. On March 23 of that year, Frank Blair, Jr., now a Representative from Missouri, rose in the House and proposed to discuss the slavery question from a point of view which, he said, had not been treated in that hall—that of "the nonslaveholding people" of the South (which, he might have added, made up the bulk of the Democratic party of the South in the forgotten days of Andrew Jackson). He then launched into a scornful attack on the Southern oligarchy. "I make no complaint . . . of having been read out of the party. I should as soon think of complaining of being read out of a chain-gang." What was the Democratic party anyway? "I have always understood," young Blair declared, "that Democracy concerns itself more about personal rights than about rights of property—the rights of individuals rather than those of monopolizing institutions." "Was the Government founded to protect rights of property in slave labor, and not to protect the rights of freemen to their own labor?"

What a position for the Democratic party to take! "There was a time when this Democratic party was not Democratic in name alone . . . when this party took ground against privileged classes, and against every attempt on the part of capitalists to usurp the power of this Government, and pervert it to their own purposes." Blair recalled the Bank War, the battles over the tariff; "now here is another question in which this struggle between capital and labor is presented in its most odious and revolting form." Here was "a colossal aggregation of wealth invested in negroes," undertaking to seize the government and prevent the freemen of the country from entering the territories except in competition with slave labor; "and the Democratic party, instead of standing where it used to stand, in opposition to these anti-Democratic measures, is as servile a tool of the oligarchy as are the negro slaves themselves."

Abraham Lincoln was amused in 1859 to note that the party supposedly descended from Jefferson had stopped mentioning his name, while the party supposedly descended from his opponents was now draping itself in his mantle. It all reminded him, he said, of a fight between two drunken men with greatcoats on. After a long contest each had fought himself out of his own coat and into the coat of the other. "If the two leading parties of this day are really identical with the two in the days of Jefferson and Adams, they have performed the same feat as the two drunken men."

YET NOT ALL JACKSONIANS WOULD ACCEPT BLAIR'S analysis. Mike Walsh as a member of Congress in 1854 powerfully stated the opposing case. "The only difference between the negro slave of the South, and the white wages slave of the North," Mike exclaimed, "is that the one has a master without asking for him, and other has to beg for the privilege of becoming a slave. . . . The one is the slave of an individual; the other is the slave of an inexorable class." He demanded that the abolitionists produce "one single solitary degradation" heaped on the slave that a Northern free laborer was not liable to suffer through poverty. "It is all very well for gentlemen to get up here and clamor about the wrongs and outrages of the southern slaves," he observed bitterly; "but, sir, even in New York, during the last year, there have been over thirteen hundred people deprived of their liberty without any show or color of offense, but because they were poor, and too honest to commit a crime." The difference between the two systems, Mike went on, was simple. "If a dozen of us own a horse in common, we want to ride him as much as possible, and feed him as little as possible. [Laughter.] But if you or I own a horse exclusively we will take good care to feed him well, and not drive him too much to endanger his health, but just enough to keep him in good traveling order."

Yet, whatever Mike's failings, there was something to be said for his argument. The Jacksonian impulse had, after all, sprung up to meet certain inadequacies of Northern society, and for all the hullabaloo over slavery, those inadequacies continued to exist. The Free Soilers might urge that the destruction of slavery was an indispensable preliminary to further reform; but the doctrinaire radicals could not but regard this as a confession of impotence, a compulsion on the part of a bankrupt reform party to escape its responsibilities at home by going on a crusade abroad. Their own sentiments, compounded of a strong sense of guilt over Northern conditions, an intellectual inflexibility and certainly a very intense desire on their own part to avoid responsibilities, drove them into sour opposition to the whole antislavery movement.

They were basically wrong. The slavery question did, in fact, embrace the Jacksonian issues of democracy and liberty: it probably did objectively, and it certainly did as soon as enough people, North and South, showed by their conduct that they felt these issues to be vitally involved. In earlier generations democratic aspirations had expressed themselves in battles over the suffrage or banking or the tariff, but in the fifties they were definitely expressing themselves in the crusade against slavery, and in no other national issue. Thus men like Walsh, despite their evident sincerity, were casting themselves adrift in national politics. By refusing to see any danger in the slave power, they were in effect supporting it. They were putting themselves outside the main stream of democratic development.

IN THE FALL OF 1860 HORACE GREELEY, TRYING TO describe the fury of the business community against Lincoln, could not but recall an earlier political crisis. "Nothing like it has been seen since the Bank controversy of 1832-8," he wrote; "and even that did not compare in the intensity and unanimity of the commercial furor." But it compared in ineffectiveness, and in November the Republicans triumphed at the polls amid gloom in the conservative clubs and mutterings of disunion from the South.

The mutterings too were reminiscent of an earlier crisis, and many Northerners began to wish that General Jackson might be once more in the White House. In December, as old Frank Blair looked down from the gallery, Charles Sumner in the midst of a speech on secession drew a letter from his pocket and held it aloft for all to recognize the free, bold scrawl. As the hall listened in uneasy silence, Sumner contemptuously hurled the blunt Jacksonian remarks about nullification at the Southern Senators. " 'Haman's gallows ought to be the fate of all such ambitious men, who would involve their country in civil war. . . The Tariff was only the pretext, and Disunion and a Southern Confederacy the real object' " Then, with sharp emphasis, the grim prophecy: " 'The next pretext will be the Negro or Slavery Question.' " (But who among the Southern Democrats still cared for the words of Jackson?)

And secession? Charles Francis Adams, Van Buren's running mate on the Free Soil ticket in '48, believed that the government could do nothing if the fifteen slave states went out together. Preston King, now Republican Senator from New York, and Sumner came to dinner in January, and over wine and cigars tried to convince Adams that compromise was impossible. The argument grew angry, and Adams soon froze Sumner into silence. But he listened to King (his clever son Henry reported that King, "the most amiable, fat old fanatic that ever existed," was "never offensive . . . even when saying things that in Sumner's mouth would be unpardonable"). Then secession came, and even Adams quickly accepted the necessity of coercion.

"Our Federal Union, it must be preserved." The obligation was as binding in 1861 as in 1830. Jacksonians everywhere, even many from the South, recognized the superior claims of nationality. All of Jackson's Southern appointments to the Supreme Court—Catron of Tennessee, Wayne of Georgia, Taney of Maryland—remained loyal to the Union. Martin Van Buren drew up resolutions for the New York state Democratic convention so antisecessionist in tone that his son felt there was no point in submitting them to the Hunker leadership. Frank Blair became one of the new President's most useful and faithful advisers. Gideon Welles, Montgomery Blair, Salmon P. Chase and Edwin M. Stanton all joined the Cabinet.

Old Amos Kendall had watched events with mounting apprehension during the fifties. In 1856 he supported Buchanan; in 1860, still clinging to the dream of a national President, he hoped that the followers of Douglas, Breckinridge and Bell would unite on a single candidate. But the reality of disunion fired him to action, and in 1861 he returned to political journalism, showing in his letters on *Secession* that his pen had lost little of its skill and none of its force. For a man used to the prompt measures of a Jackson, the uncertainty and vacillation of the Lincoln government were alarming. Kendall called for the vigorous prosecution of the war and as an example offered two of his houses for use as barracks. He pressed on Seward the need for energy, wrote spirited articles for the papers, and in February, 1862, remarked that if Jackson had been President, "the rebellion would not have occurred, or if it had, the rebels would ere this have been driven into the Gulf of Mexico." By 1864 he had turned against the administration and was writing essays, one series signed "Andrew Jackson," denouncing Lincoln for incompetence and advocating the election of McClellan, the determined waging of the war and a generous peace.

George Bancroft emerged as another leading private citizen using his influence in favor of a vigorous war. By the summer of 1862 he was urging emancipation, and in that fall he was boomed for Congress on the Republican ticket. Declining, he reiterated the Jacksonian line: "The party at the South which made this rebellion is not, and never was, a Democratic party; it was, and is, the most embittered hater of Democracy . . . by the very necessity of its nature, [it] seeks to extinguish the Democratic principles." During the war years he served as a kind of unofficial representative of loyal Democratic opinion, and after Lincoln's death he was selected to pronounce the eulogy.

Orestes A. Brownson was another Jacksonian whom the war returned to public attention. After 1844 he had retreated vociferously into the Catholic community where he carried on his stormy existence, only emerging now and then to condemn Protestantism and its works. For some years he energetically explored those lines of Catholic dogma which reject democracy and sanctify authoritarianism. In 1853 he denounced equality as "an idle dream, and empty word" and assumed pretty much the Mike Walsh position on the antislavery movement. But the arrogance of the slave power became in the end too much for his thorny nature. By the time of the Dred Scott decision he saw clearly the fatal implications of the Southern attempt to rule the nation. In 1860 he supported Lincoln with a weary conviction that the problem of Southern domination must be settled once and for all.

War mobilized his old energies. From the start he harassed the administration for its timidity and want of decision, even visiting Washington to urge on Lincoln personally the importance of emancipation. In the fall of 1862 he accepted the Unionist nomination for Congress in the third district of New Jersey. Though defeated, he kept up his tireless work for the war, writing innumerable articles, making innumerable lectures, driving himself to any sacrifice of health and of his Catholic following in order to strengthen the country. In 1864 he was involved in the conspiracy of the Radical Republicans to replace Lincoln by Frémont. In the meantime political and theological deviations caused attacks upon him within the Church; and though the charges were dismissed at Rome, the promulgation in December, 1864, of the papal encyclical *Quanta Cura*, with its wholesale proscription of liberalism, placed his recent activities under official ban. This blow, added to the collapse of the Frémont boom and the death of two sons in the war, left him sick at heart. In 1865 he dedicated a book to Bancroft "as a sort of public atonement" for the invective he had heaped on his old friend; but shortly thereafter he returned to the orthodoxies, and the last few years before his death in 1876 found him defending with vigor the most reactionary Catholic positions on almost every issue.

Frederick Robinson, the old Massachusetts radical, showed in another way how the antislavery crusade had absorbed the old Jacksonian fight. He still clung in 1862 to the basic Jacksonian convictions. "The world has always been separated into two classes. . . . and the people are divided into two parties, the aristocrats and the democrats, the conservatives and progressives." He recalled a remark he had made in the thirties—that so long as conservatism continued to denounce the Democratic party, calling it "radical, loco foco, leveller, agrarian, property dividers, setters of the poor against rich," so long the Democratic party, "would be the true rallying place of the people. But when all those vile epithets shall cease, and conservatism begins to heap its virulency upon some other name, it will be a sign that they have scented corruption in the democratic party, and have gone over into its ranks." Corruption had triumphed, and he traced its growth, apologizing for his own support of Cass in 1848, and declaring that after the Kansas-Nebraska Act "all democracy left the democratic party, and every true democrat that was too intelligent to be cheated by a name, deserted its ranks."

Even Theophilus Fisk, for all his one-time devotion to Calhoun, could not swallow secession. In January, 1846, he had departed from the *Democratic Expositor,* setting forth in bitter valedictory his disillusionment with the working classes for their contentment in servitude. In 1845 and 1848 he attended meetings of the Industrial Congress, but after 1848 he dropped out of sight till he reappeared in the fifties, with an additional "e" in his name, as editorial writer for the *Philadelphia Argus* and later for the *Pennsylvanian.* In 1856 he held a clerkship in the Philadelphia Navy Yard. During the campaign of 1860 he revived the *Democratic Expositor,* which he made a strident antiabolitionist and antisecessionist sheet. In August he tried to launch a compromise Democratic ticket, headed by Andrew Johnson, the "Mechanic Statesman of Tennessee," but when the boom got nowhere Fiske came out for Douglas and the Union and supported the war.

Of the few real Jacksonians who favored the Confederacy, John L. O'Sullivan was perhaps the most unexpected. A Barnburner in 1848, he apparently supported Van Buren without taking an active part in the campaign. But more and more his impractical imagination fed on the dreams of expansion set in motion by his own famous phrase. He tried to sell Polk the idea of buying Cuba, and during Taylor and Fillmore's administration he consorted with filibusters and vaguely conceived great imperialistic expeditions. In 1852 he was actually brought to trial for filibustering. In 1853 Pierce appointed him Minister to Portugal, where he engaged in various doubtful activities until he was removed by Buchanan in 1858.

It was probably during his return to America in 1860 that he shocked John Bigelow of the *Evening Post* by declaring himself proslavery, adding that the American Negroes ought to erect a monument by voluntary subscription to the first slave trader. He returned to Lisbon in 1861 and went to London in 1863, entertaining himself by writing prorebel letters to friends in the North. "It is the South," he blandly told Sam Tilden, "which is now fighting in defence of all the principles and rights of American liberty, for self-government and the dignity of man." He was in Paris in 1871 and back in New York by the end of that decade. He finally died in a hotel on East Eleventh Street in 1895, his services for democracy as well as his services for slavery having long receded into the forgotten past.

Ben Butler of Massachusetts, who had few convictions of his own but had a certain skill in expressing the convictions of the audience he happened at any moment to be addressing, probably uttered adequately enough the feelings of rank-and-file Jacksonian Democrats about their Northern comrades who opposed the war. "I should like to hear old Andrew Jackson say a few words about such politicians, who call themselves Democrats," Butler declared in 1863. "He'd hang them," shouted some enthusiast in the crowd. The crafty man on the platform twisted his ugly face. "No, my friend, I don't think he would hang them. I don't think he would ever catch them." The hall rang with laughter and applause.

THE AGONY OF WAR PASSED, AND IN ITS WAKE CAME the eternal disquiet of peace. The federal Union had been preserved. Now, it must be made real again, and to this task the remaining Jacksonian Democrats addressed themselves.

The new President was a Jacksonian from Jackson's own state, Andrew Johnson, fifty-six years old when he entered the White House in 1865. Born in North Carolina, Johnson moved West in 1826. From pinched beginnings he gradually became a successful and rather fashionable tailor in Greenville, Tennessee. In 1828, the year that Jackson the General was elected President of the United States, Johnson the tailor became an alderman of Greenville. His powerful personality and his frank appeal to the farmers and workingmen as against the cotton aristocrats won him steady political advancement. In 1835 he went to the state House of Representatives, in 1841 to the state Senate, and from 1843 to 1853 he served in the federal House of Representatives. A man of middle height, with strong and massive head, swarthy face and sturdy shoulders, his eyes black and belligerent, his bearing defiant and resolute, Johnson made himself felt in Washington.

Yet Johnson was able, honest and utterly fearless. Regarding himself as the spokesman of the non-slaveholding people of eastern Tennessee, he fought their battles with vigor and courage. In Congress he followed for the most part the Polk line, supporting annexation and the Mexican War, the Walker tariff and the independent treasury, opposing the Wilmot Proviso but never in Congress advocating slavery extension or defending the institution on abstract grounds. His great political contribution was the Homestead bill, which he introduced in 1846 and for which he carried on over many years a persevering and often lonely battle. This brought him to the attention of the Northern workingmen. In 1851 he received some votes in the Industrial Congress as its nominee for President, and in May, 1852, he actually addressed a New York mass meeting arranged in part by George H. Evans. In 1853, gerrymandered out of his Congressional district, Johnson ran successfully for the governorship of Tennessee, holding that position for two terms. In 1857 Tennessee sent him to the Senate.

Though Johnson never had close personal ties with Jackson or any of his immediate circle—Polk, indeed, regarded him with marked distrust—Jackson was his political idol, and his speeches had the true Jacksonian ring. He followed Cass and Douglas in their endorsement of "popular sovereignty," but he never believed, as they appeared to believe, that the achievement of political democracy exhausted the responsibilities of the democratic politician. "If, through an iniquitous system, a vast amount of wealth has been accumulated in the hands of one man, or a few men," he declared in 1864, "then that result is wrong, and the sooner we can right it the better for all concerned." The attempt to right it consumed the main part of his life. "All, or nearly all of our legislation," he said, "is for corporations, for monopolies, for classes, and individuals; but the great mass who produce while we consume, are little cared for; their rights and interests are neglected and overlooked." In 1858, when most of the South had disavowed the Declaration of Independence and was denouncing democracy, Johnson reaffirmed his faith in Jefferson and popular government, casting back into the faces of his colleagues the talk of "mud-sills" and property. "I have referred to the Declaration of Independence, and to Mr. Jefferson's Inaugural Address, for the purpose of showing that democracy means something very different from what was laid down by the distinguished Senator from Alabama. I furthermore refer to these important documents to show that property is not the leading element of government and of society."

What would war do to this faith in democracy? For Johnson there was no hesitation. Democracy had a stake in only one side of the conflict, and Jackson had charted the course for a

Tennessee man to follow when the Union was in danger. Johnson boldly denounced the seceding Senators, observing incidentally (without "intending to disparage others") that, if Jackson had been President, the rebellion would never have taken place. As War Governor of Tennessee he did his mighty best to hold the state for freedom. By 1864 he was the leading War Democrat, and in June the Union convention nominated him to run for Vice-President with Abraham Lincoln. Johnson's letter of acceptance quoted the prophecy of Andrew Jackson which Sumner had read to the startled Senate in 1860.

Yet Johnson as champion of democracy was in a sense betrayed by his private bitterness. His early life, true enough, had been hard. Still at twenty he was an alderman, at twenty-seven a member of the state House of Representatives, at thirty-five a Congressman, and others had worked up from equally desperate beginnings. But the experience was peculiarly drastic for Johnson, wounding him deeply and scarring him for life. Thus democracy was not simply for him, as it was for Jefferson and Jackson, a set of social ideals; it was that, but it was also an instrument of revenge for the grievances of childhood. His compulsion drove him relentlessly in a personal vendetta against wealth, and thus often confused and complicated the war he was waging as a disinterested public man for Jeffersonianism. His speeches, for example, were adorned with boasts of his lowly origin and calling. These neurotic feelings of inferiority burst forth most pathetically in his drunken insistence on Johnson the "plebeian" in his tragic inaugural.

They were perhaps as responsible as anything for his failure as a democratic statesman. This violence of resentment, ordinarily suppressed, under his earnest and courteous demeanor, occasionally exploded into lurid demagoguery which always harmed his cause. He lacked the instinctive restraint of the great leader who never excites the people to want more than he is able to give them. Debauching his audiences by his own excesses, he left them all the more vulnerable to assaults by more unscrupulous rabble rousers. He never knew when to stop; that inner turbulence would never permit him; and in the end he paid the penalty.

WITH JOHNSON'S ACCESSION THE SURVIVING JACKSONians made their last serious movement to recover their former influence.

But the Johnson administration was a failure, in large part because of Johnson's own defects of leadership, and with its failure collapsed the last drive of the Jacksonians.

The Democratic party meanwhile showed few signs of recovering from its misadventures of the eighteen-fifties, while the Republican party, captured during and after the war by a boarding party of bankers and industrialists, so hastily abandoned its aspirations toward freedom and democracy that some of its ablest leaders bolted in the Liberal Republican schism of 1872, eventually to rejoin the Democrats. The Democratic endorsement of the Liberal Republican candidate Horace Greeley, once one of the most active of Whigs, the inveterate foe of Jackson, Van Buren and Silas Wright, the powerful champion of the Bank of the United States, the high tariff and internal improvements, showed the evaporation of Jacksonian issues.

In 1874 John Bigelow predicted that "the original Democratical elements of the Republican party" would return to the Democratic party, with "the Whig elements" remaining as Republicans. While this may have been likely enough, the Democrats did not go very far in regaining their past vigor. In 1876 the party ran Samuel J. Tilden on an honest-government issue, and for some years this cry served as a substitute for more basic reform. Not till Grover Cleveland became President did much reform energy get in control of the Democratic party, and not till the rise of William Jennings Bryan, appealing in his Cross of Gold speech to the spirit of Jackson, did this energy assume a very radical form.

XXXVII *Traditions of Democracy*

THE TRADITION OF JEFFERSON AND JACKSON MIGHT recede, but it could never disappear. It was bound to endure in America so long as liberal capitalistic society endured, for it was the creation of the internal necessities of such a society. American democracy has come to accept the struggle among competing groups for the control of the state as a positive virtue—indeed, as the only foundation for liberty. The business community has been ordinarily the most powerful of these groups, and liberalism in America has been ordinarily the movement on the part of the other sections of society to restrain the power of the business community. This was the tradition of Jefferson and Jackson, and it has been the basic meaning of American liberalism.

YET THE TRADITION CLEARLY WENT INTO ECLIPSE FOR some years after the Civil War. They had risen up before the war a party of industrial control, with smooth-running organization, energetic leadership, an active program and a solid economic base. Then the new and more terrible problem of slavery had burst forth, mobilizing the loyalties and capacities of men of good will. The antislavery crusade thus drained off the energies, diverted the enthusiasm and destroyed the party of Jacksonian democracy.

In part, this was simply the physical consequence of facing an agonizing question and fighting an exhausting war. But in part, too, it resulted from the ineffectiveness of the Jacksonian approach to the war. The Jacksonian analysis correctly made it imperative for the radical democracy to combat the slave power with all its will; but that analysis did not sufficiently embrace all the facts of the situation to gain strength and urgency from the war, or even to arm itself for the struggle of survival.

Frank Blair, Jr., well stated the Jacksonian theory as it was extended to cover the conflict arising over slavery:—

> This is no question of North and South. It is a question between those who contend for caste and privilege, and those who neither have nor desire to have privileges beyond their fellows. It is the old question that has always, in all free countries, subsisted—the question of the wealthy and crafty few endeavoring to steal from the masses of the people all the political power of the government.

Now this was true only in part; for, in hard fact, the war *was* principally a question of North and South. Most of the humble people of the slave states rallied eagerly to the cause of slavery —the Andrew Johnsons were the exceptions—and most of the "wealthy and crafty few" in the North backed the Union. Thus many fought on Blair's side without his reasons, and many who should have accepted his reasons fought against him. In one aspect a "class" war, a war for democracy, the Civil War was primarily a sectional war; and, like all theories of war which skip the actuality of regional and national loyalties, the Jacksonian theory of the Civil War foundered on the facts.

Accordingly, as the conflict deepened, the sectional theory gained status and authority, partly because more facts and sentiments supported it; partly also because the class theory had to be soft-pedaled in the interests of national unity, and because many conservative Northerners, fearing the explosive possibilities of the class theory, did their best to destroy it. In the end, the Jacksonian analysis, powerfully expressed before the war by the Van Burens, Preston King, the Blairs, came out a fairly academic thesis, without having gained a strong emotional appeal or a wide following from the bitter years of conflict.*

The instinct of a conservative writer in the *Atlantic Monthly* in 1859 was truer than the hopes of Blair. This writer, perceiving that the slavery question had absorbed Jacksonian democracy while turning it from its main objects, observed that the emergence of the sectional issue had achieved "the freedom of our later party struggles from radical theories." "From about the year 1829 to 1841," he wrote, "there was in our politics a large infusion of Socialism," but now there was far less of "the feeling known as Agrarianism" than there had been in 1833.

This quiescence of the Jacksonian tradition, the breakup of the Jacksonian organization, the death of the Jacksonian leaders, disarmed liberalism for the postwar struggles. In the meantime the impulse of the business community toward protective coloration, begun by Seward, Weed and Greeley in the thirties, came to triumphant culmination. By capturing the Republican party the business community captured the prestige of representing freedom and democracy. The technique of "waving the bloody shirt"—that is, of freeing the slaves again every fourth year—enabled the Republicans long to submerge the fact that they were becoming the party of monopoly and wealth. Thus, for some time after the war, the pressing economic issues were kept out of national politics. When the country returned once more to the problems which had preoccupied the thirties, the radical democrats were forgotten, their experiments unknown, their philosophy sunk in oblivion. The continuities of reform had been broken.

AT THE SAME TIME NEW COMPLEXITIES, WHICH THE Jacksonians did not have to face, were weakening the faith of even some democrats in the efficacy of the radical democratic solution—in the efficacy, that is, of unlimited reliance on popular government. Of these, the most serious was the rise of a rootless, bewildered, unstable population, the creation, on one hand, of the spread of industrialism, and, on the other, of the rapid increase of immigration. Starting on a large scale in the

* It is unnecessary to point out that liberal thought has suffered a similar fate in the current world conflict. Substitute "America" and "Germany" for "North" and "South" in Blair's statement, and you get a conventional liberal interpretation of the present war, and one with the same weakness as the original. Ever since liberalism "emancipated" itself from nationalism, it has found it hard to cope with the facts of war.

eighteen-forties, thousands of Europeans, ill-educated, tractable, used to low economic standards, unused to political liberty, began flocking to American shores. There they mingled with native Americans in the large cities, and mill towns, all living a scanty and desperate life at day labor, all driven into a herd, imprinted with the same mold, and subjected to a barrage of insecurities which restricted their freedom of choice and undermined their responsibility. The "people" were being degraded into the "mass," bound together, not by common loyalties and aspirations, but by common anxieties and fears.

The political consequences of the rise of this new population were plain and terrifying. The "masses," huddled together in the slums, seemed no longer, in any real sense, to be free. As voters they were either at the beck and call of their employers, or else the dupes of unscrupulous demagogues. "Bread and circuses" appeared to be once more the formula for political success. Mike Walsh was a symbolic figure, exhibiting the good and the evil in the new mass politician: on the one hand, an honest fervor for popular rights; on the other, the methods of an accomplished political gangster—the Spartan Band and brawls in the streets and corruption at the polls ("vote early and vote often").

Yet Mike Walsh at least did, in his erratic way, have the people on his mind; but what of the men who took over Walsh's methods without his saving honesty? The rise of bosses like Fernando Wood in New York was profoundly alarming to believers in democracy.

Even more alarming in the long run were the men who took over Walsh's fervor, trumpeting their love of democracy and liberty, mainly in order to gain the power to destroy it. In New York, George Wilkes, fancy man, gossip monger, salesman of obscene literature, became an ardent Communist and wrote pamphlets extolling the Internationale and the Paris Commune. Yet the lineage from William Leggett to Mike Walsh to Walsh's pal Wilkes was straight, and much of Wilkes's appeal was couched in almost Jacksonian language. Similarly in Massachusetts the unscrupulous Ben Butler became a noisy "radical," in 1884 the presidential nominee of the Anti-Monopoly party, and he too was in direct line of descent from Jacksonianism.

Many Jacksonians, reading these portents, began to succumb to the old Jeffersonian fears of the city and the industrial proletariat. In 1864 Gideon Welles and Preston King, expressing to each other their disgust that New York City could send Fernando Wood to Congress, got into a discussion of the limits of radical democracy.

"The whole city of New York," exclaimed Welles, "is alike leprous and rotten. . . . How can such a place be regenerated and purified? What is the remedy?" He confessed a reluctant belief that "in such a vicious community free suffrage was abased, and it was becoming a problem whether there should not be an outside movement, or some restrictions on voting to correct palpable evil in municipal government."

King, as Welles put in, maintained the old faith. "The evil will correct itself," the veteran radical stoutly declared. "After they have disgraced themselves sufficiently and loaded themselves with taxes and debt, they will finally rouse to a sense of duty, and retrieve the city from misrule."

For a moment Welles felt the "old enthusiasm of former years" return with King's unquestioning conviction. He recalled those happy days "when in the security of youth I believed the popular voice was right, and that the majority would come to right results in every community; but alas! experience has shaken the confidence I once had. In an agricultural district, or a sparse population the old rule holds," he conceded; but in the large cities? The "floating mass" seemed to him no safe depository of power. "Some permanent element is wanting in our system."

Even the superb confidence of Walt Whitman was faltering. As he looked out on the post-Civil War world, as he saw "the shallowness and miserable selfism of these crowds of men, with all their minds so blank of high humanity and aspiration— then comes the terrible query, and will not be denied, Is not Democracy of human rights humbug after all?" Did these people "with hearts of rags and souls of chalk" have the grandeur of vision for self-government? He did not know; he would not "gloss over the appalling dangers of universal suffrage," but at bottom he was still convinced that the people would save themselves; he too still maintained the old faith.

Yet democracy was certainly facing a problem which no rhetoric of majority could assuage. The rise of the masses gave the democratic appeal a sinister ambivalence. It could be employed with as much passion, and with many fewer scruples, by the Fernando Woods, the Ben Butlers and the George Wilkeses, the corrupt bosses, the proto-fascists and the proto-communists, as by the honest democrat. If democratic leadership could not solve the crucial economic problems, would not the masses, seeking in despair everywhere for relief, turn in the end to the man who would provide apocalyptic promises of everything?

The returns are not yet in. But the tired liberalism of Gideon Welles clearly exaggerated the imminence of disaster. The faith of Preston King and Walt Whitman in the recuperative capacity of American democracy, in its tendency toward self-correction, was still justified (in great part, of course, because of the natural endowments of economic wealth and geographical isolation). The people have not yet altogether become the "floating mass," and the "floating mass" itself is not beyond redemption. The future thus became a race between the radical democracy, trying to build a society which would eliminate anxiety and despair, and the black infectious taint of fear, which would demoralize the people and create the drive toward security at any price—as Whitman saw it, "the battle advancing, retreating, between democracy's convictions, aspirations, and the people's crudeness, vice, caprices." Three quarters of a century after Gideon Welles's forebodings, the radical democracy in America still preserved, by some herculean exertions, a small but important advantage.

WE HAVE SEEN HOW THE GROWTH OF IMPERSONALITY in economic relations enhanced the need for the intervention of government. As the private conscience grew increasingly powerless to impose effective restraints on the methods of business, the public conscience, in the form of the democratic government, had to step in to prevent the business community from tearing society apart in its pursuit of profit. The rise of the "mass," by increasing the proportion of society only fitfully capable of making responsible decisions, added to the compulsion for state action. Yet by origin and creed the tradition of Jefferson was vigorously antistatist; and the conflict raised new problems for democratic thought.

This mistrust of government had roots deep in the American past. Many of the colonists, as Van Buren pointed out, had arrived with vivid recollections of the persecutions suffered by Puritan, Huguenot, Hussite and Dutch ancestors, which, "gradually stimulated into maturity and shape by the persevering injustice of the mother country, became political opinions of the most tenacious and enduring character." The first motive of American democracy was hostility against what was felt to be insupportable tyranny, and the war with Britain confirmed democracy in its suspicion of the state. Moreover, for people in the shadow of the Middle Ages, the history of liberty had been the history of the capture of guarantees and immunities from the state; and in the American republic itself, most interference by the central government—United States Bank, internal improvements, tariff—had been for the benefit of the business community. The instinct of democrats was thus to insist on the constitutional bounds of the state. Their experience of government and their reading of history, as Van Buren put it, destroyed all hopes that "political power could be vested in remote hands, without the certainty of its being abused."

"That government is best, which governs least," "The world is too much governed"—the mottoes respectively of the *Democratic Review* and the *Washington Globe*—expressed forcibly the prevailing antigovernmental complex. The corollary was that what government was necessary should be in the hands of the states. "The man who chiefly desires to preserve the rights of the States, and he whose interests are concentrated in perpetuating the rule of the many," as the *Democratic Review* said in 1844, "must, under our political system, use the same means to attain their ends." George Bancroft observed that it was Jackson's deep conviction that "strict construction is required by the lasting welfare of the great labouring classes of the United States."

These emotions about State rights and the evil of government were absorbed into and fortified by what may be called the "Jeffersonian myth." Every great social movement, as Sorel has reminded us, generates its "social myth"—the "body of images capable of evoking instinctively all the sentiments which correspond to the different manifestations" of the movement. Such a myth, though it purports to deal with the future, is by no means to be taken as a blueprint. It "must be judged as a means of acting on the present; any attempt to discuss how far it can be taken literally as future history is devoid of sense." The myths are "not descriptions of things, but expressions of a determination to act." It is thus idle to refute a myth, since it exists as an emotional entirety whose essential function is to mobilize men for action.

Jackson in his vindication of the presidency to the Senate displayed some of the resources of the Jeffersonian myth. It had been his purpose, he said, "to heal the wounds of the Constitution and preserve it from further violation; to persuade my countrymen, so far as I may, that it is not in a splendid government supported by powerful monopolies and aristocratical establishments that they will find happiness or their liberties protection, but in a plain system, void of pomp, protecting all and granting favors to none, dispensing its blessings, like the dews of Heaven, unseen and unfelt save in the freshness and beauty they contribute to produce." The imagery discloses the underlying pattern: the Constitution undefiled vs. the Constitution violated; plain government vs. splendid government; equal rights vs. powerful monopolies; the dews of heaven, in freshness and beauty, vs. "aristocratical establishments," with their suggestions of monarchy, wealth and decadence.

The Jeffersonian myth thus implanted and sustained in the minds of its followers a whole set of social choices: simplicity vs. ostentation; frugality vs. extravagance; rectitude vs. laxity; moderation vs. luxury; country vs. city; virtuous farmer or mechanic vs. depraved capitalist or demoralized day laborer; plain homely government vs. sumptuous complicated government; economy vs. debt; strict construction vs. loose construction; State rights vs. huge federal power; decentralization vs. concentration; democracy vs. aristocracy; purity vs. corruption.

This body of values and images animated and deepened the appeals of Jefferson, John Taylor, Jackson, Van Buren and the other Jeffersonians. They were operating in terms of a great common vision, strong, simple and satisfying, evoking the emotions which hope, memory or experience had endeared to millions of Americans, and thrusting in sharp and ugly relief the invading armies of industrialism and aristocracy. The existence of this myth in the background of the mind gave its component parts—not least the belief in the evil of government—a strong and almost sacred status.

YET CHANGE BROUGHT A GROWING DIVERGENCE BEtween the myth and the actuality. We have seen how the pat contrasts between country and city, honest farmer and demoralized laborer, were tripped up by the realities of Jacksonian politics. In the realm of government the divergence became acute with respect to the antigovernmental complex. The neat formulas of antistatism simply failed to work. Invented as protective doctrines against aristocratic despotism, they became an embarrassment when the radical party got into power itself. Jefferson ignored them when he felt strong executive action to be necessary, and in the quiet of his retirement he even developed a general rationale for overstepping the Jeffersonian limitations.*

* See Jefferson's important letter to J. B. Colvin, September 20, 1810, *Works*, XII, 418-422. "To lose our country by a scrupulous adherence to written law, would be to lose the law itself, with life, liberty, property and all those who are enjoying them with us; thus absurdly sacrificing the end to the means. . . . The line of discrimination between cases may be difficult; but the good officer is bound to draw it at his own peril, and throw himself on the justice of his country and the rectitude of his motives." Probably this statement describes accurately the necessities of leadership in a democracy. A kind of power is required in crises which would be dangerous normally and which rests ultimately on popular approval. In any case, Jefferson's statement certainly applies accurately to the behavior of himself, Jackson, Lincoln, Wilson and the Roosevelts in major crises. Jefferson evidently regarded the Constitution as an instrument to prevent bad action but not, in cases of emergency, to prevent good.

The administration of Jackson accentuated the complexities which underlay the deceptivity simple maxims of the *Globe* and the *Democratic Review*. Granted that competition free from government intervention constituted the ideal economy, what was the Jeffersonian obligation when that freedom resulted in the growth of monopolies which destroyed competition? The Jacksonian answer was government intervention—to restore the conditions of competition; that is, to "heal the wounds of the Constitution" and re-establish the principles of government in their original purity. As John L. O'Sullivan put it, "A good deal of positive government may be yet wanted to undo the manifold mischiefs of past mis-government." Thus, the Jacksonians, under the banner of antistatism, could carry on a vigorous program of government intervention, and Jackson, ruling in the name of weak government, ended up by leaving the presidency stronger than it had ever been before.

Some of the details of the Jacksonian policy, however, caused orthodox Jeffersonians distinct discomfort, even those who managed to swallow such deviations as the Nullification Proclamation or the removal of the deposits.

The struggle to reconcile the Jeffersonian myth and the Jacksonian fact was fought out most candidly in the pages of the *Democratic Review*. The first issue contained a glowing and trustful statement of the Jeffersonian position, with the theory of weak government imbedded as the keystone. But what was the status of this theory in face of an army of corporations hostile to democracy? O'Sullivan wrestled with this difficulty in a casuistical article in the second number, eventually confining the theory to the federal government alone and vehemently attacking the Supreme Court for limiting the power of state governments over business.

But was this much help? After the banks suspended in May, 1837, a trade-union meeting in Philadelphia had declared in a typical outburst, "On the question of the currency, we have no confidence in the State administrations generally . . . we hereby call upon the national administration to take all such measures as it shall judge the most expedient." Where did this leave O'Sullivan's revised theory? He perceived the difficulty, and the third number carried a somewhat embarrassed article justifying the robustness of Jackson's presidency, but hoping devoutly that "those great powers resident in the Executive arm, may never again be called forth into activity."

And so it went. Jeffersonian fundamentalists got off the bandwagon early. Even a Jacksonian like Orestes A. Brownson could in certain moods exclaim with alarm at Jackson's "tendency to Centralization and his evident leaning to *Bureaucraticy*. . . . We are making more rapid strides towards . . . Centralization and to the Bureaucratic system than even the most sensitive nullifier has yet suspected."

It is no wonder that the attempt to defend Jacksonianism in terms of that government being best which governed least excited only the derision of the Whigs. To them Jacksonian policy consisted simply, as Caleb Cushing described it, of "the meddlesome interference of General Jackson in the business of the country, his prurient tampering with the currency under the pretext of reforming it," and so on. The talk about restoring constitutional purity seemed a cynical pretext for reckless government intervention.

The vital point underlying this bandying of accusations is that "intervention" is not an absolute. It is always a question of whose ox is gored. Government *must* act; it cannot rest in Olympian impartiality. Even "governing least" is likely to be government for the benefit of the strongest group in the community. The crucial question is not, Is there "too much" government? but, Does the government promote "too much" the interests of a single group? In liberal capitalist society this question has ordinarily become in practice, Is the government serving the interests of the business community to the detriment of the nation as a whole? This has been the irrepressible conflict of capitalism: the struggle on the part of the business community to dominate the state, and on the part of the rest of society, under the leadership of "liberals," to check the political ambitions of business.

The real issue between the Whigs and Jackson was, thus, not freedom of enterprise. Both parties would concede that enterprise should be free, would claim always to be acting to protect this freedom, and each, when in possession of the state, would unhesitatingly intervene in business, on its own behalf and in the name of "freedom," by destroying United States Banks or establishing protective tariffs. The champions of Jeffersonianism were eager for government to suppress small notes and institute a ten-hour day, while the Hamiltonians would flourish free-trade principles when questions of trade-unionism or corporations control were brought up. If the men of the thirties and forties really accepted the antistatist maxims they constantly invoked, they would not have been in political parties at all, but in lonely huts around country ponds like the one man of the day who believed radically that that government was best which governed least.

The question was not principles but power: was a "liberal" government, in fact, strong enough to act contrary to the wishes of the business community? And in the struggle over this basic question conservatism or liberalism would adopt any myth, and has adopted most which promised to promote its cause. This is not to impugn the honesty of belief in the visions excited by the myth, for no great social movement can exist without such stimulus and support. The myth, it should never be forgotten, expresses only the "determination to act." The ends of action lie necessarily in an inscrutable future.

THERE WERE, IN FACT, CERTAIN "STRONG GOVERN-ment" strains implicit in Jeffersonianism from the start. Jefferson himself could refer to "the protecting hand of the legislature." Speaking of the distresses caused by paper money, he would declare that they could not fail to "engage the interposition of the legislature." The decisions of Marshall's Court, safeguarding corporations from the operations of state laws, intensified the Jeffersonian tendency to aggrandize the state governments. "The restoration of public supremacy," observed Charles Jared Ingersoll, arguing for legislative control over charters of incorporation, "is the great desideratum." A Democratic Justice from Virginia, Philip P. Barbour, firmly and emphatically expanded the police power of the states against the disciples of Marshall.

Once government was conceded some virtue in the states, it was difficult not to extend a little of the exoneration to the federal government. Some functions were simply too important to be confided to the states. As Thomas Hart Benton remarked of the currency, it should not be trusted to any authority "but the highest and most responsible which was known to our form of government"—the people's government at Washington. The experience of the eighteen-thirties, when, from a Jacksonian point of view, state governments were exceedingly unreliable and the federal government was the stronghold of democracy, increased the tendency toward tolerance.

The pivotal conception in this redirection of the liberal tradition was expressed very ably by Taney in his Charles River Bridge decision. "The object and end of all government," he declared, "is to promote the happiness and prosperity of the community by which it is established; and it can never be assumed, that the government intended to diminish its power of accomplishing the end for which it was created."

Now this remark appalled no Jacksonians and delighted no Hamiltonians; yet it foreshadowed a basic shift in the Jeffersonian theory, in the direction of Hamiltonianism. For Taney's maxim could hardly be distinguished from observations made by Hamilton and Marshall:—

> Now it appears to the Secretary of the Treasury that this *general principle* is *inherent* in the very *definition* of government, and *essential* to every step of the progress to be made by that of the United States, namely: That every power vested in a government is in its nature *sovereign,* and includes, by *force* of the *term,* a right to employ all the *means* requisite and fairly applicable to the attainment of the *ends* of such power, and which are *not* precluded by restrictions and exceptions specified on the Constitution, or not immoral, or not contrary to the *essential ends* of political society.
>
> Let the end be legitimate, let it be within the scope of the Constitution, and all means which are appropriate, which are plainly adapted to that end, which are not prohibited, but consist with the letter and spirit of the Constitution, are constitutional.

Jeffersonianism, if it were to follow the lead of the Taney formula, must abandon a good deal of its abhorrence of the state. And what other lead could it follow? Was not Jackson's administration—was not Taney's very decision—a confession that Jeffersonianism required Hamiltonian means to achieve its ends?

Jacksonian democracy lacked, however, a great creative political philosopher, who would perceive the essential drift of the Taney doctrine, formulate its implications and restate basically the principles of the liberal faith. The Jeffersonian myth was so persuasive, and Jacksonian action could be so plausibly explained as hewing the way back to original principles that few were prepared to face the vital gap in the Jeffersonian argument. Yet this gap had to be faced. For if, in the ideal state, government was to be confined to the narrowest possible sphere, what was there to prevent the proliferation of the very monopolies that would, at some later date, require the active intervention of the government? Without a strong government, in other words, how could the people ever hope to deal with the business community? A Jeffersonian would answer that at least the "aristocracy" could do less harm in control of a weak government than a strong one. But under a weak government would not economic power gain the aristocracy all the control they needed? And was not the whole moral of the Jacksonian experience that only a strong people's government could break up the power of concentrated wealth?

But the Jeffersonians refused to admit this final step. Each energetic employment of the government for Jeffersonian ends was for them an exception, a transition stage, irrelevant to theory. In fact, they dared not acknowledge the true answer. They had to suppress it. The birth of democracy in revolt against tyranny had a traumatic effect on Jeffersonian democracy, coloring it with morbid fears of despotism, conditioning it to hate the state, inducing a whole complex of fantasies about government, which made it impossible for Jeffersonians to accept its necessity and drove them to hide what they were doing under a cabalistic repetition of the slogans of antistatism.

This persistence of the Jeffersonian myth during the Jacksonian period had, moreover, great immediate advantages. Indeed, the very fact of its persistence was presumptive proof of its necessity. It corresponded more accurately and profoundly to the needs of the people than any alteration could have. In particular, it united, for more or less harmonious action over a long period, two essentially unfriendly groups: on the one hand, those opposing the business community from the point of view of the *rentier* class, the landed aristocracy, North as well as South; and on the other, those opposing it from the point of view of the small farmer and workingman. Their differences in interest, social status and ultimate hopes were concealed by their common absorption in the slogans and images of Jeffersonianism.

Small points occasionally betrayed the basic divergence. The first group, for example, exulted in the word "conservative," like Calhoun, Cooper, Taney, Hawthorne, the middle Brownson, and regarded themselves primarily as guardians of the sacred flame, cherishing the purest essence of the Jeffersonian past. The other group exulted in the word "radical," like Van Buren, Bancroft, Blair, Benton, the early Brownson, and regarded themselves as crusaders, out to realize the full values of the Jeffersonian tradition. The first group was defensive in outlook, fundamentally oriented in favor of a vanishing order, and on its behalf assisting in assaults on the aggressive sections of the existing order, while the second was itself aggressive, interested above all in transforming the existing order according to the Jeffersonian faith. The alliance broke down when the emergence of slavery, presenting the basic challenge, called the bluff of the "conservative" Jeffersonians.

BUT, IN THE LONG RUN, THE FAILURE TO CODIFY THE Jacksonian deviations was unfortunate for American liberalism. With Jackson's mighty personality removed and the lessons of his presidency unlearned, his party tended to relapse into the antistatist formulas. The Jeffersonian myth was allowed to linger on, gaining a certain venerability and sanctity; and as a strong government became more clearly the necessary instrument of greater democracy, the business community rushed to fortify itself behind the antigovernmental parts of the Jeffersonian tradition. Ever since, conservatives have been turning to the Jeffersonian myth for weapons to defeat Jefferson's essential purposes. When the antistatist formulas are invoked today, it is ordinarily in defense of the very interests which Jefferson was urging them to attack.

After the Civil War, conservatism, draping itself in the mantle of Jefferson and assuming the credit for destroying slavery, stared down the pretensions of any other group to stand for "democracy." Liberalism, deprived of the social myth which had united and sustained it before the war, was left uncertain and incoherent. Men of liberal inclination had nothing with which to mobilize their forces against the rule of the business community.

It was this sense of democratic impotence, intensified by the cynicism of post war politics, which caused Walt Whitman to define "our fundamental want to-day"—a new faith, "permeating the whole mass of American mentality, taste, belief, breathing into it a new breath of life, giving it decision . . . radiating, begetting appropriate teachers, schools, manners, and, as its grandest result, accomplishing . . . a religious and moral character beneath the political and productive and intellectual bases of the States."

Whitman was demanding, among other things, a new social myth, which would serve the liberal tradition as the Jeffersonian myth had served it before the war. He recognized keenly how "the great literature," as he called it, "penetrates all, gives hue to all, shapes aggregates and individuals, and, after subtle ways, with irresistible power, constructs, sustains, demolishes at will." Unless radical democracy could thus inaugurate "its own perennial sources, welling from the centre for ever, its strength will be defective, its growth doubtful, and its main charm wanting." He announced the time had come for "a native expression-spirit . . . sternly taking command, dissolving the old, sloughing off surfaces, and from its own interior and vital principles, reconstructing, democratizing society." Whitman himself made the greatest sustained attempt to create the "single image-making work," but the need he had perceived could be filled only secondarily by literature. As he saw at other times, "the exercise of Democracy" contained the greatest promise for salvation. The very struggle for liberty and equality was immensely valuable; "strength it makes & lessons it teaches," and from it would emerge the great men who would renew and incarnate democratic ideals.

In the end, exercise rather than literature saved democracy. A century of bitter experience in the democratic fight finally led liberalism to uncover what the Jeffersonians had buried: the need for a strong government. The impotence of the Jeffersonian state to realize Jeffersonian ends first became clear in the economic field, as it grew increasingly apparent that workingmen required protection from the mercies of their employers. Jackson and Van Buren sponsored the ten-hour day and worried over the power of businessmen to drive wages below subsistence. As George Bancroft declared in 1854, *laissez faire* might solve problems of international trade, "but its abandonment of labor to the unmitigated effects of personal competition can never be accepted as the rule for the dealings of man to man. . . . The good time is coming, when humanity will recognise all members of its family as alike entitled to its care; when the heartless jargon of overproduction in the midst of want will end in a better science of distribution."

Such aspirations, in last analysis, called for government to take a much more active role in economic life. One of the first to acknowledge the inadequacy of the Jeffersonian view was the rascally but thoroughly intelligent Ben Butler of Massachusetts. While he had been "dazzled with the brilliancy of Jackson's administration," he wrote in his autobiography, "I early had sense enough to see that it conflicted, in a very considerable degree, with the teachings of Jefferson." The conclusion seemed obvious. "As to the powers and duties of the government of the United States, I am a Hamiltonian Federalist. As to the rights and privileges of the citizen, I am a Jeffersonian Democrat."

Slowly the liberal tradition was overhauled, and the twentieth century saw the final disapearance of the Jeffersonian inhibitions. The Hamiltonian progressivism of Theodore Roosevelt ushered in a period of energetic government. Woodrow Wilson understood even more plainly the need for executive vigor and government action. Franklin D. Roosevelt carried out these tendencies more decisively than Wilson, and the New Deal achieved the emancipation of liberalism from